365
Daily

Whispers of Wisdom for
Busy Women

365
Daily

Whispers of Wisdom for
Busy Women

A YEAR OF INSPIRATIONAL READINGS

BARBOUR
PUBLISHING

© 2008 by Barbour Publishing, Inc.

ISBN 978-1-60260-137-6

Published by Barbour Publishing, Inc., P.O. Box 719, Uhrichsville, Ohio 44683, www.barbourbooks.com

Our mission is to publish and distribute inspirational products offering exceptional value and biblical encouragement to the masses.

Member of the
Evangelical Christian
Publishers Association

Printed in the United States of America.

Introduction

You're a wonder woman, balancing every area of your life—home, work, school, ministry, the list goes on. The hours are long, but the days are too short to get everything accomplished. What's the first thing that usually suffers when life gets too busy? Time spent with God.

The Father knows what it is to be busy, and He understands the stress we suffer when our schedules are bursting at the seams. Even when we don't take the time to hear His voice, He's still there—encouraging and supporting us every step of the way.

These 365 whispers of wisdom come to you straight from the Father Himself. Make it a priority to meet Him every day in His Word, through a devotional thought, and in prayer. Even on the days you feel like you don't have a second to spare, dedicate a minute or two to time with God—and He'll bless the rest of your day immeasurably.

The Publishers

REBIRTH

Create in me a clean heart, O God. Renew a loyal spirit within me.
PSALM 51:10 NLT

$\mathcal{D}$onna sighed as she watched the Times Square ball drop on TV. It had been a rough year. She was in a slump emotionally, spiritually, and physically. Exhaustion was her constant companion. Peace seemed far away and God even farther.

"Heavenly Father," she prayed, "Help me find You again."

As she changed for bed, a still, small voice filled her head, as real as if someone spoke aloud. *Renavatio.* What was that? Vague memories of high school Latin assignments flickered through her mind. *Renavatio.* What did it mean?

Donna found the definition—"rebirth; discarding the old and embracing the new"—just as the words of a song came to her:

New life stirs within me now.
Like a soft breeze, transforming me now.
It's a miracle of love
Precious blessing from above
My heart has taken wings. . .like a dove.

And suddenly she knew: God had been right there all along. The Giver of Life was also the Renewer of Hope, and He was ready and waiting to fill her with new life, new hope—to transform her heart and lift her out of her pit. All she had to do was ask.

Breath of Life, breathe into me Your sweet joy and peace.
Help me see the coming year as an opportunity to discard the old,
embrace the new, and fly on the wings of a dove. Amen.

NEEDED:
A STRONG SPRING

*My voice shalt thou hear in the morning, O Lord; in the morning
will I direct my prayer unto thee, and will look up.*
PSALM 5:3 KJV

When he bought a watch in an army supply in Japan in 1946, Lonnie never thought it would still be running today, more than sixty years later. Sometime back, however, he saw that his watch wasn't keeping time as well as it once did. He took it to a watch repairman.

"When do you wind it?" the man asked.

Lonnie told him he winds his watch when he assumes most people wind theirs—if they haven't gone digital.

"Every night before retiring."

"There's your problem," the repairman said. "Your watch gets its hard knocks during the day. That's when it needs to be running on a strong spring. Wind it in the morning and you won't have any problem with it."

And he hasn't.

We need to begin our busy days on a strong spring, too. Not with just a good cup of coffee, but some time spent with our source of strength. Taking five minutes or an hour—or more if we're really disciplined—in prayer and Bible reading can make the difference in our day. No matter if we're facing wresting kids out of bed or fighting traffic all the way to work, that special time can give us a "spring in our step" today.

*Thank You, Lord, for another day. Be my source of strength today.
In Jesus' blessed name. Amen.*

BLESSED ASSURANCE

Day 3

"Don't be afraid," he said, "for you are very precious to God.
Peace! Be encouraged! Be strong!"
DANIEL 10:19 NLT

$\mathcal{D}$aniel was a man of strength and character. Taken to the conquering enemy's land, he remained faithful to God, refusing to yield to the pressures around him. He insisted on eating vegetables instead of the rich food of the king, and God blessed him with good health. Daniel would not bow down before the king, and when Daniel was thrown into the den of lions as punishment, God protected him by closing the lions' mouths.

God continually blessed Daniel with the favor of the king and with the ability to see and interpret visions. Nevertheless, during Daniel's last recorded vision, he confessed that he was afraid and weak. He nearly fainted but was revived and comforted with the strengthening words above.

Faith and commitment to God are as challenging today as they were when Daniel lived. Temptation surrounds us, and even when we obey the Word of God and stand firm, we sometimes grow weak and afraid. Coming face-to-face with the power of God may be even more overwhelming than dealing with the pressures of life. These words spoken to Daniel so long ago are words that still apply to us today. Are you afraid, troubled, or weak? Do not fear. Be at peace. Take heart and be strong. You are deeply loved by God!

Dear Lord, thank You for Your love and mercy.
Please give me Your peace and strength today. Amen.

OUTSIDE OF TIME

*"Only I can tell you the future before it even happens.
Everything I plan will come to pass, for I do whatever I wish."*
ISAIAH 46:10 NLT

Time ticks away, fleeting past as we go about our busy day. How often have you wished time would stop—stand still for moments, hours, or even days? It's normal to want to capture the good times in our lives and hold them tightly.

As an eternal being, God stands outside of time. He *was*, *is*, and always *will be*. We live in the moment—the sliver of time we call today, and that is where our focus often stays. But what if we looked at our lives from God's perspective? He created us to live for all eternity with Him. He didn't intend for us to live our lives here on earth, die, and *then* begin eternity with Him.

Eternity is now! It starts with the realization that your salvation has granted you a never-ending story—a life without end. Sure, you'll leave this earth at some point, but you'll carry on as a child of God with Him forever and ever. You can live outside of time knowing there is really no end to your time with Him.

God, help me to live each day with an eternal focus. Amen.

LISTENING VS. TALKING

"My sheep listen to my voice; I know them, and they follow me."
JOHN 10:27 NIV

It has been said that the Lord gave us two ears and one mouth for a reason: We need to listen twice as much as we speak. However, talking seems to come easier for most of us. Our interaction with others becomes the model for our relationship with the Lord. We can become so busy talking to Him during our prayer time that we forget He has important wisdom to impart to us!

Jesus is our Good Shepherd. As His sheep, we have the ability to distinguish His voice. But are we taking the time to listen? It seems much of our prayer time is devoted to reciting our wish list to God. When we stop and think about it, doesn't God already know our needs before we utter one word? We need to learn to listen more instead of dominating the conversation. God is the One with the answers. He knows all things and possesses the wisdom we yearn for.

Learning to listen takes time. Do not be afraid to sit in silence before the Lord. Read His Word. He will speak softly to your heart. He will impart truth to your hungry soul. He will guide you on the path you should take. Listen.

*Dear Lord, help me learn how to listen and distinguish Your voice.
Grant me time to be silent in Your presence. Speak to my
heart so that I may follow You. Amen.*

PATTERN OF WORDS

*What you heard from me, keep as the pattern of sound teaching,
with faith and love in Christ Jesus.*
2 TIMOTHY 1:13 NIV

Have you ever listened to the conversations going on around you without contributing—not listening so much to the words, but to the pattern of the discussion? A person can tell just from listening whether an exchange will end in argument, laughter, gossip, or a myriad of other possibilities. The way words are shared leads the listener to know what is forthcoming.

If you are involved in the conversation, you can change the course by inserting something encouraging or discouraging. A person's words have great power to subtly shift the direction of any dialogue.

In the Bible, God speaks to us in "patterns of sound words," words we can trust. God uses these words to guide, chastise, and encourage His people. The underlying message throughout the Bible shows God's complete love for His children.

From the beginning in the Garden to the end in a new, heavenly home, God's dialogue with us always consists of His love reaching out to draw us to Him. The truth of God's love was shown when His Word became flesh and Jesus Christ walked among us. Be encouraged in His love and share that assurance with others when their pattern of words becomes discouraged.

*Father, thank You for the words You've given to show us Your love.
Help my conversation to always reflect the reality of Jesus' love. Amen.*

CARE ENOUGH
TO CONFRONT

Better is open rebuke than hidden love.
PROVERBS 27:5 NIV

*F*riendships don't always go smoothly. Some days we're in close accord, sharing the most personal emotions and feeling as if we agreed on everything. Other days, little seems to go right, and misunderstanding easily comes between us.

But even those times of disagreement may benefit friends. Perhaps when friendships aren't so touchy-feely, we can be more honest with each other. The hidden irritants that sometimes crop up in relationships can be confronted and dealt with.

Whatever rebuke we receive, isn't it better from a friend who cares for our feelings than from a stranger or enemy? Even if that friendship remains tense for a while, caring can return. What if that friend neglected to tell us an unpleasant truth we really needed to hear?

Let's listen to the courageous love of friends and avoid those who only want to please. The rebuke we face could change our lives for good.

Lord, I don't need a bunch of yes-women as my friends. Give me relationships with those who care enough to confront me. I need Your truth in all my friendships. Amen.

ONE THING

*One thing I ask of the LORD, this is what I seek: that I may dwell
in the house of the LORD all the days of my life, to gaze upon the
beauty of the LORD and to seek him in his temple.*
PSALM 27:4 NIV

David understood what it takes to "dwell" with God. He continually gazed at God's beauty. At this time, David was living on the run—not in the lavish palace of a king but finding beauty and richness in the starkest of environments.

Do we seek God's beauty in our environment, which is not quite so bleak? Isn't His beauty reflected in the smiling toddler in the grocery store line? What about the church couple who, after fifty years of marriage, still hold hands throughout the service? This is the beauty of God. When we bite into an apple crisp, sweet, and naturally loaded with nourishment, or when we see the grace and agility of a dancer, or listen to the intoxicating notes of a flute—we learn more about God. Where did all this beauty originate? Whose power and creativity is behind it all? Creation points to God's power and awesomeness! Like David, these ordinary things draw us into God's presence, where we can praise Him, enjoying His beauty and greatness all the days of our lives.

*Magnificent Creator, Your greatness and beauty surround me. May my eyes gaze
at You, seeking You, that I may dwell in Your presence continually. Amen.*

GOD OF HOPE

I pray that God, the source of hope, will fill you completely with
joy and peace because you trust in him. Then you will overflow with confident
hope through the power of the Holy Spirit.
ROMANS 15:13 NLT

*I*n our busy, fast-paced lives, we may feel exhausted at times. Our culture fosters frenzy and ignores the need for rest and restoration. Constantly putting out fires and completing tasks, working incessantly, we may feel discouraged and disheartened with life. There is more to life than this, isn't there?

Our God of hope says, *"Yes!"* God desires to fill us to the brim with joy and peace. But to receive this gladness, rest, and tranquillity, we need to have faith in the God who is trustworthy and who says, "Anything is possible if a person believes" (Mark 9:23 NLT). We need to place our confidence in God who, in His timing and through us, will complete that task, mend that relationship, or do whatever it is we need. The key to receiving and living a life of hope, joy, and peace is recounting God's faithfulness out loud, quietly in your heart, and to others. When you begin to feel discouraged, exhausted, and at the end of your rope, *stop*; go before the throne of grace and recall God's faithfulness.

God of hope, I recount your faithfulness to me. Please fill me with your joy and
peace, because I believe you are able to accomplish all things. Amen.

LOSING INTEREST

Do not wear yourself out to get rich; have the wisdom to show restraint.
Cast but a glance at riches, and they are gone, for they will
surely sprout wings and fly off to the sky like an eagle.
PROVERBS 23:4–5 NIV

*E*very season of dangerous weather brings uncertainty. Normally meteorologists can track a storm's progress, but even if everyone is told to evacuate early, not every possession can be taken or protected. The aftermath of hurricanes, tornadoes, floods, and other natural disasters proves that possessions can be gone in seconds.

Some people stake their identities on acquiring possessions. Others live to make names for themselves. Even living for family members and friends can feel unsatisfying and empty.

Having money and possessions isn't wrong. Even having high-priced possessions isn't wrong. But there is something missing when our desire for wealth outweighs our desire for God. We may hold on too tightly to things that don't have eternal value and not cling closely enough to the One who does.

God has asked us to use wisdom as we work for Him. Wisdom plans for the future, but it also recognizes that even plans fail. Finances and storms come and go. Our trust in God can be a firm anchor.

Lord, help me to give back to You what You have given to me. Amen.

FUTILE FAITH?

*"My righteous ones will live by faith. But I will
take no pleasure in anyone who turns away."*
HEBREWS 10:38 NLT

*W*e clean the windows and wash the car, and a day later it rains. We sweep the kitchen floor, and hours later the crunch of cookie crumbs resounds under our feet. Some tasks seem so futile.

So it is with our spiritual life. We pray unceasingly and no answers seem to come, or we work tirelessly and problems entrench us. In frustration we wonder, *Why did this happen? What purpose is there to all of this?* It all seems so pointless.

To the skeptic, logic must pervade every situation. If not, there is no basis for belief. But to the person of faith, logic gives way to faith—especially during the most tumultuous, nonsensical times.

So even when our prayers remain unanswered, we continue to pray. Even when God is silent, we continue to believe. And though we grope for answers, we continue to trust.

When our chaotic lives turn upside down and we labor to find rhyme and reason, God asks us to hold fast to our faith. For no labor of love is pointless, no prayer is futile.

*Dear Lord, please forgive me for allowing my problems to undermine my faith.
I trust in You, knowing that my faith in You is never futile. Amen.*

SHARING TROUBLES
LIGHTENS THEM

Yet it was good of you to share in my troubles. Moreover, as you
Philippians know, in the early days of your acquaintance with the gospel,
when I set out from Macedonia, not one church shared with me in
the matter of giving and receiving, except you only.
PHILIPPIANS 4:14–15 NIV

The three lists hanging on the refrigerator seemed to grow longer every day, but they were a necessity of life. The young mom checked them one more time before herding her kids to the garage. Carpool schedule, after-school activities, the list of home chores for her family.

The tasks would be overwhelming except for the three other families whose names were on the lists. All four stayed in touch and shared transportation and child care. They even helped each other clean. Sharing tasks enabled them to get everything done.

Not even the apostle Paul took on the world alone. As our lives become more hectic and crowded, finding a way to help others—and be helped by them—can open the door to blessings for everyone, including more time with our children and trusted friends, and more rest for our minds, bodies, and souls. God never meant for us to face our days alone.

Father God, You have brought so many good people into my life. Help me
remember to offer my help to them and to ask for help when I need it. Amen.

HONEST FRIENDS

*Perfume and incense bring joy to the heart, and the pleasantness
of one's friend springs from his earnest counsel.*
PROVERBS 27:9 NIV

A woman clicked on an e-mail from one of her oldest and best friends.
She had been thinking about this friend and had been meaning to call
her, but it seemed life had just gotten in the way recently. She opened
the e-mail thinking it would contain her friend's usual newsy musings
about family, church, and the latest happenings. Instead, her friend
made the stunning announcement that she believed their friendship
had soured and she was wondering why. She explained that she hadn't
received an e-mail, phone call, or a visit in months, and she wondered if
she had done something—unwittingly—to offend her friend.

After the woman got over her shock, she began to feel defensive.
"She's exaggerating. . .oversensitive. . .completely wrong!" she cried.
A little time and a lot of prayer revealed the truth—that she not only
owed her friend an apology, but she would need to prove her worth as
a friend once again.

God uses our relationships to make us better people, better
Christians. An honest friend full of forgiveness and grace can open
our eyes to our faults so we can then start making positive changes
with God's help. The woman who admonished her friend was a true
friend, and she valued the friendship so much that she was willing to
risk rejection.

Does this kind of friend remind you of anyone?

*Thank You, Jesus, for the example You have set for a true friend.
Help me to be a better friend as I follow You. Amen.*

CONTENTMENT
IN CHRIST

But godliness with contentment is great gain.
I TIMOTHY 6:6 KJV

In the midst of a conversation, the young woman was caught up short.

"Will you ever be content?" her friend asked.

"I don't know," she said. "I don't think so. I always want things to be better than they are."

The question echoed as the years passed. A career melted into marriage and motherhood. With each challenge, she worked harder to make things better. Nevertheless, she often felt empty. She wondered if there was a better way to live.

There is. True profit and gain lie not in toiling for money, but in being content with one's situation.

How can we learn contentment?

We must start looking to Jesus. If we take hold of all we have as joint heirs with Christ and as partakers of grace, we will have no desire for the world's riches.

According to the Bible, we are raised up with Jesus and are seated in the heavenly places with Him. We have His constant presence through the indwelling Holy Spirit. He has given us all things that pertain unto life and godliness. What more do we need?

We need a fresh vision for who we are in Christ. Therein we will find contentment.

Father, I am so foolish. I have everything in You, yet I try to find more in the world and in myself. Thank You for the true riches I have through Jesus Christ. Amen.

A COFFEE FILTER

Let no corrupt communication proceed out of your mouth, but that which is good to the use of edifying, that it may minister grace unto the hearers.
EPHESIANS 4:29 KJV

A coffee filter serves an important role in the brewing of a fine cup of coffee. It holds back the bitter grounds while allowing the soothing, aromatic drops of rich coffee to flow into the pot. When you remove the filter, it contains nothing but soggy, dirty coffee grounds that no longer serve any good purpose.

Imagine what would be found if a filter were placed over your mouth to capture all that is distasteful before it left your lips. How full would that filter become before the day ended?

Our Father desires that our words be soothing and inspiring, never bitter or distasteful. In fact, His message of love cannot flow from a bitter mouth. We can ask the Holy Spirit to be our filter in order to keep the bitter grounds out of the tasty brew that God intends to come forth from our mouths. With the filter of the Holy Spirit in place, He can use us to bring His message of love to those around us.

Heavenly Father, please forgive my harsh and bitter words of the past. Help me to use a fresh filter on my tongue each day so I may bring Your comfort and joy to those whose lives I touch. Amen.

MISUNDERSTOOD?

*[Martha] said to Him, "Yes, Lord, I believe that You are the Christ,
the Son of God, who is to come into the world."*
JOHN 11:27 NKJV

*W*hen we think of Martha, we remember Jesus telling her to pay
more attention to spiritually important things than to her preparations
for guests. Or perhaps we remember that she questioned Jesus about
why He didn't arrive in time to save her brother's life. Based on these
events, most people probably remember Martha as something of a
spiritual failure.

But do we remember that even before Jesus' death, this woman
understood just who Jesus was? Many religious leaders of her day
hadn't a clue—or they only began to understand after the Resurrection.
Martha wasn't as spiritually unsophisticated as we often consider her.

Like Martha, we may be misunderstood—people might assume
that because we're single we can't be in charge of the nursery, or
because we're married, our husbands should be considered first for any
important position in the congregation. Or maybe because we've made
one mistake, people have locked us into a certain low level of spiritual
maturity.

Sometimes people's perceptions of us are inaccurate, and that can
hurt. But that shouldn't stop us in our tracks. Jesus knows both our
failures and successes. By His standards, Martha was never a failure—
and neither are we.

*Lord, I believe, and You know where I stand in my faith.
Don't let me be distracted by what others think of me. Amen.*

The Sin of Sloth

Whatever your hand finds to do, do it with all your might.
ECCLESIASTES 9:10 NIV

*D*id you ever wonder why some people, though blessed with health and stamina, fail to perform their responsibilities or carry their load in the workplace while others less fortified accomplish twice as much?

The book of Proverbs calls it laziness and defines slothful persons as those who procrastinate (6:9–10), fail to finish what they start (12:27), and follow the least difficult course of action (20:4).

The Bible gives us a simple solution to conquer the sin of sloth. Namely, God admonishes us to do our best in whatever task we undertake, no matter how large or menial the job. A strong work ethic emerges from steadfastness and a determination to give our all.

Theodore Roosevelt once said, "It is only through labor and painful effort, by grim energy and resolute courage that we move on to better things." Only as God's people are faithful in the small tasks can He move them forward to greater things.

As we give our best, God returns the gesture. He blesses us with a centered life, a successful career, and a more meaningful, productive existance.

Dear Jesus, Please forgive me for the times I have been guilty of the sin of slothfulness. Empower and remind me to give my best in everything I do, just as You give Your best to me. Amen.

IN HIS ARMS

I will both lay me down in peace, and sleep:
for thou, LORD, only makest me dwell in safety.
PSALM 4:8 KJV

$\mathcal{S}$ally read until her eyes could no longer stay open. She closed her book, shut off the light, and let her head sink into the comfort of her pillow.

As her eyes closed, Sally's mind began to roam free. *Will seven hours be enough sleep tonight? Lord, can You make sure I'm up by six tomorrow morning? I didn't get nearly enough done today. . . . I wonder if my car will pass inspection next month. I can't afford a new one. What if it doesn't pass? Maybe I could borrow some money. . . .*

Sally shook her head, frustrated at the turn of her thoughts, the worries that crept in, fueling insecurities and fears. *This will not do!*

She rose up and turned her light back on. Reaching for her Bible, Sally opened up to a favorite verse—Psalm 4:8: "Lay me down in peace, and sleep. . .makest me dwell in safety." The words turned over and over in her mind. She smiled, closed her Bible, and turned off the light. Letting God's Word saturate her mind, Sally fell asleep, cradled in His arms.

Don't let the thoughts of days past and future keep you from catching those forty winks. Fall asleep in God's Word, rest easy, and rise refreshed.

God, with Your Word in my thoughts, I can lie down in peace and sleep. You will keep me safe, now and forever, as I rest and then rise in Your power. Amen.

PERSISTENCE

*"For the past twenty-three years. . .the LORD has been giving me his messages.
I have faithfully passed them on to you."*
JEREMIAH 25:3 NLT

The Bible is full of persistent people, people who persevered despite problems and difficulties, long after the time most people would consider such persistence wise. Noah spent one hundred years building the ark. Abraham waited twenty-five years for Isaac, the son of promise. And by the end of his life, Jeremiah had preached God's message to an unbelieving audience for forty years. Israelites called him a traitor, threw him in prison, and left him to die, but he continued preaching God's message. Nothing slowed him down.

Jeremiah's faith enabled him to persevere. The writer of Hebrews could have had Jeremiah in mind when he wrote, "Still others were chained and put in prison. . . . They went about. . .destitute, persecuted and mistreated—the world was not worthy of them" (Hebrews 11:36–38 NIV).

God expects the same persistence of us. He calls for persistence, also known as perseverance, over a dozen times in the New Testament. He means for the trials that come our way to increase our perseverance. When we successfully pass small hurdles, He may put bigger ones in our way. Why? Because He doesn't love us? No—because He does.

Persistence results in faith that is pure, molten gold.

*Lord, we can only persist because You are unchanging.
We pray that we will keep our eyes fixed on You and keep moving forward,
regardless of what happens around us. Amen.*

SHATTERED GLASS

But he was pierced for our transgressions. . .by his wounds we are healed.
ISAIAH 53:5 NIV

*B*renda stepped outside for her morning walk and discovered that someone had partied in the night and thrown bottles into the middle of her street. Glass had shattered helter-skelter across the road. Concerned for children in bare feet and for passing motorists, Brenda grabbed a broom and began sweeping up the glass.

As she swept, she thought about how people's lives are like shattered glass. Out of brokenness, we often jab others with the jagged edges of unhealed wounds. Brenda recalled a colleague who proudly invited office personnel to her daughter's wedding. Everyone was excited except for one person who said, "I don't do weddings." The statement immediately dampened the joyful atmosphere. The comment was not meant to hurt, but it did. The comment reflected the speaker's own deep hurt and shattered dreams.

As a child, Brenda had loved to go to Disneyland and watch the glassblowers in Fantasyland. The craftsmen deftly shaped fragments of colored glass into charming creatures that delighted onlookers. In much the same way, our heavenly Father patiently waits for us to come to Him with the fragments of our shattered lives. For "He was pierced for our transgressions," and it is "by His wounds we are healed" (Isaiah 53:5 NIV). When we bring our brokenness to the foot of the cross, He provides a life-giving transfusion, healing the hurt and shaping His children into healthy, whole vessels.

Lord, I bring my shattered remnants and broken dreams to the foot of the cross.
Bring healing and wholeness to my life. Amen.

ANY OTHER NAME

*By faith Moses, when he had grown up, refused to be known as the son
of Pharaoh's daughter. He chose to be mistreated along with the people
of God rather than to enjoy the pleasures of sin for a short time. He regarded
disgrace for the sake of Christ as of greater value than the treasures of Egypt,
because he was looking ahead to his reward.*
HEBREWS 11:24–26 NIV

Mary grew up hearing the labels the world put on her: unwanted trash, orphan, illegitimate, scum. It wasn't easy living in no fewer than a dozen foster homes and being shuffled from school to school. She had no close friends, no family ties, and—worse yet—no identity.

Mary eventually was adopted at age eleven by a loving couple. They offered her the attention, love, and understanding she needed to feel she belonged. Mary's parents introduced their faith to her, and soon she began to find her identity in the family of God.

As a teenager, Mary volunteered at an after-school program for at-risk kids. She spent time playing with and tutoring many students who were orphans or who came from abusive situations. Many of the kids wanted to know why she wasn't sad or angry that her biological parents didn't want her.

"Biological parents take what they get," she would explain, "but my parents chose me. They weren't the only ones to choose me, either. God chose to be my heavenly Father. I'm His kid, too, and He'll love me forever."

Lord, thank You for being my family. Amen.

PRICEY OR
PRICELESS?

O LORD, you preserve both man and beast. How priceless is your unfailing love!
PSALM 36:6–7 NIV

After her introduction, the keynote speaker assumed her place behind the microphone.

"This is the first time I've attended this conference as a speaker and not a listener. So I thought I'd splurge and buy a new suit," Megan said. She told how she had gone to an upscale women's clothing store for the first time in her life. Although she wasn't used to such pampering and accessorizing by a sales associate, the clerk had found her the perfect outfit.

"And it's on sale!" the sales clerk gushed.

"Really?"

"Twenty-nine ninety-five!"

Megan couldn't believe her good luck. "You're kidding! Thirty dollars?"

The sales woman's face contorted slightly. She lowered her voice. "No, miss. That would be $2,995."

Megan stepped out from behind the podium and waved her hand down the front of her suit.

"This," she said to her audience, "is not that suit."

Those of us in the audience that day don't remember Megan's keynote speech. But we remember the story of her suit.

Many things in life are pricey. Name-brand clothing, cars—even cosmetics. But they will wear out or be used up before long, no matter what the price tag. By contrast, God's preserving, unfailing love is priceless. His amazing love was costly, but it's not pricey.

Thank You, Father, that no price tag can be put on
Your lavish love for me and for all of creation. Amen.

THREE LITTLE WORDS

"Why do you look for the living among the dead? He is not here; he has risen!"
LUKE 24:5–6 NIV

The car ride home was a solemn one. In a formal graduation ceremony, the Fisher family had presented Arbor, a guide dog raised in their home since a small pup, to his new nineteen-year-old blind partner, Jon.

Six months earlier, Arbor had been recalled to Guide Dogs for the Blind for formal training before being matched to a blind student. The Fishers knew that Arbor would help Jon achieve the independent life he desired, yet saying good-bye was still hard. They felt a keen loss. Most likely, they would never see Arbor again.

The very next day, Jon's mother sent them an e-mail. "Jon walked Arbor to his friend's house," she wrote. "I can't even remember the last time he had the confidence to make that walk."

With that piece of news, their focus changed completely. In just twenty-four hours, Arbor was changing Jon's life. Loss was transformed into gain.

The right information, at just the right time, can be powerful.

Two thousand years ago, imagine how those women felt as they arrived at Jesus' tomb to anoint His body with spices. They focused on loss, heads bowed low, until the triumphant angel interrupted their mourning with the greatest words ever declared: "He is not here. He has risen!"

Three little words, "Jesus has risen!" and loss was transformed into gain.

Giver of all that is good, help me to keep praying, to joyfully expect the best. Remind me to focus on Your end to this world's story. Amen.

THE PROMISE OF JOY

Weeping may endure for a night, but joy cometh in the morning.
PSALM 30:5 KJV

Have you experienced suffering? Perhaps you are hurting even now. Tough times are a reality for all of us.

The psalmist David was well acquainted with hardship. He used phrases such as "the depths," "the pit," and even "the grave" to describe them. Although he was known as a man after God's own heart, at times David was pursued by his enemies and forced to run for his life. He also lived with the consequences of committing murder and adultery, even long after receiving God's forgiveness.

God is faithful, and suffering is temporary. This is a promise we can claim, as David did, when facing difficulty or depression. David experienced God's faithfulness throughout the ups and downs of his life.

King Solomon, one of the wisest men who ever lived, concludes in the third chapter of Ecclesiastes that there is a time for everything, including "a time to weep and a time to laugh" (v. 4 NIV).

Some trials are short-lived. Others are more complex. As believers, we can find joy in the Lord even as certain trials remain a backdrop in our lives. All suffering will end one day when we meet Jesus. The Bible assures us that in Heaven there will be no tears.

Your loving heavenly Father has not forgotten you. You may feel that relief will never come, but take courage. It will.

God, where there is anguish in my life, may Your joy enter in. I ask for grace to face my trials, knowing that in time You will replace weeping with joy. Amen.

REFLECTIONS OF LIGHT

*"Arise, shine, for your light has come,
and the glory of the LORD rises upon you."*
ISAIAH 60:1 NIV

*G*od said, "Light, be," and light came into existence. Light appeared from the lips of God so He could see all He was about to create—and His creation could see Him.

When you gave your heart to God, His light came on inside your heart. Christianity lives from the inside out. When your heart is right, then your actions truly portray the influence that God and His Word have in your life.

Your life should then begin to reflect the character and nature of the One who created you and should oppose all darkness. You are a reflection of His light to everyone around you. From within, you shine on the lives of others around you and become a light to the world.

As you point others to God, to His light—His goodness, mercy, and love—your light shines, repelling darkness and giving comfort to everyone God brings across your path.

How encouraging to know your life can brighten the whole room. You have the power to open the door of people's hearts for the Holy Spirit to speak to them about their own salvation. Don't miss a moment to let your life shine!

Jesus, show me what I can do and say to let my light shine brightly. Amen.

ALWAYS SEARCHING, NEVER SETTLED

For of this sort are they which creep into houses, and lead captive silly women laden with sins, led away with divers lusts, ever learning, and never able to come to the knowledge of the truth.
2 TIMOTHY 3:6–7 KJV

"I am strong. . .I am invincible. . .I am woman."

Since women first uttered this mantra in the 1970s, Christian women have come to embrace it. If the world's woman is strong, we reason, God's woman is stronger still.

But that's not what God says. While He desires us to be women of strength, He says some women are silly. Silly women are those who listen to the wrong voices and can't make up their minds.

We are silly when we are so open-minded that we believe things we know are too good to be true—a slick sales pitch, the false teaching of a charismatic leader, or the unexamined claims of someone offering us something larger, better, or easier.

If we are to be truly strong, we must listen to God alone and settle our hearts in the truth of His Word.

Father, I have been confused by many voices in this world. Open my ears to Your voice alone. Settle my heart in Your Word, because I know it is truth. Amen.

Unbroken Promise

In hope of eternal life which God, who cannot lie,
promised before time began.
TITUS 1:2 NKJV

The walkway of our lives is littered with broken promises—both those we've made and those that have been made to us. Each time the commitment was given with wonderful intentions of carrying through, but something happened to make it impossible for the vow to be completed.

When we are the one who breaks the promise, guilt becomes our companion. Knowing we've hurt others is painful. We often vow to ourselves never to make another pledge, yet even that oath isn't kept.

The results of other people's broken promises to us are usually disappointment and hurt. Perhaps we didn't get the raise we counted on or an old friend backed out of a get-together. We feel that the other person lied to us or that we weren't worthy of his or her commitment.

God always keeps His word. The Bible is filled with the promises of God—vows to us that we can trust will be completed. God never lies. Lying is not in Him. He sees us as worthy of His commitment.

The promise of eternal life—given even before time began—is one of God's most wonderful gifts. No matter how disappointed we are with ourselves or with others, we only have to look at the pledge God has made to be filled with a heart of praise and gladness.

God, thank You that Your Word is trustworthy and true.
Praise You for the promise of eternal life. Amen.

SHARING OUR LIVES

We loved you so much that we shared with you
not only God's Good News but our own lives, too.
1 THESSALONIANS 2:8 NLT

*W*hy do people choose to spend time with other people? Perhaps taking an important client out for dinner will seal a big business deal. High school students may choose their friends based on popularity status. Unfortunately, loneliness drives some women to seek the companionship of the wrong type of men. The greatest motivator for the development of any relationship, however, is love.

Paul says in this verse that he and Timothy loved the Thessalonians so much that they shared their lives with them. A popular Christian song a few years back had the following lyrics *"People need the Lord. When will we realize that we must give our lives, for people need the Lord?"* Paul realized that, didn't he? He knew that investing in the lives of others and sharing his life with them were important aspects of leading them to the Lord.

Unbelievers may hear Christians talk about Jesus. What they may not experience is unconditional love from those who call themselves Christ followers. This week, practice sharing your life with those around you. Through reaching out in friendship to those around you, doors may be opened for you to share the gospel as well.

God, help me to share my life with those around me.
Let others see Jesus in the way I live and the way I love. Amen.

CONTAGIOUS LAUGHTER

*And Sarah said, "God has made me laugh,
and all who hear will laugh with me."*
GENESIS 21:6 NKJV

Nothing brings more joy to our hearts than when God blesses our lives. Like Sarah, we may at first laugh with disbelief when God promises us our heart's desire. For some reason, we doubt that He can do what we deem impossible. Yet God asks us, as He did Sarah, "Is anything too hard for the LORD?" (Genesis 18:14 NKJV).

Then when the blessings shower down upon us, we overflow with joy. Everything seems bright and right with the world. With God, the impossible has become a reality. We bubble over with laughter, and when we laugh, the world laughs with us! It's contagious!

When Satan bombards us with lies—"God's not real"; "You'll never get that job"; "Mr. Right? He'll never come along"—it's time to look back at God's Word and remember Sarah. Imbed in your mind the truth that with God, nothing is impossible (see Matthew 19:26). And then, in the midst of the storm, in the darkness of night, in the crux of the trial, laugh, letting the joy of God's truth be your strength.

*Oh God, Your Word says that You will give us the desires of our hearts
(Psalm 37:4). I trust in that, Lord. I trust in Your Word. I believe You
can do the seemingly impossible. Help me to rest in that assurance
and to laugh with Sarah, who was given her heart's desire. Amen.*

MIRIAM:
A GIFTED LEADER

*Miriam the prophetess, the sister of Aaron, took a timbrel in her hand;
and all the women went out after her with timbrels and with dances.
And Miriam answered them, Sing ye to the LORD, for he hath triumphed
gloriously; the horse and his rider hath he thrown into the sea.*
EXODUS 15:20–21 KJV

*M*oses' older sister, Miriam, kept careful watch over her baby brother as he floated in a basket among the bulrushes. When Pharaoh's daughter found him, the quick-thinking girl asked the princess if she needed a nurse for the crying baby—and brought their own mother! Because Miriam took the initiative, Moses survived cruel Egyptian edicts, staying with his own family during his early years before Pharaoh's daughter claimed him as her son.

But Miriam played other key roles as an adult. A prophetess, she spoke God's messages to His people, a solemn responsibility. Miriam also excelled in the arts. When God brought Israel safely through the Red Sea, she led thousands of women in dancing, playing timbrels, and singing praise to Him. Like many strong, godly women, she struggled with ego issues, especially in relation to her little brother. But God used Miriam to help Moses lead Israel through the wilderness.

*Lord God, thank You for Miriam's example. Help me use the leadership gifts
You have given me to bless Your people and help them grow. Amen.*

God's Business or Busyness?

Solid food is for those who are mature, who through training
have the skill to recognize the difference between right and wrong.
HEBREWS 5:14 NLT

As growing Christians, we want to improve our faith, moving from the milk of easy spiritualism to the solid food of real faith. So we study our Bibles even when we'd rather not, make time for prayer in a busy schedule, and take on more church projects than really fit into our lives.

But sometimes even all those spiritual disciplines don't give us exactly what we want. We end up feeling dried out, like a creek bed during a drought.

Maybe, for all our busyness, we're not quite going about God's business. The Bible encourages us to do good works. But the description of a mature believer in this verse doesn't focus on how she has filled her calendar, but on her ability to distinguish good from evil.

Sometimes distractions look so good. They may be dressed up in their Sunday clothes and sitting in church. But even in God's house, disruptions of His will or outright sins exist. Living in faith is a challenge, even within a spiritual congregation.

Mature faith relies more on living as God wants us to live than on filling our calendars to overflowing. Are we just doing good things or doing the things God wants us to do?

Lord, help me fill my days with Your will,
not all the works that come my way. Amen.

STOP ANALYZING

*I press on to reach the end of the race and receive the heavenly
prize for which God, through Christ Jesus, is calling us.*
PHILIPPIANS 3:14 NLT

𝒥udy lay awake recounting all the conversations she'd had at the office
that day, *Was I too harsh when I made that comment? What if Jerry misunderstood
what I said? What about the decision to move forward on the Tyson account? Was
that too. . . ?* Judy's mind was racing with questions, overanalyzing the
decisions and commitments she made at work and in her personal life
that week.

Suddenly, her sister's words came back to her. "You pray every day
for God to help you do the very best you can. Don't you trust Him
to complete that work?" Her sister was right, and she was wasting
precious time when she could be getting some much needed sleep. She
slipped down beside her bed and kneeled to ask God to help her let go
of thoughts that seemed to hold her captive each night.

As women, we often want to cover our bases, assuring ourselves
that our decisions are right, but we must not lose ourselves in the
analysis. Find your strength in the leadership of the Holy Spirit and
then relax and enjoy peaceful sleep.

*Lord, help me to trust You in the decisions I make throughout my day. Help me
to stop second-guessing myself and trust who You created me to be. Amen.*

REJECTION

*Cleanse thou me from secret faults. Keep back
thy servant also from presumptuous sins.*
PSALM 19:12–13 KJV

Sarah and Walt had struggled with infertility for some years before they finally had their first daughter. Not until Bethany was a very young toddler did they take their first extended trip without her. Sarah's best friend, Ann, and her family kept Bethany with them for the week. They loved having a little one in the house for all of them to spoil! By the end of the weeklong trip, Sarah was almost tearful in anticipation of seeing Bethany again.

When Sarah arrived at Ann's house, she eagerly reached for her daughter. Bethany took one look at her mother then turned away from Sarah and clung to Ann. Sarah understood Bethany's reaction—but the understanding didn't make her daughter's initial rejection hurt any less.

When we knowingly sin against God, we're often hesitant to seek His face for forgiveness. Even in those rare instances when we sin in ignorance, we must still humble ourselves before Him. But we never need fear that He'll turn away from us. God will never say to us, "I won't let you hurt me like that again." Whenever we reach for Him, He eagerly receives us. Such total forgiveness should bring us running back to Him on a daily basis.

*Heavenly Father, forgive me for both secret and presumptuous sins.
Help me to live consistently as a godly woman. Amen.*

TRUST TEST

Hear my prayer, O LORD, and let my cry come to You.
PSALM 102:1 NKJV

*H*ave you had days when your prayers seemed to hit the ceiling and bounce back? Does God seem distant for no reason you're aware of? Chances are good that if you've been a Christian for more than a short time, you've experienced this.

The psalmist experienced it as pain and suffering became his lot. At night insomnia plagued him. During his tired days, enemies taunted him. His was a weary life, and in earthly terms, he hardly could see the outcome.

But once the psalmist described his plight, his psalm turned in a new direction, glorifying God. Suddenly, life wasn't so bad anymore because he trusted in the One who would save him.

When prayer hits the ceiling, it's time to remind ourselves of God's greatness, not complain about what we think He hasn't done. As we face trials that threaten to undo us, let's remind ourselves that He has not forgotten us, and our ultimate security is never at risk.

As we feel the dangers of life, let's trust that God is still listening to our prayers. He will never fail us. All He asks is that our reliance on Him remains firm. At the right hour, we'll feel His love again.

Even when I don't feel Your presence, Lord, You have not deserted me.
Keep me trusting and following You, O Lord. Amen.

HELP FOR THE TOUGH TIMES

"I will not leave you as orphans; I will come to you."
JOHN 14:18 NIV

Joan stared at the envelope in her hand. Another wedding invitation, this time from her cousin's daughter. She set it aside, annoyed that it made her feel so alone.

Joan knew all too well that she was *not* alone. Her days were filled with work, church commitments, and the buzz of her two teenagers in and out of the house. Friends constantly dropped by just to chat or help themselves to coffee. Sometimes her days were nonstop from dawn to bedtime, leaving her barely enough time to breathe.

Yet the loneliness created by her husband's death never quite left her, no matter how active her life. There were times Joan struggled to move on to the next task, the next responsibility, when all she wanted to do was grieve. Only when she remembered God's promise to always be there did she feel any relief.

God never, ever abandons us. No matter how busy we are, He never forgets us. He promised his followers that He would always help and support them, a promise He still keeps today.

Lord, You sent your Holy Spirit as a helper and guide.
No matter how tough our world becomes, let us remember
Your presence in our lives. Amen.

SOUL
SATISFACTION

All my longings lie open before you, O Lord; my sighing
is not hidden from you. . . . My soul thirsts for God.
PSALM 38:9; 42:2 NIV

Trina found herself sighing again. She couldn't help it—it seemed as if the weight of the world was on her shoulders, but she wasn't able to pinpoint exactly what it was that troubled her so.

But God knew exactly what her sighs were all about. He knew the weight on her heart. She couldn't verbalize it to anyone. These deep longings pressed in on Trina as she tossed and turned at night. She prayed that they'd subside or that God would provide a distraction—or better yet, satisfy this longing deep within once and for all, whatever it was.

Scripture guided Trina to the heart of the problem. "My soul thirsts for the living God." She could think of several troubling issues that worried her, and she had cried out to God to fix them—the finances, the car, and broken relationships. But, really, she needed more of Him—more of His presence, His Word, His consolation, His hope. Nothing material or relational would fill the void—just her living God, breathing fresh life into her aching soul.

Holy Comforter, fill my deepest longings with Your quenching presence.
Keep me looking only to You for soul satisfaction. Amen.

JOY IS JESUS

*And even though you do not see [Jesus] now, you believe in him
and are filled with an inexpressible and glorious joy, for you are
receiving the goal of your faith, the salvation of your souls.*
1 PETER 1:8–9 NIV

As children we find joy in the smallest things: a rose in bloom,
a ladybug at rest, the circles a pebble makes when dropped in water.
Then somewhere between pigtails and pantyhose, our joy wanes and
eventually evaporates in the desert of difficulties.

But when we find Jesus, "all things become new" as the Bible
promises, and once again, we view the world through a child's eyes.
Excitedly, we experience the "inexpressible and glorious joy" that
salvation brings.

We learn that God's joy isn't based on our circumstances; rather,
its roots begin with the seed of God's Word planted in our hearts.
Suddenly, our hearts spill over with joy, knowing that God loves and
forgives us and that He is in complete control of our lives. We have joy
because we know this world is not our permanent home and a mansion
awaits us in glory.

Joy comes as a result of whom we trust, not in what we have. Joy
is Jesus.

*Dear Jesus, thank You for giving me the joy of my salvation.
Knowing You surpasses anything and everything else the world offers.
Never allow the joy in my heart to evaporate in the desert of difficulties. Amen.*

REMEMBERING
TO FORGET

*J*essica Shaver and her two brothers grew up with a strong, critical father. Nothing any of them ever did pleased him. In frustration, one brother left home as a teenager. The other withdrew into his own world. When Jessica became a Christian, her father rejected her. He thwarted Jessica's attempts at reconciliation.

Then Alzheimer's disease changed everything.

Jessica's dad's crusty strength deteriorated into frequent weeping. Did he take cream in his coffee? What happened to his vast book knowledge? What was Jessica's name again? Mostly, Jessica's aging father forgot past hurts.

After a thirty-five year hiatus, the three grown children came together to spend a day with their memory-debilitated father. Jessica saw her father grasp his estranged son in a bear hug. He reached for his younger son. He called Jessica to join in their (first ever) group hug. Her dad had forgotten the years of separation. He had forgotten that he had cruelly rejected his children. With no memory of the years of hurt he had caused, he joyfully embraced his grown children.

Some things we need to remember. Others we need to forget. When we can put away past hurts, we look more like our forgiving Father. When the Lord provides unexpected healing in fractured relationships, we can thank Him for such marvelous grace.

Lord God, I praise You for the blessedness of forgotten hurts. Amen.

ADVICE FROM MOM

Quiet down before GOD, be prayerful before him.
PSALM 37:7 THE MESSAGE

*P*eggy's mother lived overseas, so when she visited, it was for lengthy stretches. She had an opportunity to see Peggy's life on a daily basis. In particular, she noted how busy Peggy was with six children heading off in six different directions.

"You sign these children up for too many activities," complained her mother. "Life was never this busy when you were growing up."

"Maybe not," Peggy replied. "But when I was growing up, there were school buses to take kids home from school. And sports weren't as serious for kids as they are now."

"But how will they ever learn to be still?" her mother asked.

Peggy had a nagging feeling that there was wisdom in her mother's observation. She had assumed that it was part of her job as a mom to provide opportunities for her children to develop skills and talents. She decided to limit each child to one activity during the school year.

"Be still and know that I am God," urged the psalmist. How can our children learn to be quiet and meditate on God's Word when their schedules are hectic and every minute is committed? It's easy to crowd out the things that matter most to God: worshiping Him, listening to Him, and seeking His presence.

Heavenly Father, as my children grow up, I pray they will learn not just how to stay busy but how to stay still. And within that stillness to hear Your quiet voice. Amen.

LIVING A LIFE
OF FORGIVENESS

Be kind and compassionate to one another,
forgiving each other, just as in Christ God forgave you.
EPHESIANS 4:32 NIV

*C*hristina recalls that when she would recite the Lord's Prayer she would omit the words, "And forgive us our debts as we forgive our debtors." With all she had been through in life, it was so difficult to say those few words. However, even though Christina was a Christian, she could not be fully used by the Lord until she forgave and began living a life of forgiveness.

Our God in Christ has forgiven us. Jesus, as He was dying on the cross for our sins, spoke the words, "Father, forgive them" (Luke 23:34 NIV). As we come to understand what Christ has done for us, we become more willing to forgive. That does not mean forgiveness is easy. However, forgiveness is not impossible with help from the Lord Jesus.

As believers, we have the Spirit of God within us, "who is able, through his mighty power at work within us, to accomplish infinitely more than we might ask or think" (Ephesians 3:20 NLT). The Lord desires for us to have relationships founded on kindness, tenderheartedness, and forgiveness. As we, through the Holy Spirit in us, are able to live this kind of life, we model Christ to others. Our purpose in life is to become more like Him. Why not begin today by living a life of forgiveness?

Forgiving Lord, I desire to be more like You. Enable me to forgive
those who have hurt me and to live a life of forgiveness. Amen.

Spiritual Health

"If your right eye causes you to sin, gouge it out and throw it away."
Matthew 5:29 niv

$\mathcal{D}$ianne was an extremely responsible person who worked hard. At one point in her career, she realized she had been working far too hard. She worked such long hours that she began skimping on her quiet time. The more she skimped on time in the Word and prayer, the more she became impatient about her work responsibilities.

She called out in frustration, "I hate working in this place!" Her emotional and spiritual deficit stemmed from allowing overwork to supersede spiritual health.

Jesus said in Matthew that if some part of your body causes you to sin, you should tear it out (5:29). If you work so hard at your job that you don't have time for God, then alter your responsibilities, hours, or perspectives on your work *immediately*.

You cannot minister to others when you are spiritually bankrupt. Effective ministry emerges from vast resources bestowed upon you as the Lord shapes you through quiet, contemplative prayer, Bible study, and the voice of the Holy Spirit—not from a frenetic lifestyle. A frenetic lifestyle *distorts*; whereas, a balanced, spiritually nourished lifestyle *shapes* one into the image of God.

O God, assist me in keeping life balanced so that my
walk with You might be first and foremost. Amen.

JUST DO IT

Be joyful in hope, patient in affliction, faithful in prayer.
ROMANS 12:12 NIV

*T*he words seem to readily roll off our tongues, "I'll be praying for you." Words may come easy, yet are we faithful to actually pray? Praying for someone is different than simply thinking about them or wishing them well. Prayer is hard work because it requires time and discipline. Prayer is spiritual warfare.

Whenever we commit to pray for someone, the enemy schemes to prevent it. Why? Even Satan knows that prayer unleashes God's power. Prayer is a spiritual weapon at our disposal. It has the power to demolish strongholds and defeat Satan. Prayer gives us access into the spiritual realm so we can communicate with our heavenly Father through Jesus Christ, His Son. We claim the promises and victory we have been given. We submit our hearts and ask that God's will be done.

Nothing draws us closer to other people than praying for them. Asking for God's intervention in their lives is an awesome privilege. We experience matchless rejoicing when our prayers are answered. We may not understand how, yet we realize that somehow our prayers have made a difference. Let's not just promise to pray for someone. Let's be faithful to do it!

Dear Lord, often I have good intentions to pray for others but fail to follow through. Help me to be faithful in prayer so that I may see Your power at work.
Amen.

AN EXHORTATION

Then David continued, "Be strong and courageous, and do the work.
Don't be afraid or discouraged, for the LORD God, my God, is with you.
He will not fail you or forsake you."
1 CHRONICLES 28:20 NLT

*I*n 1 Chronicles 28:20, King David has just given his son Solomon and the people of Israel detailed instructions for building the Lord's temple. Can you imagine how awed and overwhelmed the people felt as they heard the plans for the temple's design? First Kings 5 and 6 tells us that it took *tens of thousands* of skilled workmen *seven years* to complete the temple! No wonder David exhorted his people to be strong and courageous! No wonder he urged them to resist discouragement and fear!

God knew His people could complete the undertaking He had set before them, but He also knew they would be overwhelmed by the enormity of the task. Perhaps you, too, are feeling disheartened by the sheer size of your responsibilities. Maybe you feel like giving up. David's words still offer us encouragement in the face of the seemingly insurmountable: Be strong and courageous! Do the work! Don't be afraid or discouraged by the size of the task. The Lord God is with you, and He will not fail you or forsake you!

Dear Lord, give me strength and courage to do the work You have called me to do. Take away my fear and discouragement, and help me to lean on You. Amen.

ARE YOU GETTING SQUEEZED?

By his divine power, God has given us everything we need for living a godly life.
2 PETER 1:3 NLT

*D*oes your schedule ever get so full you feel like you can't breathe? Maybe your boss demands meeting on top of meeting, or your children's extracurricular activities have you going in circles. Somehow you keep moving forward, not always sure where the strength comes from, but thankful in the end that you made it through the day.

In those situations, you're not just stretching your physical body to the limit but your mind and emotions as well. Stress can make you feel like a grape in a winepress. The good news is that God has given you everything you need, but it's up to you to utilize the wisdom He has provided. Don't be afraid to say no when you feel you just can't add one more thing to your to-do list. Limit your commitments, ask someone to take notes for you in a meeting you can't make, or carpool with someone who shares your child's extracurricular activity.

Alleviate the pressure where you can and then know that God's power will make up for the rest.

Lord, help me to do what I can do; and I'll trust
You to do for me those things that I can't do. Amen.

BELONGING

A wife belongs to her husband instead of to herself,
and a husband belongs to his wife instead of to himself.
1 CORINTHIANS 7:4 CEV

Shawna grinned as she finished lettering "I Love You" in ketchup atop the heart-shaped meatloaf. Wouldn't Glen be pleased with his Valentine surprise?

She thought back to last year, their first Valentine's Day as a married couple. She'd rushed home from work to create a heart-shaped pizza, tomato sauce creating a fitting crimson background for black olives forming the words, "Forever Yours." Glen hadn't even noticed as he wolfed down a slice with one eye on the ballgame blaring from the television.

Later that evening, Shawna had given Glen her carefully selected gift: an autographed jersey of his favorite player. He'd presented her with a baking dish. He seemed completely flabbergasted when she burst into tears.

She knew things would be better this Valentine's Day. After she'd lovingly explained how his insensitivity hurt her, Glen had diligently turned off the TV during meals to give her his undivided attention. For holidays, he'd selected personal gifts that demonstrated forethought.

Suddenly, Glen burst through the door carrying a mop tied with an enormous red bow. Laughing, they wrapped their arms around each other, and Glen reached behind her neck to clasp a necklace with a dangling silver heart pendant.

Lover of my soul, thank You for soul mates here on earth.
Give us loving patience to learn to belong to each other. Amen.

AN UNCHANGING BOSS

*The sleep of a laborer is sweet, whether he eats little or much,
but the abundance of a rich man permits him no sleep.*
ECCLESIASTES 5:12 NIV

God created work to be good! Even before the Fall, Adam and Eve worked. God told them to care for the Garden of Eden, name the animals, and even rule over the area. Only after sin entered the picture did Adam and Eve come to realize that their work was no longer 100 percent enjoyable but quite difficult at times.

The earth's soil refused to cooperate, and weeds immediately sprang up. Pain from childbearing intensified, and later Cain would kill his brother Abel. With an ancestral history such as this, how are present-day Christians supposed to enjoy and profit from the work we do?

A key factor behind our work is not our identity but our motivation. When Adam and Eve worked, they were working for God. Just because sin entered the world doesn't mean we have a different boss. God doesn't require us to be slaves. In fact, He allows us to take a righteous pride in the work we do for Him. Our projects and daily tasks are a reflection of what we can give back to Him.

*Lord, thank You for giving me the work I have.
Give me a passion for reflecting You in it. Amen.*

CHECKLIST

*I am glad to be weak or insulted or mistreated or to have troubles
and sufferings, if it is for Christ. Because when I am weak, I am strong.*
2 CORINTHIANS 12:10 CEV

The apostle Paul suffered from an unknown "thorn in the flesh."
He begged God to take it away. He didn't stop asking until God
revealed an important spiritual truth: God's strength is made perfect
in weakness.

Paul searched for words to explain this principle to the Christians
at Corinth. *What are the things that keep them from serving God? How can I help
them understand that God will use those very weaknesses to make them strong?* He
came up with a checklist.

Weaknesses. What area do we struggle with constantly, whether it is
physical, mental, or emotional?

Insults. What hurtful things do others say about us, whether true
or not?

Hardships. What physical and financial catastrophes have happened
to us recently?

Persecutions. Do neighbors, family, or coworkers make fun of our
faith?

Calamities. What natural or manmade disasters have impacted our
world?

Paul stopped struggling against his thorn in the flesh when he
realized it was God's gift to make him rely on God's strength. God
wants us to do the same with our weaknesses. Each day we should
check our inventory. Where do we feel weak today? When we turn that
area over to Him, God will demonstrate His strength.

*Christ Jesus, You are all-powerful. Step into our weaknesses, take over, and
demonstrate Your power and care on our behalf. Amen.*

BEST PAYCHECK

"The LORD repay your work, and a full reward
be given you by the LORD God of Israel."
RUTH 2:12 NKJV

Stepping back, the woman reviewed the kitchen she had finished cleaning. The dishes were washed, the cabinets and oven were wiped down, the floors were swept and mopped, and the flowers on the table added a spot of brightness. Her shoulders slumped as she noted the rain and mud outside. Before long her spotless room would need cleaning once again.

Many jobs have to be done over and over, and they become tedious and repetitive—dishes, laundry, vacuuming, dusting. The work doesn't end, and sometimes we get so tired we want to complain about our drudgery. We don't stop to consider how God has given us these chores to teach and perfect us.

When God created the heavens and the earth, He paid great attention to all the little details. Every day, all day, He is there to listen to our needs, to answer prayers over and over. He never complains. He never thinks we aren't worth His effort. He loves being there and providing for us.

We have chosen to seek refuge in the Lord. He has given us a work to do. Sometimes the labor is new and exciting. Sometimes the job is repetitive. Both types are given to us for His purpose. We can look forward to the reward God has for us when we complete the tasks He has set before us.

Thank You, Lord, for the work I can do. Give me joy as I serve. Amen.

POISONOUS DARTS

No man can tame the tongue. It is an unruly evil, full of deadly poison.
JAMES 3:8 NKJV

𝓔llen, the church secretary, sat at the table with three other leaders, waiting for more board members to appear. Her pen poised above the steno pad, she turned off the thoughts careening through her mind and tuned into the pastor saying, "It shouldn't be a long meeting because the list of discussion items is relatively short. We should be out of here in an hour or so."

"Well," said the treasurer, "you know what they say: 'It ain't over till the fat lady sings.'"

The portly pastor, having a good sense of humor, began singing. When he stopped, Ellen, without thinking, said, "No, Pastor, it's not over till the fat *lady* sings." As soon as the dart was thrown and the target hit, Ellen cringed with remorse as an unsettling silence filled the room.

We've all experienced those moments when the words are out of our mouths before we know it. If we would stop and *think* before speaking, we wouldn't hurt the feelings of others as often as we do. As Abe Lincoln said, "Better to remain silent and be thought a fool than to speak out and remove all doubt."

Weigh your words carefully before using them. And if, in those "thoughtless" moments, you've said something you cannot take back, be quick to ask forgiveness.

Dear Lord, I want to glorify You and edify others, not cut them down. Help me to think before I speak, and may my words be filled with compassion and love.
Amen.

AVAILABLE 24/7

I call on you, O God, for you will answer me;
give ear to me and hear my prayer.
PSALM 17:6 NIV

*N*o one is available to take your call at this time, so leave a message and we will
return your call—or not—if we feel like it. . .and only between the hours of 4:00
and 4:30 p.m. Thank you for calling. Have a super day!

We've all felt the frustration of that black hole called voice mail. It
is rare to reach a real, honest-to-goodness, breathing human being the
first time we dial a telephone number.

Fortunately, our God is always available. He can be reached at
any hour of the day or night and every day of the year—including
weekends and holidays! When we pray, we don't have to worry about
disconnections, hang-ups, or poor reception. We will never be put on
hold or our prayers diverted to another department. The Bible assures
us that God is eager to hear our petitions and that he welcomes our
prayers of thanksgiving. The psalmist David wrote of God's response
to those who put their trust in Him: "He will call upon me, and I will
answer him" (Psalm 91:15 NIV). David had great confidence that God
would hear his prayers. And we can, too!

Dear Lord, thank You for always being there for me. Whether I am on a
mountaintop and just want to praise Your name or I am in need of Your
comfort and encouragement, I can count on You. Amen.

MARGIN

*For anyone who enters God's rest also rests from his own work,
just as God did from his. Let us, therefore, make every effort to enter that rest,
so that no one will fall by following their example of disobedience.*
HEBREWS 4:10–11 NIV

Imagine a busy person's planner or calendar. More often than not, it
is bursting with notes and reminders and is well-worn from frequent
use. Seldom is there an opening in the day's schedule for unexpected
things that may arise, let alone a few minutes set aside for rest. But
God instructs us to plan for rest in our schedule and to leave ourselves
some breathing room in order to accommodate last-minute things.

Hebrews 4 refers to the final, eternal rest that we will enter into
with Christ. But in the meantime, we are called to lead an uncluttered
life so we are ready for service to God. We are not to busy ourselves
with the cares of the world, completely filling our margins.

Does your life have a clean margin, or have you filled your page
completely, leaving no room for additions or corrections? Is there
room in your life for the plans God has for you?

*Lord, correct my thinking and clear my clutter. Help me to work a
margin into my day so that Your plans, last-minute notes, corrections,
and additions can find a place in my life. Let me not be so busily focused
on my own agenda that I miss Yours. Amen.*

TREASURE VAULT

"For where your treasure is, there your heart will be also."
LUKE 12:34 NIV

*W*here is your greatest treasure? Do you own something so valuable it sits in a safe-deposit box in your bank? Maybe you take it out once in a while then return it for safekeeping.

If that's really your life's greatest treasure, you're in trouble, for according to this verse, your heart is locked up in a narrow, dark safe-deposit box, where it's awfully difficult to love others and enjoy the world God has given you.

Maybe you don't own that kind of valuable, but you're inordinately proud of the vehicle you drive. Would you really want your heart to sit out in all weather, where it could eventually rust away? Even the best care will never make a car last forever. Hide it in a garage, but it still has a limited life.

But when your best treasure is your relationship with Christ and His eternal reward, you don't have to worry about where your heart is. It's safe with Jesus, free to love others, and valuable to both you and the people with whom you share Christ.

Are you gathering earthly treasures or eternal ones? Those on earth won't last. Sending treasures before you to heaven is the wisest thing you can do. Worldly goods fade, but not those in Jesus' treasure vaults.

*Lord, help me send treasures ahead of me into eternity
instead of grabbing all the earthly items I can get. Amen.*

DO FOXES MAKE YOU FUME?

"Catch for us the foxes, the little foxes that ruin the vineyards."
SONG OF SOLOMON 2:15 NIV

*W*hat makes you fume? You know, those bothersome little annoyances that drive you up the wall? We all have them—like losing our keys when we're in a hurry, missing the train home from work, or losing five pounds only to gain back six over the weekend.

The Bible teaches that the "little foxes" in life "spoil the vine." The real joy-robbers aren't the big catastrophes but the trivial, petty annoyances we encounter daily. One or two consecutive foxes have been known to hurl the best of us into an all-out tailspin, ruining an otherwise perfect day.

So how do we harness little foxes? The psalmist said, "When anxiety was great within me, your consolation brought joy to my soul" (Psalm 94:19 NIV). God understands our human frailty. Wherever we are, whatever we are doing, He is eager to administer calm, peace, and joy! As we turn to the Lord in prayer and praise, He begins to "catch for us the foxes."

God's antidote to our flailing emotions is simple: Prayer plus praise equals peace.

Still fuming?

Dear God, please give comfort to my disquieted soul and drive away the little foxes of aggravation. When I'm tempted to fret and fume, remind me of Your antidote to keep my emotions in balance. Amen.

THE PRIORITY
OF PRAYER

*Very early the next morning, Jesus got up and
went to a place where he could be alone and pray.*
MARK 1:35 CEV

*S*andy rubbed the sleep from her eyes and stared at the glowing red numbers on the alarm clock. *Yep. Time to get up.*

She glanced over at her dog, which had crept into her bed after she'd gone to sleep, and envied his simple world. Eat, sleep, fetch the ball, sleep. That was his routine. But hers—yikes! Her days were so filled, it was hard to find even a moment's peace. Yesterday nothing had gone right. And today? Who knew? The only thing she did know was that for strength to face the day, she needed to spend some time alone with God. Before her feet touched the floor, she sat up, turned on the light, and grabbed her bedside Bible. In the quiet of the morning, Sandy was determined to spend time with God. Otherwise, how would she ever find her way?

We are to walk as Jesus did. And so we arm ourselves with God's truth and wisdom *before* our feet hit the floor.

Find your own quiet place where you can be alone. Find a reading plan that will help guide your way through God's Word. And then open up your spirit, heart, and mind to the true reality—life in Christ!

*Hello, Lord! What a beautiful morning You have made! Be with me
as I spend these moments alone with You. And remain with me as
I live in You throughout this glorious day. Amen.*

CALLED TO REST

But Jesus often withdrew to lonely places and prayed.
LUKE 5:16 NIV

*C*hristians often make the mistake of believing the Lord wants us to be busy about His work constantly. We sign up for everything and feel guilty saying no to anything that is asked of us. This is perhaps especially true of women. We feel it is our duty to serve.

Certainly, we are called to be about God's work. We are His hands and feet in this world, and He can use us in mighty ways. But we are also called to rest and pray. Jesus put a priority on this, frequently leaving the crowd to seek solitude. He encouraged His followers to do the same. One day when they had been busy meeting the needs of people all day, Christ insisted that the disciples come away with Him to rest and to nourish themselves.

There is no denying that our lives are busy. All sorts of demands are placed on women today. You may find yourself in a station in life that pulls at you from every angle. Make time to rest. Find a place that is quiet where you can pray. Jesus modeled this for us. He wants us to find rest in Him.

Father, show me the importance of rest. Allow me to say no to something today in order that I might say yes to some quiet time with You. Amen.

A DAY OF REST

Six days thou shalt do thy work, and on the seventh day thou shalt rest:
that thine ox and thine ass may rest, and the son of thy handmaid,
and the stranger, may be refreshed.
EXODUS 23:12 KJV

If there is one scriptural principle that women routinely abandon, it is that of the Sabbath. Because Christ has become our rest and because we now worship on the Lord's Day, we often disregard the idea of a Sabbath rest.

Rest was at the heart of the Sabbath. One day out of seven, God's people were not to work or to make others work, so they could all be refreshed.

God Himself started the work-rest pattern before the earth was a week old. God didn't rest because He was tired; He rested because His work of creation was finished.

But a woman's work is never done! How can she rest?

It's not easy. There are always more things that can be done. But most of those things can wait a day while you recharge.

God's design for the week gives rest to the weary. Let's not neglect His provision.

Father, help me to rest from my labor as You rested from Yours.
Refresh me this day. Amen.

CHECK YOUR MOTIVES

People may be pure in their own eyes, but the LORD examines their motives.
PROVERBS 16:2 NLT

$\mathcal{D}$uring a Bible study prayer request time, a woman asked for prayer for an absent member of the group. She then proceeded to say some very personal things about the reasons for that group member's absence. They were so personal that the leader actually had to stop the discussion.

Prayer request: good! Gossip: bad! It is God alone who can judge the true motives behind any action. In the case of that Bible study, the behavior that was construed as gossip needed to be dealt with to avoid further hurt for the absent group member, but it was up to God to determine whether the wrongdoing was innocent or impure.

The Lord examines the motives of the heart. That can be both a blessing and a challenge. We all make mistakes, so errors made with a pure motive will be seen as such. However, good actions made with an impure motive will not be rewarded.

Even though we can't always judge another person's motives, we can always take stock of our own. Even right behaviors can become wrong when the motive is impure. Ask Jesus to reveal your true motives to you before you fall into sin.

Heavenly Father, forgive me for the dishonesty behind impure motives.
Please help me to recognize the truth of my motives before I hurt others
or cause myself to sin. Thank You for leading me into all truth. Amen.

SAYING YES
TOO MUCH

Above all else, don't take an oath. You must not swear by heaven
or by earth or by anything else. "Yes" or "No" is all you need to say.
If you say anything more, you will be condemned.
JAMES 5:12 CEV

The children's ministry meeting had come to a standstill again. Looking at her watch, Liz volunteered, "I'll make the calls to get the ball rolling." The team had heard these "commitments" from Liz before. More than likely, Liz would drop the ball rather than get it rolling.

Liz was sincere in her offer. She knew the spiritual growth this project could bring to the kids. She fully intended to get started that very afternoon. But the project had to wait, because yesterday she'd promised Jordon's teacher she'd make three dozen cupcakes for the class party. In line at a fast-food drive-thru for the family dinner, she called Kate, her accountability partner, to tell her they would have to reschedule because she was too busy to meet.

Many women can easily identify with Liz's plight. We see a need and think we're the ones to fill it. We say yes when our plates are already full. This may compromise family time, personal devotions, or adequate sleep. One urgent task may get accomplished, but two other important priorities may get overlooked. We must learn that it is okay to say no so we can make our yes a sure yes.

All-knowing Father, help me to know when I need to say no.
Let me be a woman of my word. Amen.

GOD IN THE DRIVER'S SEAT

I will instruct thee and teach thee in the way which thou shalt go:
I will guide thee with mine eye.
PSALM 32:8 KJV

*H*annah came to a fork in the road. She had to make some life-changing decisions. The hardest part was that the decisions she made would significantly affect the lives of her loved ones. What was she to do?

God tells us that whenever we have a decision to make, He will instruct and teach us. He will not let us flounder, but as we seek His face, He will provide direction, understanding, wisdom, and insight. He will teach us the way—the road, the path, or journey we need to take that is in our best interest. We can clearly comprehend the way we should walk because God is guiding, with His eye upon us. He is omniscient, which means He knows all things. He knows our past, our present, and our future. He sees and understands what we are not able to comprehend in our finite beings. What a blessing that an all-knowing Lord will guide us!

All-knowing Lord, I praise You that regardless of the decision,
You know what is best for me and will direct me in the path I should take.
Amen.

CONVENIENT LOVE

Jesus replied: "'Love the Lord your God with all your heart and with all your soul and with all your mind.' This is the first and greatest commandment. And the second is like it: 'Love your neighbor as yourself.'"
MATTHEW 22:37–39 NIV

Christians have been given two assignments: Love God and love each other.

People say love is a decision. Sounds simple enough, right? The fact is that telling others we love them and showing that love are two very different realities. Let's face it—some people are harder to love than others. Even loving and serving God can seem easier on a less stressful day.

Think about convenience stores. They're everywhere. Why? Because along the journey people need things. It's nearly impossible to take a long road trip without stopping. Whether it's gas to fill our vehicles, a quick snack, or a drink to quench our thirst, everyone needs something. Gas station owners realize this—and we should, too.

It may not always be convenient to love God when the to-do list stretches on forever or when a friend asks us for a favor that takes more time than we want to give. But God's love is available 24/7. He never puts us on hold or doles out love in rationed amounts. He never takes a day off, and his love is plentiful.

Lord, I promise to love You and my neighbor with my whole heart. Amen.

STEP UP TO THE PLATE!

Moses said, "Who am I to go to the king and lead your people out of Egypt?"
God replied, "I will be with you."
EXODUS 3:11–12 CEV

*A*s Suzanne gingerly stepped onto the bobbing Star Ferry in Hong Kong's Victoria Harbor, she wondered again, "Lord, *what* am I doing here?"

Just one month earlier, her husband had come home with the news that he had been transferred to Hong Kong. Suddenly, she was living in a skyscraper that clung precariously to the harbor's edge and was trying to adjust to a new culture on a bustling island with seven million Chinese people.

Soon God provided an answer to her question. Someone was needed to start a prayer group at the school—and a women's Bible study at the church. She could almost hear God whisper to her, "Step up to the plate." So she did. And those activities have carried on since she repatriated, continued by other women who have stepped up to the plate.

God often plucks people out of their comfort zone and sets them down elsewhere to carry out His purposes. Moses' tranquil day of shepherding was interrupted by God's announcement that he had a job to do in Egypt. Five times Moses objected. Five times! But God persisted. To ease the anxieties of the very reluctant, freshly appointed leader of the Israelites, God tenderly assured him, "I will be with you."

And nearly four thousand years later, those words are still true. We can trust that God will be with us wherever we go.

Thank You, Lord, for being the same yesterday, today, and tomorrow. Amen.

To Be or
to Do?

*They did not conquer the land with their swords; it was not their own strong
arm that gave them victory. It was your right hand and strong arm and the
blinding light from your face that helped them, for you loved them.*
PSALM 44:3 NLT

$\mathcal{S}$he stared out the window, misty-eyed. *What's wrong with me?* she
wondered. *I should do more for the Lord, but I'm so tired.* Unfounded guilt
weighed upon her spirit. The young woman seldom felt that she did
enough, though she gave of her time and talents regularly.

Still immersed in thought, she sensed the gentle nudge of the
Holy Spirit. *"I don't want you to* do, *as much as I want you to* be.*"

Women are conditioned to "do it all." And most of the time, we
do! But our personal expectations are unreasonable and self-defeating
if we think we must accomplish all tasks by our own strength and
skills.

As Christian women, we must remember the basic precepts of our
walk with God. Namely, Jesus saved us because He loves us. God cares
more about who we are and what characteristics we develop through
the work of the Holy Spirit than what we do in the work of ministry.

God requires us to *be.* To be faithful to Him through Bible study
and prayer. To be obedient. And to be ourselves. That makes God
smile.

*Dear Lord, sometimes I forget to be what You want me to be and
I do what I think You expect of me or what I expect of myself.
Help me to be all that You want me to be. Amen.*

EYEWITNESS ACCOUNT

We did not follow cleverly invented stories when we told you about the power and coming of our Lord Jesus Christ, but we were eyewitnesses of his majesty.
2 PETER 1:16 NIV

It's not uncommon to run into people who don't want to believe in Jesus, who claim the Bible is a collection of fairy tales. Often they treat Christians like the most naive people in the world. "How can you believe that?" is the message they impart, even if they'd never say such words.

It's difficult to get through to people with hard hearts. They're blinded to the truth. So explaining Jesus to them may be like trying to describe the color blue to a blind person. But remember, you, like the apostles, are an eyewitness. You were there when Jesus saved you. And you have testimonies from those who actually observed Jesus' ministry. So it's not as if you're an "airy-fairy" person who believed without checking out the truth of what you believe.

One day all will be eyewitnesses to Jesus' majesty. Every knee will bow before Him and confess that He is Lord. So when people wonder why you believe, tell them. Christians aren't the ones reading fairy stories, and someday everyone will know that.

When others act as if I'm crazy to believe in You, help me not to be offended, Lord. Instead, help me show them Your truth. Amen.

CHANGE AGENT

*"For I am the LORD, I do not change;
therefore you are not consumed, O sons of Jacob."*
MALACHI 3:6 NKJV

As a girl traversing the globe with her military family, she looked forward to new schools, new friends, and a chance to reinvent herself with every move. In Indiana, she called herself Jackie, and in Germany, Jacqueline—because she imagined it made her elegant and sophisticated.

Today, even as an adult, Jackie needs change. We all do. We change our hair color every time the wind changes direction. Our hemlines are up one minute and down the next. We take classes and go to seminars to learn how to change behaviors we don't like. Most of the time, change is healthy, and we should be seeking to make considerable changes in our lives—such as repenting of sin, walking more closely with God, and loving our neighbor as ourselves.

We can trust Jesus, who is "the same yesterday and today and forever" (Hebrews 13:8 NKJV) to be the change agent in our lives. He is always faithful to work in us when we want to make a sincere change. He is always loving—never condemning. He is always merciful when we fall and need to be helped back up. What a miracle that the God who never changes can make the greatest changes in us!

You are my change agent, Lord. Help me to change those things about myself that are displeasing to You so that I may serve You more fully. Amen.

A BETTER WORLD

*Encourage one another daily, as long as it is called Today,
so that none of you may be hardened by sin's deceitfulness.*
HEBREWS 3:13 NIV

*F*irst, the good news: You have been saved by Christ. You can live in His power. You can revel in the joy of this life. And in the end, you will be with Him in heaven.

Now for the bad news: There's still a lot of sin in this world. People hurt each other, countries are at war, and at times, even the godly give the Christian faith a black eye. So how can we live with the right perspective? How can we make this world a better place?

Begin by encouraging at least one person every day. Find something encouraging to say to someone you love. Do something special for an absolute stranger. Stretch out your hand and touch someone else's life. And do these things selflessly, without expecting anything in return.

Need ideas? How about buying a coworker a cup of iced coffee with a shot of hazelnut creamer? Or pray for a loved one before he or she walks out the door to begin the day. Write out a word of encouragement and place it in someone's mailbox at church. Pay the toll for the car behind you.

Make this a better world by doing something nice for someone else. Start today.

*Father God, I want to make this world a better place. Show me whom
You want me to bless today. Allow me to be Your conduit of love.
And I'll praise You for it! Amen.*

SPENDING LIMITS

The more you have, the more people come to help you spend it.
So what good is wealth—except perhaps to watch it slip through your fingers!
ECCLESIASTES 5:11 NLT

$\mathcal{D}$eidre's income has risen 50 percent over the past eight years. She expected such a dramatic increase would allow her to pay all her bills and even save some. Instead, finances have remained a constant struggle.

Along with the raise in income, Deidre bought a car instead of riding the bus, watched gasoline prices skyrocket, and moved from a one-bedroom apartment to the larger place she had needed for years. She continued to spend to the limits of her income and beyond.

Making more money doesn't result in financial stability. We buy more of what we consider needs but may actually be "wants." Whatever the level of our income, as Americans, we spend more than we make. Many of us struggle with getting out of debt. Another medical emergency arises; we have to replace an appliance that stopped working; we buy new models to replace the old. Wealth runs through our fingers, and we wonder how we will pay for everything.

It's time for us to put the principles we know into action. We can start by investing in the eternal—God's work and people.

God gives us joy in our possessions. He only asks us to use them wisely.

Jehovah Jireh, the Lord who provides, we thank You for Your provision.
Teach us to value the eternal over the temporal. Amen.

Sabbath Queen

"Observe the Sabbath day, to keep it holy."
Exodus 20:8 THE MESSAGE

*W*eekends are a time to catch up on chores. A time to get some sunshine and to work in the yard. A time to sort laundry and wash clothes. A time to grocery shop and plan menus. A time to sort paperwork and pay bills.

For Sharon, weekends are also a time to do a little extra work for her job, to get ahead by responding to work e-mails and phone calls, to sort through papers, set goals, and prepare presentations.

But something has gone wrong. Sharon is worn out. Joy has been wrung from her soul. Her forty-hour work week has grown to sixty—and she is burned out.

What happened to the Sabbath?

Nan Fink, in *Stranger in the Midst*, wrote, "Shabbat is like nothing else. Time as we know it does not exist for these twenty-four hours, and the worries of the week soon fall away. A feeling of joy appears. The smallest object, a leaf or a spoon, shimmers in a soft light, and the heart opens. Shabbat is a meditation of unbelievable beauty."

Lauren F. Winner, a messianic Jew and author of *Mudhouse Sabbath*, wrote, "We spoke of the day as *Shabbat haMalka*, the Sabbath Queen, and we sang hymns of praise on Friday night that welcomed the Sabbath as a bride."

Shabbat. Quiet. Holy. Worship.

Welcome the Sabbath Queen to your home this week.

Lord, help me practice a rhythm of rest and restoration, weekly welcoming the Sabbath, restoring order and worship to my weary soul. Amen.

ANTICIPATED
PRAYERS

I will answer their prayers before they finish praying.
ISAIAH 65:24 CEV

Alaire, a busy wife and mom of five girls, waved to her oldest daughter as she walked to the airliner that would take her off to her first year of college. Days later Alaire sent her youngest off to grade school. For the first time in eighteen years, her house reverberated with. . .silence.

This stay-at-home mom was just about to take her long, quiet days to the Lord in prayer when the telephone rang. A woman from her church asked if she would be willing to lead a women's Bible study.

As Alaire shared all this with the women's leadership team during their kick-off organizational meeting, she smiled broadly. "God did just what He says He will do in Isaiah! I got that telephone call just before I was going to call on the Lord about my empty mornings."

God alone knows what we need before we ask. He even knows what we need before *we* know the need. Life may take us by surprise, but never the Lord God who knows the end from the beginning. He knows what's behind, what's ahead, and what's now. Whether we're sending children away to school, taking in ailing parents, or going it alone for the first time—or for yet another season—"the LORD surrounds his people" (Psalm 125:2 NLT).

I praise You, Lord, that You surround me through all of life.
Keep my eyes of faith on You and not on my changing circumstances. Amen.

CLIMBING HILLS

*And though the Lord give you the bread of adversity, and the water
of affliction. . .thine ears shall hear a word behind thee,
saying, This is the way, walk ye in it.*
ISAIAH 30:20–21 KJV

The woman walked every day for exercise. She loved the quiet of
the early morning plus the way the workout improved her health. As
she grew stronger, she began to take more challenging paths. At first,
climbing the steeper hills was hard. The loose rocks would cause her
to stumble. The sharp grade made her legs ache, and she had trouble
catching her breath. But eventually she felt her body strengthening and
her ability to navigate improving even though the path got no easier.

In our Christian walk, we have times when the path is easy. We know
God is there, and we enjoy our time of fellowship with Him and with
others. However, there are times when God allows us to experience trials.
These are hard times, when the Christian walk is tough. Sometimes we
may want to give up, saying the path is too rough, causing us to stumble.
If we persevere, calling on God for help, the path may not be easier, but
we will be strengthened in our faith and our fellowship with God.

*Thank You, Lord, for allowing hardships and tests that make me stronger as a
Christian. Help me to trust You when the path becomes difficult. Amen.*

GOD AND FIVE GIRLS

*The LORD spake unto Moses, saying, The daughters of Zelophehad
speak right: thou shalt surely give them a possession of
an inheritance among their father's brethren.*
NUMBERS 27:6–7 KJV

Zelophehad left Egypt during the Exodus but died as the Israelites wandered in the wilderness. He left five daughters: Mahlah, Noah, Hoglah, Milcah, and Tirzah. According to law, they could not inherit their father's estate. Why? Because they were girls.

This injustice blew them away. Not only had they lost their father, but they found themselves stuck in the desert with no financial resources—unless they married. The only solution for young women of that era: grab a man, any man. But Zelophehad's daughters brought their case before God.

Doing so took a lot of courage. Mahlah, Noah, Hoglah, Milcah, and Tirzah had to appear before Moses, other leaders, and the entire congregation at the door of the tabernacle. But they didn't back down.

"Our father didn't join in rebellion against God," they insisted. "Why should our father's name disappear? We are his children. Please give us the property due us."

No doubt some found the young women pushy, even radical. But when Moses asked God for a ruling, He affirmed the fairness of their cause.

*Father, when these young women called for justice, You did not turn a deaf ear.
Thank You for listening and acting on their behalf—and ours. Amen.*

A MATTER OF PRIORITIES

To everything there is a season, a time for every purpose under heaven.
ECCLESIASTES 3:1 NKJV

*C*hange is a regular part of modern life, as routine as an afternoon thunderstorm—and often just as messy. Jobs shift or disappear. Friends move. Babies are born, and children graduate and marry. On top of lives already crammed to the brim with responsibilities and stress, change comes to all of us.

Only one thing in our lives never changes: God. When our world swirls and threatens to shift out of control, we can know that God is never surprised, never caught off guard by anything that happens. Just as He guided David through dark nights and Joseph through his time in prison, God can show us a secure way through any difficulty. He can turn the roughest times to good. Just as He supported His servants in times past, He will always be with us, watching and loving.

Lord, help me remember Your love and guidance when my life turns upside down. Grant me wisdom for the journey and a hope for the future. Amen.

IT'S YOUR MOVE

The LORD God Almighty will be with you, just as you say he is.
AMOS 5:14 NIV

Sometimes we have trouble feeling God's presence, especially in troublesome situations. In those times, we may ask, "Where are You, God?"

God has told us that He will never leave us nor forsake us (see Deuteronomy 31:6). So if we feel as if God is not near, perhaps the distance is of our own choosing.

We need to believe God is always with us (see Matthew 28:20). We need to have the knowledge firmly implanted upon our heart, soul, and mind that when we seek Him, He is near.

God warns us, "My people are destroyed from lack of knowledge" (Hosea 4:6 NIV). How true that is! The destroyer revels in the idea of us moving away from God, becoming unfamiliar with Him. The evil one celebrates when we abstain from reading God's Word, praying, and praising Him.

Each day, tell yourself the truth: that God is always with you; then He "will be with you, just as you say he is."

And during those times when you feel as if God's presence has slipped out of your life, take a look around. See where you are standing. Then make your move. Look into the goodness of His Word. Seek His face. Don't let Him out of your sight. Proclaim that He is standing there, right by your side. And there He will be, just as you have said.

Thank You, Lord, for always being with me. With You by my side, I will live!
I will not be destroyed. I will overcome all. Thank You for being immovable.
Amen.

HOSPITALITY AND FRIENDSHIP

Cheerfully share your home with those who need a meal or a place to stay.
1 PETER 4:9 NLT

*W*hen Anne was young, having company meant frenetically cleaning the house from floor to ceiling, shopping for groceries, and cooking elaborate meals. Company meant trying to make a good impression. As Anne anticipated company, her heart raced and she focused all her energy to make things perfect.

After several years of anxious entertaining, Anne heard her mentor describe how she did not worry what the house looked like when company came over. All that mattered to Anne's mentor was that when people were invited into her home, they would come as they were and she would receive them as she was. Anne's mentor put up no pretenses, cast aside anxiety related to "making impressions," and focused solely on *ministering* to her guests, as opposed to *impressing* her guests.

Shortly after this discussion, Anne had ten women coming to her home for the day, and she barely had time to cook or shop. Instead of panicking, Anne kept things simple. She left the floors as they were and simply cleaned the bathrooms and kitchen where cleaning really counted. Instead of planning elaborate meals, she prepared a simple breakfast—bagels, cream cheese, string cheese, fruit, orange juice, and coffee. Delicious. And instead of cooking lunch, she had a simple, hearty meal delivered by a local restaurant. Everyone enjoyed it. The day could not have gone better, and Anne relaxed and enjoyed the day as well.

Lord, help me focus on relationships and cultivate authentic friendships. Help me invite my friends into my life as it is, rather than orchestrating impressions. Amen.

TO DO OR TO BE?

And God said unto Moses, I AM THAT I AM: and he said,
Thus shalt thou say unto the children of Israel, I AM hath sent me unto you.
EXODUS 3:14 KJV

*S*ome women work themselves into a frenzy about the many things they have to do. Others moan about the tasks they are unable to get done, while yet others fret over what they still need to do. The woman who constantly lives with past regrets and future anxieties can be quite unpleasant in the present.

God is not like this. He doesn't regret or fret. Although He existed in eternity past and will be in eternity future, God is neither past nor future. His most revered name is I Am. God is eternally present.

God *is*. Women *are*. And women are what they are, where they are, and how they are because God *is*.

Life is not about doing. Life is about who we are in relationship to who God is.

God's first call to us is to Himself, not to His service. "Come unto me, all ye that labour and are heavy laden, and I will give you rest," Jesus said (Matthew 11:28 KJV).

Be the woman God wants you to be—rest in Him.

Oh Father, I want to accomplish so much in my life, but sometimes
I'm so busy that I don't have time for You or for others. Teach me
to rest in You, to be all that You want me to be. Amen.

BE A WISE
BUILDER

*Every wise woman buildeth her house:
but the foolish plucketh it down with her hands.*
PROVERBS 14:1 KJV

*E*very wise woman builds her house.

No matter the season of her life, no matter what house she is in, a woman should be about the business of building a home and a family.

An unmarried daughter can help build her father's house. A wife must build the home she and her husband have established. Even a widow can continue building her house for her children's children.

While home building is the highest calling of womanhood, we sometimes turn aside from it, thinking the world offers something better. We sometimes think the world's view of personal achievement is better than God's view of submission and self-sacrifice.

Don't be fooled—real wisdom is found as we apply scripture to the many tasks of homemaking. Teaching kindness to a two-year-old is more difficult than teaching economic theory to graduate students. Clearly explaining salvation to a preschooler is more challenging than convincing a bank to finance a business plan.

When done well, home building will yield rewards for many generations. When done thoughtlessly, generations suffer.

Let's not neglect this great task for the Lord.

Let us be wise builders.

*Father, even though I know building a home is my most important job,
sometimes I don't see the value. Let me labor in my home with diligence
and grace, knowing it is truly my best work. Amen.*

OUR SECRET LIFE

"Then your Father, who sees what is done in secret, will reward you."
MATTHEW 6:6 NIV

$\mathcal{W}$e live two lives. Our visible life is lived before others. Our secret life is lived solely before the Lord. Are they consistent? Many times the motives behind our actions are to impress others. Our real heart is revealed by what we do in secret, when only the Lord is watching.

How do we choose to spend our time and money? Do we pray aloud to look spiritual in the eyes of others? Are we generous to attain a certain reputation? Do we mention tithing and fasting to appear devout? When we look closely at our motives, we must admit that sometimes we are more concerned about gaining the applause of people than of God.

Perhaps your behind-the-scenes sacrifices are going unnoticed by the world. Do not be discouraged. God knows. He hears your prayers and sees what you are doing in secret to serve Him. Eternal treasures are being stored up in heaven. Your selfless acts will be rewarded. Do not give up and think it doesn't matter. It matters to God. Seek to please Him above anyone else. Live before an audience of One so that your life will honor Him.

Lord, help me walk consistently in Your truth. May what I do in secret bring glory to You. May I not seek man's approval, but Yours alone. Amen.

RUN TO
RELATIONSHIP

"This is how much God loved the world: He gave his Son, his one and only Son. And this is why: so that no one need be destroyed; by believing in him, anyone can have a whole and lasting life."
JOHN 3:16 THE MESSAGE

*P*roductivity carries a lot of weight in business these days. It often weighs heavily in performance reviews that determine promotions and salary increases. With that in mind, it can sometimes seem difficult to balance productivity with the relationships we have with other people—especially those we work with each day.

We can become so wrapped up in the task we are trying to achieve that we forget that life is about the people—the relationships—God has put around us. We must be cautious not to be so focused on a task that we discount the value of others. We must disconnect from the task and focus on the person, and sometimes that means letting go of the work for a minute or two—long enough to really listen to what someone is saying. We need each other—as friends, family, or just passing acquaintances—in order to live successful lives.

God measures His wealth in souls. That should be our focus, too.

Lord, help me to know when it's time to drop the task and run to the relationship. Amen.

LIKE A TREE FROG

*The soul of Jonathan was knit with the soul of David,
and Jonathan loved him as his own soul.*
1 SAMUEL 18:1 KJV

*I*nterior designer Ali works among some of the wealthiest women in Palm Beach, Florida. Her flair for decorating to suit the personality of her clients regularly takes her into multimillion-dollar homes. But Ali's interest in her business contacts goes beyond antique furniture, fine art, and elegant tapestries. She's looking for women who may be as empty in soul as she was before she met Jesus Christ.

Toni, a real-estate agent who works among the same clientele as Ali, kept crossing paths with the attractive decorator. Ali kept inviting Toni to church. Or she'd ask her to come to her weekly Bible study. Toni kept refusing, but Ali kept inviting her. Toni says Ali was like a Central American red-eyed tree frog. Once those frogs latch their sucker-equipped feet onto something, they stick like glue.

Ali didn't give up. Eventually, Toni acquiesced. Soon after she heard the life-changing message of the gospel, Toni became more than a friend of Ali's. She became a Christ follower.

God brings people into our lives with whom we sense a binding, just like Jonathan to David or Ali to Toni. Like Ali, we may be spiritual tree frogs—valuing our relationships with others while gently pointing them to the Creator of everything—including exquisite art and iridescent tree frogs.

*Father, help me to love my friends enough to lovingly share the gospel with them.
Amen.*

DESERT FLOWER

"Do not grieve, for the joy of the Lord is your strength."
NEHEMIAH 8:10 NIV

*F*riday dawned gloomy and overcast. *A fitting end to a miserable week,* Cheryl thought. Her husband had wrecked the car, and her daughter had broken her thumb in a tumble at school. A beloved friend had been diagnosed with an aggressive form of uterine cancer.

As Cheryl stared at a sky the color of bruises, she blinked back tears and fell to her knees. Second Timothy 4:6 (NIV) came to mind: "I am already being poured out like a drink offering." She could relate to Paul's expression of helplessness. Cheryl felt empty. She cried out to the Lord; then she just cried.

And a strange thing happened. A sensation of warmth started in her toes and spread throughout her body, infusing her with something totally unexpected—joy! She enjoyed a refreshing time of praise-filled fellowship with the renewer of her soul.

Not to be confused with happiness, joy is not dependent on external circumstances. It's a Holy Spirit-inspired mystery that defies all reason. During the times we should be downcast or depressed, the joy of the Lord bolsters us like a life preserver in a tumultuous sea.

Living joyfully is not denying reality. We all have hurts in our lives. But even in the midst of our parched desert times, our heavenly Father reaches in with gentle fingers to lift and sustain us.

*Giver of strength, fill me with Your joy in the midst of
sorrow like the bloom of a desert flower. Amen.*

LOVING ENEMIES

Love your enemies, bless them that curse you, do good to them that hate you,
and pray for them which despitefully use you, and persecute you.
MATTHEW 5:44 KJV

Catherine was filled with jealousy and hate. It seemed that from the moment she awoke she thought to herself, *Whose life will I make miserable today?* She continually had conflict with everyone who crossed her path. She delighted in spreading lies about colleagues behind their backs and stirring up strife, trouble, conflict, dissension, and discord. Do you know anyone like that?

Our natural response to the Catherines of our world is to retaliate with anger and hatred. However, Jesus encouraged us to love and pray for our enemies. Jesus experienced the Catherines of this world during His stay on earth and responded in a supernatural manner. He modeled how to show tangible acts of goodness with forgiveness, kindness, mercy, grace, and compassion.

We too can respond in a supernatural manner by surrendering the situation to the Lord Almighty, forgiving our enemies, inviting the Holy Spirit to reign through us with acts of love and goodness, and praying specifically that our enemies would be blessed.

Lord, I meet Catherines every day. Please help me not to retaliate in kind,
but to live a life of forgiveness, love, goodness, and blessing. Amen.

EVAPORATED DREAMS
OR POOLS OF BLESSING?

*What joy for those whose strength comes from the LORD, who have set
their minds on a pilgrimage to Jerusalem. When they walk through
the Valley of Weeping, it will become a place of refreshing springs.
The autumn rains will clothe it with blessings.*
PSALM 84:5–6 NLT

*W*illem had a goal. At age twenty-five he wanted to devote his life
to others and to the Word of God. So he traveled the coal mines of
southern Belgium after a disaster struck a small mining town. Tirelessly,
he ministered to the hungry and hurting, and the community packed
his church each Sunday.

After the tragedy ended, however, a jealous church official dismissed
Willem from the church he loved. But God didn't dismiss him.

Passionately, Willem began to sketch figures of the miners and
townspeople. Through his art, he captured their torment, triumph, and
dignity. Those he no longer could reach through the pulpit, he instead
reached through the canvas. For God had another plan for one of the
greatest artists ever known—Vincent Willem Van Gogh.

Have you ever questioned God when, through unforeseen
circumstances, your goals and plans were altered? We all have had
disappointments and failures, but God never fails us. Our "Valley of
Weeping" will form pools of blessings when we continue on God's
path despite our dashed dreams. As the river of one dream evaporates,
the tributaries of a new goal will flow.

*Heavenly Father, Help me to surrender my dreams and goals to You. When
my dreams evaporate, please turn my Valley of Weeping into pools of blessings.
Amen.*

PRACTICAL CHRISTIAN ADVICE

Finally, all of you, live in harmony with one another;
be sympathetic, love as brothers, be compassionate and humble.
1 PETER 3:8 NIV

*P*eter has spent the last few verses addressing masters, slaves, husbands, and wives. He now turns to practical advice for the Christian community as a whole.

Peter intentionally lists godly traits in a particular order. First, live in harmony. In other words, get along. When we can live in peace with each other, we have already learned something about putting away our own selfishness. Second, be sympathetic. Sympathy implies that we feel sorry for those of our community in pain. Third, we must love as a family. Once we have begun to be sympathetic, natural love will spring up between us. Fourth, be compassionate. Compassion takes sympathy to the next level. We not only recognize hurt in our brothers and sisters and feel sorry for them from afar, but we long to relieve them of their burdens and pain. Finally, living together in harmony, being sympathetic and compassionate, and loving each other as brothers and sisters inevitably leads to humility. Humbling ourselves is putting aside our selfish natures and living for each other—the very thing Peter asks us to do.

When we embody these Christian attributes, imagine how we will revolutionize our relationships with our families, friends, coworkers, peers, and all those in between!

Dear Lord, Please teach me to embody each of these traits and transform my relationships. Humble me and help me to cast aside my selfishness today. Amen.

WHERE IS YOUR TREASURE?

"But store up for yourselves treasures in heaven, where neither moth
nor rust destroys, and where thieves do not break in or steal;
for where your treasure is, there your heart will be also."
MATTHEW 6:20–21 NASB

Treasure maps show up regularly in children's stories and pirate movies. What is so intriguing about a treasure map? It leads to treasure! People have gone to great lengths in search of treasure, sometimes only to find in the end that the map was a hoax and no treasure existed.

Imagine a treasure map drawn of your life, with all its twists and turns. Where do you spend your time? How do you use your talents? Would the map lead to heaven, or is your treasure in earthly things?

Each day consists of twenty-four hours, regardless of how we use them. We make choices about the priorities in our lives. The world sends messages about how we should spend our time; however, if we listen to the still, small voice of God, we will learn how to "store up treasures in heaven."

Nurturing relationships and sharing Christ with others, as well as reading God's Word and getting to know Him through prayer, are examples of storing up treasures in heaven. Using our gifts for His glory is also important. The dividends of such investments are priceless.

Eternal God, help me to store up treasures in heaven with the choices
I make today. Give me opportunities to show Your love. Remind
me of the importance of time spent with You. Amen.

WHAT NEXT?

Fig trees may no longer bloom, or vineyards produce grapes; olive trees may be fruitless, and harvest time a failure; sheep pens may be empty, and cattle stalls vacant—but I will still celebrate because the LORD God saves me.
HABAKKUK 3:17–18 CEV

Have you ever had a day when everything has gone wrong? The neighbor's dogs bark all night, so you don't get any sleep. You spill coffee on your favorite blouse. The car has a flat tire. You're running late, so you get a ticket for speeding. You end up wondering what next—what else can go wrong?

On days like this it's hard to find any reason to be joyful. How can we be happy when every time we turn around another disaster strikes? Instead of greeting everyone with a smile, on these down days we tend to be cranky or snarly. We tell anyone willing to listen about our terrible lot in life.

Rejoicing in the Lord is not a matter of circumstances but of will. We can choose to remember the God of our salvation and be content with His love for us. No matter how much goes awry, we have so much more to be thankful for because of the grace of God.

God is sovereign. With His help we can rise above the worry of our circumstances to find peace and contentment. Then, no matter what is happening in our lives, other people will see the joy of God.

Thank You, God, that You have provided for my salvation and my joy. Help me to look to You instead of dwelling on my momentary troubles. Amen.

INTIMACY

*Aware of this, Jesus said to them, "Why are you bothering this woman?
She has done a beautiful thing to me. . . . When she poured this perfume
on my body, she did it to prepare me for burial."*
MATTHEW 26:10, 12 NIV

The woman who anointed Jesus understood who He was and what
was about to happen. Even the men who walked daily with Jesus didn't
get it. To her, no gift was too lavish. No words were adequate to express
her gratitude for what He was about to relinquish—His life!

The beauty of it all? He knew her very soul! He knew her heart
longed to give more. He knew her message, beyond any words, was
a pale reflection of her gratitude. He knew her soul so wholly, so
intimately, so deeply. What a connectedness they shared. That is why
He said, "What she has done will always be remembered."

This intimate loving Lord is the same Lord today. He hasn't
changed. He knows the depths of our hearts. He knows what we try to
express but fall short. He sees our intentions. Take comfort in His level
of understanding and in the intimate relationship He wants with us.
Its depth is beyond any friendship, parental devotion, or even earthly
marital union. It is a spiritual melding of souls. An amazing truth of
a perfect, loving Bridegroom becoming one with His bride by laying
down His life for her.

*Lover of my soul, You know my every thought. As my soul thirsts
for You, so You desire realness and oneness with me. Remove all that
hinders that intimacy. May my heart be solely Yours. Amen.*

RUN YOUR OWN RACE

I have fought the good fight, I have finished the race, I have kept the faith.
2 TIMOTHY 4:7 NIV

A young woman began running her first 10K race side-by-side with her dad. Soon it became apparent that they had different needs. She needed to run faster to maintain her endurance on the hills, and he needed to run at a slower and more measured pace to even have a hope of finishing. They decided to separate so they could run their own races more effectively.

Although she had wanted to finish with her dad, she crossed the finish line well ahead of him. She was proud of herself and reveled in her moment, but something was missing. She turned and ran back through the finish line, the way she had already come, hoping to find her determined, but likely weakened, father. When she successfully caught up with her dad, she proudly turned to finish his race with him.

It is important to run your own race, at your own pace—not too fast, but not too slowly, either. It's also necessary to take others into account and be an encouragement to them as they run their races. Try not to compare yourself too closely with others. We are all at different stages on our own courses. You can learn from those who have gone before, and you have the privilege of teaching those who come behind.

Lord, give me the strength I need to finish my race and the wisdom I need to run it well. And help me to be an encouragement to others. Amen.

CONSIDER THIS

*When I consider your heavens, the work of your fingers, the moon
and the stars, which you have set in place, what is man that
you are mindful of him. . .[and] care for him?*
PSALM 8:3–4 NIV

*W*hen we reflect on the world around us—the beauty of trees,
mountains, streams—it staggers the imagination. Looking up into the
heavens, gazing at planets and stars light-years away, we are humbled.
Just think: God, in His infinite wisdom, has created all these things
with His mighty hands, just as He created us.

Viewing and considering such magnificence puts everything into
perspective. Our problems seem miniscule in comparison to the heavens
above, the majesty of the mountains, and the grandeur of the trees.
Knowing that God has favored us with His grace, mercy, and love, and
has given us the responsibility to care for those things He has put into
our hands fills us with songs of praise.

If life is getting you down, if your problems seem insurmountable,
take a walk. Look around, below, and above you. Take a deep breath.
Draw close to a tree and touch its bark, examine its leaves. Look down
at the spiders, ants, and grass. Feel the wonder of the earth. Thank
Him for the heavens—the sun, moon, and stars—above you. This is
what God has created for us, for you. Praise His worthy name.

*Lord, the beauty of this earth is so awesome. In the glory of all You have created,
thank You for caring so much about me, for creating the magnificence that
surrounds me, and for giving up Your Son Jesus for all our sakes. Amen.*

REMEMBER ME?

*What does the worker gain from his toil? I have seen the burden God
has laid on men. He has made everything beautiful in its time. He has
also set eternity in the hearts of men; yet they cannot fathom what
God has done from beginning to end.*
ECCLESIASTES 3:9–11 NIV

*H*ow many times have we heard someone declare, "If I weren't getting
paid, I wouldn't work at all"? It's a frustration almost everyone feels
sooner or later. When we're asked to do just one more task, handle just
one more errand, oh, and "Would you mind handling the refreshments
for tomorrow?" the urge to quit and stare at the stars for a while
becomes utmost in our minds.

The more exhausted we are, the harder it is to remember that God
has a plan for us and that we are living that plan every day. We are
unable to see "the big picture" of our lives, what God has in store for
us, and how what we do every day fits into His plan. Instead, we have
to trust in His wisdom and keep on the journey He has set before us.
The final reward will be well worth every frustration.

*Lord, be with me as I focus on my work. Guide my steps so that everything
I do reveals my love for You and my faith in Your plan for my life. Amen.*

THINKING OF OTHERS

Do nothing out of selfish ambition or vain conceit, but in humility consider others better than yourselves. Each of you should look not only to your own interests, but also to the interests of others.
PHILIPPIANS 2:3–4 NIV

The apostle Paul, along with Timothy, founded the church at Philippi. Paul's relationship with this church was always close. The book of Philippians is a letter he wrote to the church at Philippi while he was imprisoned for preaching the gospel.

Paul knew the Philippians had been struggling with jealousy and rivalry. He encouraged them in his letter to think of others. He reminded them that this was the attitude of Jesus, who took on the role of a servant and humbled Himself for us, even to His death on the cross.

In the final chapter of Philippians, we read the well-known verse, "I can do everything through him who gives me strength" (Philippians 4:13 NIV). We can do *everything* through Christ Jesus who gives us strength. That includes putting others before ourselves. That includes replacing "I deserve. . ." with "How can I serve?"

When you start to look out for "number one," remember that your God is looking out for you. You are His precious daughter. As you allow Him to take care of you, it will free up space in your heart and allow you to look to the needs of others.

Father, You have made me to be a part of something much larger than myself. Focus my attention on those around me and not only on my own needs. Amen.

ALL BY MYSELF

Thou say in thine heart, My power and the might of mine hand hath gotten me this wealth. But thou shalt remember the LORD thy God: for it is he that giveth thee power to get wealth.
DEUTERONOMY 8:17–18 KJV

Little Logan set up a lemonade stand. He stirred the mixture into a pitcher of water and floated ice cubes with lemon slices his mom cut. Logan designed a sign with brightly colored pasteboard and markers: ICE COLD LEMONADE—75¢. Now he was ready for business!

At first, only Mom came. Soon members of a neighboring family each bought a glass. Grandma and Grandpa came! Grandpa said he was awfully thirsty and drank two glasses. Aunt Shelly drank a couple of glasses, too.

By lunchtime, Logan had sold ten glasses of lemonade. He yelled, "Mommy, I'm rich! And I did it all by myself!"

Logan did not consider his mother's investment in lemons, lemonade mix, napkins, cups, and pasteboard—or her time. It never crossed his mind that she tipped off his customers on the phone about the stand while he waited for business to magically appear!

We smile at a little boy's self-centeredness, but sometimes we adults act as if financial accomplishments live and die with us. God showers us with health, intelligence, education, and opportunity. Every breath and heartbeat are gifts from Him! Like Logan, we never suspect the roles He plays behind the scenes to encourage and prosper us.

Father, please forgive me when I take credit for blessings You give because of Your generous heart. Help me use them for Your glory. Amen.

MUSIC ON
THE GO

I will sing of your strength, in the morning I will sing of your love;
for you are my fortress, my refuge in times of trouble. . . .
I sing praise to you. . .my loving God.
PSALM 59:15–17 NIV

*S*usan identified with David, who was doggedly pursued by enemies in Psalm 59. "My enemy, Satan, has been snarling at me lately," she noted, thinking of the temptations that had come out of the blue. She thought she'd dealt with them years ago, once and for all. "Wouldn't the enemy love for me to fall prey to them again?"

In the final verses of Psalm 59, David's focus turns from enemies to music and singing. Thinking on this, Susan was reminded of the role music once played in her spiritual life. "Christian music once filled my home, but the main stereo has been broken for years. In the car? Well, silence is good—it leaves me to my thoughts."

Soon musical scripture CDs turned her car time into foot-tapping, finger-drumming focus on God. She brought out a small stereo to play Christian music while cooking and even turned on Christian music stations on cable TV to echo around the house. Her enemy of destruction didn't hunt with all that praise going on! She empathized with how David could go from cowering in the shadows to singing praises. Her music helped her do the same.

Mighty Father, thank You for the wonder of music. Help me to sing of Your strength and love daily, that I can continue to live victoriously. Amen.

ANCHOR YOUR SOUL

Take the sword of the Spirit, which is the word of God.
EPHESIANS 6:17 NLT

*A*n anchor is usually made out of metal and is used to hold a ship to the bottom of a body of water. It is interesting to note that wind and currents are not the largest forces an anchor has to overcome, but the vertical movement of waves.

God gave us the Bible to serve us much as an anchor serves a boat. The Bible is filled with valuable information for your mission on earth. God's Word can set your mind at peace and hold you steady through life's storms. The truth found within its pages is your assurance that no matter what you face in this battle of life, God will bring you safely home.

Take a new approach to God's Word. Let it breathe new revelation—new life into your heart. Expect knowledge and understanding of God's Word to become personal, written just for you. Anchor your soul by believing what you read, and know that the promises from God assure that the victory belongs to you.

God, I know the Bible is true and full of wisdom for my life.
Help me to grow and understand what I read and apply it to my life. Amen.

Simple Disciplines

Don't you realize that your body is the temple of the Holy Spirit, who lives in you and was given to you by God? You do not belong to yourself, for God bought you with a high price. So you must honor God with your body.
1 Corinthians 6:19–20 nlt

In New Testament times, lifestyles were quite different than they are today. The required tasks of the day were so physically demanding that it was unnecessary to set aside periods for concentrated exercise. Meals consisted of homegrown and gathered fruits, vegetables, and meats.

Today we are not nearly as naturally healthy. We avoid physical exertion by using cars, escalators, elevators, moving sidewalks, riding lawn mowers—the list goes on. We have turned a once-healthy diet into an overprocessed, sugar-laden diet, high in sodium, fat, and other unthinkable chemicals.

God, in His infinite wisdom, created us with certain bodily needs to teach us discipline. We need to institute simple, physical disciplines like exercise, diet, and rest to properly care for the temple of the Holy Spirit—our bodies. While those actions will attend to the needs of the body, spiritual disciplines such as prayer, fasting, and fellowship will attend to the spirit.

*Father, forgive me for not caring for Your temple as I should.
Help me to make time in my life for those simple disciplines that
You require for a healthy body and spirit. Amen.*

THE SAME STYLE

*Your path led through the sea, your way through
the mighty waters, though your footprints were not seen.*
PSALM 77:19 NIV

Marnell Jameson, who works from her home office, tells a story of her three-year-old daughter, Marissa. One early evening Marnell started to set the table for supper. She moved a few of Marissa's crayons while her daughter was coloring at the table. Marissa spread her tiny frame across her "work space."

"Stop it!" she protested. "This is my office!"

Marnell's husband barely looked up from what he was doing.

"Hmm. I wonder where she learned that."

Sometimes our children don't look like us physically as much as they "look like us" in their actions, attitudes, or mannerisms. Often when we meet a good friend's mother for the first time, we "see" our friend in the way her mom uses her hands or laughs. They have the same style.

That's not unlike the Lord Jesus and His Father.

"Anyone who has seen me has seen the Father," Jesus told His disciples (John 14:9 NIV).

When we read about God making a path through the mighty waters, we shouldn't be surprised when the Son does the same thing. Christ's disciples saw Him walking through the rough waters to them (John 6:19). What a blessing to know that when rough waters come into our lives, they can't stop the One whose unseen footprints lead right to us.

I praise You, Lord Jesus. You've shown me my heavenly Father. Amen.

FAST LANE

An argument started among the disciples as to which of them would be the greatest. Jesus, knowing their thoughts, took a little child and had him stand beside him. Then he said to them, "Whoever welcomes this little child in my name welcomes me; and whoever welcomes me welcomes the one who sent me. For he who is least among you all—he is the greatest."
LUKE 9:46–48 NIV

No one likes to wait in a line—especially at the grocery store. Inevitably the shortest line ends up in the longest wait.

Whether shoppers realize it or not, almost every one has a checkout strategy. People attempt to avoid long waits by evaluating the shoppers in each line, the number of items they are attempting to buy, and the cashier's alertness and speed. A teenage boy wanting to buy a single DVD is going to think twice before getting behind a mother of two with a full grocery cart. A rushed businesswoman likely won't get behind a slow-moving grandmother.

People often huff and make annoyed faces, but in reality, their impatience probably doesn't stem from a life-or-death matter requiring check-out in the next five minutes. The real reason has to do with pride. Just as the disciples argued over who would be the greatest, people view themselves and their daily activities as more important than someone else's.

Jesus' mentality was the exact opposite. He promised that the last would be first. Glorify Him today by humbling yourself enough to give up your space in line to someone who needs it.

Lord, give me humility as I interact with people today. Amen.

THANKFUL ROMANCE

*Among you there must not be even a hint of sexual immorality,
or of any kind of impurity, or of greed, because these are improper
for God's holy people. Nor should there be obscenity, foolish talk
or coarse joking, which are out of place, but rather thanksgiving.*
EPHESIANS 5:3–4 NIV

*M*any Christians would view sexual immorality as a "big sin,"
certainly of higher importance than obscenity or crude joking. But the
apostle Paul warns against them all—especially jesting about those
"big sins."

When we're at work or in a family or community gathering and not
surrounded by strong Christians, the talk may go in such directions. We
hear things we'd rather not listen to and have to resist them. Sometimes
even Christians can stumble, laughing about things that God takes very
seriously. Or, less obviously, we might get caught up in worldly pop
psychology or bad theology, saying unwise or silly things about the
male-female relationship God Himself created for our benefit.

The Lord's attitude is that humans should be thankful for the gift
He's given. Human sexuality is a wonderful thing when it's used as God
planned it to be, in marriage. But we should never laugh at the world's
misuse of sex. And we shouldn't denigrate the gift with "foolish talk or
coarse joking," even when our own romance isn't everything we'd like
it to be.

Some kinds of laughter imply disrespect and ingratitude. But those
attitudes are "out of place"—so replace them with thanksgiving.

*Thank You, Lord, for making men and women and the attraction between us.
Thank You for the joy it brings. Amen.*

UNAPPRECIATED BLESSINGS?

*Daniel answered and said: "Blessed be the name of God
forever and ever, for wisdom and might are His."*
DANIEL 2:20 NKJV

*W*hen God brings us through a trial, do we worship Him with great thankfulness, or do we take that blessing as our due? Though God is great, He doesn't appreciate being taken for granted any more than we would.

Required to describe King Nebuchadnezzar's bad dream to him or face imminent death, Daniel didn't worry or have a pity party. Instead, he called a prayer meeting of his three best friends. In the middle of the night, God answered their prayers, revealing Nebuchadnezzar's dream to Daniel, the wisest of the Babylonian king's wise men.

Daniel's first and very grateful response, in the midst of his relief, was to praise the Lord who had saved his life. He gave God recognition for His saving grace even before he went to see the king who had threatened to kill him.

We may believe that our Lord answers in such life-and-death situations, but do we have confidence that He takes care of smaller troubles, too? And when He does respond to an ordinary situation, do we give thanks?

*Make me thankful, Lord, for all the ways in which You bless and care for me.
I don't want my life to become laden with ungratefulness. Amen.*

BAD WORK DAY?

Then the king ordered the guards at his side: "Turn and kill the priests of the
LORD, because they too have sided with David. They knew he was fleeing,
yet they did not tell me." But the king's officials were not willing
to raise a hand to strike the priests of the LORD.
1 SAMUEL 22:17 NIV

There are bad days at work, and then there are disastrous ones. For the priests of Nob, this was the ultimate in disasters. Because they'd hidden David from Saul, the king wanted them dead.

Priest Ahimelech had bravely asked the king, "Who of all your servants is as loyal as David?" (1 Samuel 22:14 NIV). Not the politically correct response to give an angry sovereign. Those words cost the spiritual leader his life. Though the king's guard refused to kill priests, pagan Doeg the Edomite didn't quaver. He took the lives of eighty-five men.

You may have a less-than-perfect boss, but chances are slim anyone is trying to murder you. It's unlikely you'll have to pay for unwise words with your life.

Though you pay a lesser price than Ahimelech, can you stay faithful? Sometimes even very minor challenges seem so important in the workplace. Will they stop your love for Jesus in its tracks? The day that denies Jesus is disastrous, too.

Help me recognize what is really important, Lord,
and serve You wholeheartedly through every challenge. Amen.

No Turning Back

"Remember Lot's wife."
LUKE 17:32 KJV

In the Gospels, Jesus commands us to remember the nameless wife of Lot.

What kind of woman was she?

Lot's wife was a woman who lacked faith. While the Bible is silent on her origins, she may have been a heathen from the plain, whom Lot married after he separated from his uncle Abram. She apparently did not know the God of Abram, and she learned little about Him from her husband.

She was a woman who lingered. Instead of responding immediately to the instructions of the angels, she waited, causing them to drag her out of town.

Lot's wife had an independent spirit. We never see her beside her husband. Lot didn't take his wife by the hand; the angels did. She was behind—not with—him when she looked back.

She was a woman who disobeyed. Few women get such clear direction from the Lord: "Escape. . .look not behind thee" (Genesis 19:17 KJV). When the going got tough, she forgot or disbelieved the words of the angels. She stopped and looked back.

Jesus implied that she wanted to save her own life. But in so doing, she lost it, becoming a pillar of salt.

When we turn back from the narrow road Christ calls us to walk, we can also be hardened. Not in body, but in heart and mind.

Be soft, tender, obedient.

And remember Lot's wife.

Father, let me not forget the lessons of Lot's wife. Teach me to obey, and to not look back but to press on toward the high calling of God in Christ Jesus. Amen.

REMEMBER THIS

Keep your eyes on Jesus, who both began and finished this race we're in.
HEBREWS 12:2 THE MESSAGE

$\mathcal{J}$t can happen in a split second. Your life is suddenly turned upside down. Your mother is rushed to the emergency room. Your doctor utters the word *cancer.* Layoffs leave you jobless. Dark clouds quickly obscure your vision. Emotions reel out of control. Questions without answers rush through your mind. Life has been dramatically altered in the blink of an eye.

If you have not encountered such an experience, it's likely that someday you will. Prepare yourself now. Remember that when life throws us curveballs, we may be caught off guard, but God never is. He knows all things; past, present, and future. Since He knows what lies ahead, He can safely navigate us through the chaos.

When our heads are spinning and tears are flowing, there is only one thing to remember: focus on Jesus. He will never leave you nor forsake you. When you focus on Him, His presence envelops you. Where there is despair, He imparts hope. Where there is fear, He imparts faith. Where there is worry, He imparts peace. He will lead you on the right path and grant you wisdom for the journey. When the unexpected trials of life come upon you, remember this: focus on Jesus.

Dear Lord, I thank You that nothing takes You by surprise. When I am engulfed in the uncertainties of life, help me remember to focus on You. Amen.

MADE TO LAUGH

Our mouths were filled with laughter, our tongues with songs of joy.
PSALM 126:2 NIV

*C*omedians live their lives to make people laugh. From famous actors on the movie screen to the class clown at a local high school, we take a moment to celebrate with them. Sometimes the many worries in life keep us from letting our guard down, relaxing and enjoying the little things in life that bring us great joy and laughter.

It feels good to laugh—from a small giggle that you keep to yourself to a great big belly laugh. It is a wonderful stress reliever or tension breaker. How many times have you been in an awkward situation or in a stressful position and laughter erupted? It breaks the tension and sets our hearts and minds at ease.

As children of the Creator Himself, we were made to laugh—to experience great joy. Our design didn't include for us to carry the stress, worry, and heaviness every day. When was the last time you really had a good laugh? Have you laughed so hard that tears rolled down your cheeks? Go ahead! Have a good time! Ask God to give you a really good laugh today.

Lord, help me rediscover laughter. Help me to take every opportunity You bring to see the joy in life and the comedy that it brings to my world every day. Amen.

FOOTRACE

I have fought the good fight, I have finished the race, I have kept the faith.
2 TIMOTHY 4:7 NIV

Celia felt a growing anxiety about her future. She'd been raising kids for many years, but now her youngest child was heading off to school. Celia talked her husband into selling their house and buying a fixer-upper.

Ah! A new focus. Celia felt relieved.

It took a tremendous amount of work to pack up the old house and prepare it to sell. Then the fixer-upper became all-consuming. Celia stopped many of the activities she had participated in with her other kids—a moms' prayer group and volunteering at school. She didn't have time!

Only afterward, as she looked back, did she acknowledge that year had become a blur. She couldn't remember a thing about her kids' school year! And she hadn't avoided what she most feared—an empty house. Sadly, Celia realized she had bolted forward without consulting God. She had let a fear of the future steal her present, which included time with her children that she would never get back.

The apostle Paul often compared the journey of faith to a race. We need to finish the race well, Paul admonished. The race of motherhood, the race of filling our lives with important things, the race of trusting God with our future.

Lord, one day we want to be able to say, with a satisfied sigh,
just like Paul, "I have finished the race. I have trusted in God." Amen.

WHERE ARE YOU?

Day
103

*Adam and his wife hid themselves from the presence of the
LORD God amongst the trees of the garden. And the LORD God
called unto Adam, and said unto him, Where art thou?*
GENESIS 3:8–9 KJV

Throughout the Bible, God asks us questions, inviting us to dialogue with Him. The very first question God asked called Adam and Eve to self-awareness. *"Where are you?"* Of course God knew where the couple was that night. He asked to make them aware of where they were.

God waits for us at the appointed hour. He hovers over the latest Bible study guide and the beautifully illustrated prayer journal. He longs to listen to the words that pour out from our hearts. He remains eager to speak to us through His written Word and the Holy Spirit. But too many pages of the journal remain blank, and the Bible bookmark doesn't change places.

Today God still whispers, *Where are you?* God wants to spend time with us, but too often we hide among the trees of our gardens, the routines of everyday life. We have e-mails to answer, car repairs to see to, clothes to wash, phone calls to answer—and another appointment with God gets broken. The more appointments we break, the easier it becomes to forget.

Take a moment to answer God's question. He will meet you wherever you are.

*Dear heavenly Father, teach me the discipline of spending time with You.
Let me listen and answer when You call. Amen.*

CHILD'S PLAY

"Unless you change and become like little children,
you will never enter the kingdom of heaven."
MATTHEW 18:3 NIV

The famous biographer James Boswell recounted with fondness his memory of a boyhood day when his father took him fishing. Boswell gleaned important life lessons from his dad that day as they sat on the creek bank waiting for a bite on their fishing lines.

Having heard Boswell's fishing experience so often, someone thought to check the journal that Boswell's father kept to determine, from a parental perspective, what he recorded about the father-son excursion. Turning to the date, the inquirer found one sentence: *Gone fishing today with my son; a day wasted.*

Though hard to admit, have you ever felt the same? Like when you played catch with a nephew rather than catching up on housework, or when you took your child to the zoo although you had errands to run?

As our to-do list grows, it becomes harder to engage in child's play. But often what we need most is to enter the world of make-believe where clocks and adult responsibilities are as extinct as the toy dinosaurs with which children play.

Spending time with a special child in our lives affords us the opportunity to influence him or her for God's kingdom. So don't waste another moment; seize the day and play!

Father, help me to learn to play and enjoy the children You have brought into my
life. I want to influence them for Your kingdom. Bless them and use me today.
Amen.

ANGER AND RECONCILIATION

Day 105

Be ye angry, and sin not: let not the sun go down upon your wrath:
Neither give place to the devil.
EPHESIANS 4:26–27 KJV

Renee lived with anger that permeated all her relationships. Many could not blame her, with all she experienced in life. However, many did not want to be around Renee, for without warning, they often became the recipients of her wrath.

God tells us it is okay to be angry, but we are not to sin. The words "let not the sun go down upon your wrath," mean we are not to let a great deal of time go by before we reconcile. We need to have a spirit of reconciliation, making amends and compromising, even when we think we are 100 percent right. When we don't have this perspective of quickly resolving conflict, our anger festers and we become embittered, hard-hearted, and resentful. We end up making room for the devil, allowing Satan a foothold in our lives. The unresolved anger will poison us and destroy relationships with others, leaving us lonely, afflicted, and alone in our wrath.

Surrender your anger to the Lord, asking the Holy Spirit to empower you to forgive and be reconciled to the offender. In this liberation, enjoy the abundant life Jesus came to give us (John 10:10).

Forgiving Lord, I surrender my anger to You. Please give me a spirit of reconciliation and the opportunity to make amends with the offender. Amen.

TRUE FRIENDSHIP

Most people would not be willing to die for an upright person, though someone
might perhaps be willing to die for a person who is especially good.
ROMANS 5:7 NLT

$\mathcal{F}$ew may recognize the name of Liviu Librescu. Liviu survived the Holocaust, even though he was imprisoned in a Nazi labor camp. Professor Librescu taught at universities the world over, including Israel's Tel Aviv University. He published numerous scientific papers and received grants from NASA for his work in aeronautics. But what this brilliant septuagenarian did on April 16, 2007, overshadows all his other accomplishments.

On that day Professor Librescu did what he had done for numerous Mondays in his lifetime—he taught. On this April day, he was teaching at Virginia Polytechnic Institute and State University. Gunshots reverberated outside his classroom door. As his students bolted for the windows and began jumping to safety, Liviu Librescu blocked the doorway.

Chances are none of those students had ever thought of seventy-six-year-old Professor Librescu as their friend. It's just as unlikely he called his students his friends. But that day at Virginia Tech, Liviu Librescu proved to be the best friend any of them had ever had.

We don't know when or if such a sacrifice will be asked of us. But a life lived for others, even to death, will be a life lived well. Liviu Librescu did it. So did Jesus Christ. Will we?

Lord Jesus, I know that You're my best friend.
Teach me be a true friend to You and others. Amen.

ACTION-FIGURE EASTER

*We will not hide these truths from our children; we will
tell the next generation about the glorious deeds of the LORD.*
PSALM 78:4 NLT

*M*ichelle opened the big picture Bible to Jesus' donkey-riding entry
into Jerusalem and smiled down at her children busily assembling
their props. Seven-year-old Michael spread palmetto fronds across the
toothpick road he'd carefully laid across the living room carpet. Five-
year-old Kyla mounted the Jesus doll on My Little Pony and began
the trek down the winding path amid cries of "Hosanna!" from her
dad, who had lined a battalion of green army men along the roadside.
Toddler Josh clutched the round pillow that was to become the stone
rolled in front of the shoe-box tomb after Jesus' crucifixion on a cross
formed from pencils rubber-banded together.

The Good Friday tradition of acting out the Easter week story
had begun when Michael was in diapers and had evolved into a much-
anticipated family production. A real Jesus doll had been purchased,
but the rest of the cast was assembled—with much imagination—from
the toy box. As Michelle read the Easter story aloud, beginning with
Palm Sunday and ending with Jesus' glorious resurrection, the children
acted out each scene.

Michelle treasured her children's delight each Easter morning
when they sprang from their beds to find the grave handkerchief
discarded and Jesus miraculously sitting atop the shoe-box tomb, his
little plastic arms raised triumphantly in the air.

*Risen Savior, help us use every opportunity to instill in
our children the marvelous truths of our faith, so that Your love
may be as a precious heirloom to future generations. Amen.*

FRIENDSHIPS
TAKE TIME

A friend is always loyal, and a brother is born to help in time of need.
PROVERBS 17:17 NLT

*P*atty frowned as she hung up the phone. She knew that a one-hour get-together really meant three hours. She didn't have that kind of time in her day! Her to-do list was already two pages long. But Patty could tell by the tone in her friend's voice that she was troubled and needed to talk.

Oh, why can't friendships be more efficient? Patty wondered to herself, not for the first time. She loved her friends, but her spare time was in short supply. It was so valuable!

But relationships are valuable, too. And they take time to be nourished so they will develop into a satisfying experience. Isn't the entire Bible an analogy of God's patience, wooing us into a deeper relationship with Himself? God knew that nothing can satisfy us like a relationship with Him. To woo us, He gives us His time and attention, the kind of focus that can touch our hearts.

True intimacy cannot be rushed or scheduled or abbreviated or economized. It just takes time.

Lord Jesus, what a friend You are! All who know You can look to
You in need. Show me how to be a friend to others as if I were representing
You—not just because I have to, but because I see them through Your eyes.
Help me to love my friends at all times, for Your glory. Amen.

PRICKLY PEARS

*If anyone thinks himself to be religious, and yet does not bridle his
tongue but deceives his own heart, this man's religion is worthless.*
JAMES 1:26 NASB

*T*wo friends strolled through a desert habitat and noticed dozens of
prickly pears at the base of a cactus. Drawn by curiosity, the women
picked them up to examine them, carefully avoiding the larger needles
and not paying attention to the tiny, nearly invisible clusters of smaller
needles.

Suddenly, one cried out, "Ouch! I think I have a needle in me."

Then the second friend yelled even louder, "OUCH!" realizing
she had dozens of small, hairlike needles stuck in her fingers as well.
For the next thirty minutes, the pair stood there tediously removing
needles from each other's fingers.

As with prickly pears, it is important in relationships to heed all
warning signals, large and small. Larger needles are easier to identify
and avoid, but smaller, hairlike needle clusters are insidious. Like
the less visible clusters of hairlike needles, some life situations and
relationships are webs of entrapment—they appear harmless at first,
perhaps even fruitful on the surface, but actually lead to severe pain.

When you see the warning signs of gossip, do not associate
yourself with the situation or the person(s), lest you be drawn in by
the allure of "juicy" (poisonous) information or prideful associations.
Do not become part of a subgroup that makes its entertainment the
downgrading of others. Remain as shrewd as serpents, but as innocent
as doves (Matthew 10:16), because life is filled with prickly pears.

Oh Lord, help me bridle my tongue and associate with those who bridle theirs.
Amen.

GET MOVING!

Do not be wise in your own eyes;. fear the LORD and shun evil.
This will bring health to your body and nourishment to your bones.
PROVERBS 3:7–8 NIV

*F*eeling run down? Has your spiritual fervor left? Do you need a boost in your body and spirit?

Obeying and living by God's principles produces life and health. Just as we exercise to strengthen our bodies, we must use our spiritual muscles to attain the strength, peace, and prosperity we all need and desire.

An ancient proverb reads: "He who has health has hope; and he who has hope has everything." As we pray, read, and meditate on God's Word, we increase our spiritual stamina. Although our circumstances may not change, the Lord gives us a new perspective filled with the hope and assurance that we may have lacked before. Exercising our faith produces character and a stronger foundation of trust in the Lord.

Consider this: Medicine left in the cabinet too long loses its potency; masking tape loses its adhesiveness with time; old paint hardens in the can. So when was the last time you shook out the old bones and got moving? A workout for the body and spirit may be just the medicine you need!

Dear Lord, please help me out of my spiritual and physical rut. As I seek Your strength, revive my soul and touch my body with Your healing power, I pray.
Amen.

TOUGH LOVE

Day
111

Dear children, let's not merely say that we love each other;
let us show the truth by our actions.
1 JOHN 3:18 NLT

The relationship between speech and actions is seen throughout the Bible. Joseph's brothers *tell* Jacob they are sad that their brother is dead, yet they are the ones who staged his death and sold him into slavery. Saul *says* he loves David, but he tries over and over again to kill him. Pontius Pilate *declares* that he thinks Jesus is innocent, but he gives the order to crucify Him anyway. As the old adage goes, "Actions speak louder than words."

We are called to intentionally love one another, not with our meaningless words, but with our quantifiable actions. We discover that the command to love actively is much more difficult than loving with words. Loving with words requires little thought and no commitment. Loving with actions requires firm purpose and devotion.

Jesus is the embodiment of active love. He loved those who most thought were unlovable, talking to, touching, healing, and eating with them, and in the ultimate act of love, dying on the cross to save every one of us from our sin. The author of 1 John is asking us to love as Jesus loved. We must push our selfishness aside and give ourselves fully to others with active and truthful love.

Dear Lord, teach me to love like You love. Let me be intentional, active, and
willing to put aside my own desires so that I can love others better. Amen.

CRISIS
COUNSELOR

Offer unto God thanksgiving; and pay thy vows unto the most High: And call upon me in the day of trouble: I will deliver thee, and thou shalt glorify me.
PSALM 50:14–15 KJV

$\mathcal{W}$e all experience moments of panic when we are almost overwhelmed with the need to talk to someone. Perhaps someone we know has developed a devastating illness, we've been in an accident, we experience the death of a friend or family member, or our character has been maligned. The pain is often so great that the only relief we can think of comes through sharing with someone we love or a confidant we feel can help us.

Often the person we want to talk to is not available. She or he may be busy, not at home, or it could be late in a different time zone. When that help or counselor is not available, discouragement or depression can result.

God is always there. He never sleeps; He's on call twenty-four hours a day, seven days a week. He is willing not only to listen but to give wise counsel. He gives peace beyond our understanding and joy in the midst of trials.

The next time you find yourself hurting or in a panic, call on God. Ask Him to listen and help you. You'll find He is the only Counselor you need.

Thank You, Lord, for being there whenever I need You.
Help me to learn to rely on You, not on anyone else. Amen.

Unswerving Faith

Let us hold unswervingly to the hope we profess,
for he who promised is faithful.
HEBREWS 10:23 NIV

*D*o you remember your first bicycle? Maybe it was a hand-me-down from an older sibling or one found at a neighborhood garage sale. Or maybe you remember the joy of discovering a brand-new bike on Christmas morning. In your delight, you never wondered how Santa got it down the chimney!

Do you remember learning to ride your bike? What a process! While mastering putting it all together—the pedaling, the steering, the balance—did you ever lose control? When you started to swerve, it was a lost cause. Regaining momentum was practically impossible. Almost inevitably, the bike tipped over, and you ended up in the grass.

"Keep it straight!" parents call out when they see their child headed for yet another bike crash. "Look where you're going! Hold it steady!" Similarly, the author of Hebrews challenges us to hold *unswervingly* to our hope in Christ Jesus. Certainly we fail to do this at times, but life is much better when we keep our eyes fixed on Him.

Sometimes just a whisper from Satan, the father of lies, can cause shakiness where once there was steadfastness. Place your hope in Christ alone. He will help you to resist the lies of this world. Hold *unswervingly* to your Savior today. He is faithful!

Jesus, You are the object of my hope. There are many distractions
in my life, but I pray that You will help me to keep my eyes on You.
Thank You for Your faithfulness. Amen.

FREE AT A PRICE

The Spirit and the bride say, "Come!" And let him who hears say,
"Come!" Whoever is thirsty, let him come; and whoever wishes,
let him take the free gift of the water of life.
REVELATION 22:17 NIV

Have you noticed lately that a lot of "free" things have many strings attached? Search the Web, and you'll discover scores of ads that offer a supposedly free item *if* you'll do something. In our world, very few people really want to give anything away.

But Jesus gave His earthly life away without our asking Him to or paying Him beforehand. Love led Him to give all He could to draw some to Himself. Though He knew many would deny His gift, Jesus offered Himself freely.

The benefits are all on our side: new life and a relationship with our Creator. What can we offer the Omnipotent One? What could He require that we could fulfill for Him? Our Creator doesn't really need us. He simply chooses, out of His own generous nature, to give us new life.

As we drink deeply of the water of life, we recognize God's great gift. Grateful, we seek out ways to serve Him. But even if we gave all we had, we could never repay God. His gift would still be free.

Do you know people who could use the best, really free gift in the world? Tell them about Jesus!

Thank You, Lord, for giving me a really free gift—
the best anyone could offer. Amen.

IN HIS CONTROL

For You are my hope, O Lord GOD;
You are my trust from my youth.
PSALM 71:5 NKJV

*E*verything about Jan's life was organized and beautiful. She called herself a professional organizer and, in fact, she earned a good living helping others organize and beautify their own homes. She had been featured in the local media and was making a name for herself on the speaking circuit as well.

Most assuredly, Jan had talents and skills that her friends admired— even envied—and when they came for a visit, they often enjoyed playing little tricks on her, sometimes rearranging her silverware drawer or hanging the guest towel in the bathroom upside down before leaving her house. Days later, she would call up her friends and they would share a laugh about their silly pranks.

Sobering news came, however, the day Jan was diagnosed with cancer, and like an upended sock drawer, her life was turned upside down. Jan had a decision to make. She could keep a tight hold on her life, or she could let go and lean into her Savior. Because Jan loved the Lord more than anything else, it was no contest. She admitted to Him that she was incapable of organizing her life and asked Him to take control of it all, including her cancer. Her friends and everyone she met—even strangers—marveled at her grace and peace in the face of adversity.

Lord, in times of trouble, help me to follow
Jan's example to let go and to lean into You. Amen.

Joy in the Ride

Yes, there will be an abundance of flowers and singing and joy!
ISAIAH 35:2 NLT

What if we viewed life as an adventurous bicycle ride? With our destination in focus, we would pedal forward, but not so swiftly as to overlook the beauty and experiences that God planted along the way.

We would note the tenacity of a wildflower in bloom despite its unlikely location for growth. We would contemplate God's mercy and savor the brilliance of a rainbow that illuminated a once-blackened sky.

At our halfway point, we would relax from the journey, finding a spot in life's shade to refresh and replenish ourselves for the return trip. We wouldn't just ride; we would explore, pausing along the way to inhale the fresh air and scent of wildflowers.

In life, however, sometimes the road gets rough, and we are forced to take sharp turns. When that happens, we miss the beauty that surrounds us. But if we savor the ride and keep moving forward despite the bumps in the road, then "flowers and singing and joy" will follow.

So when your legs grow weary and your pathway seems long, brace yourself, board your bike, and keep on pedaling. Joy awaits you just around the bend.

Oh Lord, pave my pathway with song, even when the road is rough.
Remind me to stop and appreciate the scenery along the way.
Only then will I experience the joy awaiting me. Amen.

STRENGTH FOR THE JOURNEY

An angel touched him and told him, "Get up and eat!"
1 KINGS 19:5 NLT

*F*ran rushed through the kitchen door, messenger bag and commuter mug in hand. She tossed the bag onto the table, threw the plastic mug in the sink, and ran over to the fridge. *Hmm. . .dinner. Chicken.* She grabbed the boneless breasts out of the fridge and removed the frying pan from a base cabinet. *Now some oil.*

As she ran over to the pantry, Fran's elbow hit a glass sitting on the counter, and *crash*! She stopped in her tracks, staring at the million little pieces of glass at her feet. Slumping into a kitchen chair, Fran just sat there, tears running down her face. Sniffling, she cried, "Lord, help me! I can't do this anymore!"

Some days we eat the bear. Some days the bear eats us, and we find ourselves feeling like Elijah, who ran and ran and ran before finally slumping down beneath a solitary broom tree. Depleted, exhausted, spent, Elijah prayed, "I have had enough, LORD" (1 Kings 19:4 NLT). Then he gave himself up to sleep. But God, having heard his cry, sent an angel to touch him. Through God's ministrations, Elijah was given the strength he needed.

Isn't it great to know that God is there, just waiting to hear our cry and respond, encouraging us to rest and take nourishment, strengthening us for the journey? Praise the God who replenishes us!

*Thank You, God, for enabling me to face each day. Help me when
I feel I can go on no longer. Touch me, and replenish me with
Your Word and strength as I rest in You. Amen.*

PATIENCE, NOT FURY

Do not be quickly provoked in your spirit,
for anger resides in the lap of fools.
ECCLESIASTES 7:8–9 NIV

It had been one of those days when everyone wanted something *now*. The boss left early, depositing three projects on Marsha's desk that had to be finished before 5:00 p.m. Her husband had to work late and couldn't pick up their two teens at ball practice. Marsha's cell phone buzzed constantly during the afternoon, breaking her concentration. Her kids were furious, and her mother called, needing to talk "right now; it can't wait." The bank wanted her car payment, but when Marsha checked her bank balance, her paycheck had not been deposited. Again.

That's when her friend walked up and asked if she'd like a coffee break. "No!" Marsha wanted to scream. "I have too much to do!"

When the world dumps everything in our lap at once, anger is a natural, human response. Yet the Bible warns us not to become angry too quickly (James 1:19). Quick anger leads to foolish actions, such as shouting at an innocent colleague. Instead, step back, take a couple of deep breaths, and remember that you can place all burdens at the feet of Christ. Ask for help, prioritize, then tackle your duties one at a time.

Lord, help me remember that You always provide a way of
handling all troubles. Guide me as I find the right path and
hold on tightly to my tongue—and my temper. Amen.

FIRSTFRUITS

*Honor the LORD from your wealth and from the first of all your produce; so
your barns will be filled with plenty and your vats will overflow with new wine.*
PROVERBS 3:9–10 NASB

*P*erhaps you think this verse doesn't apply to you because you don't
consider yourself *wealthy*. The only *produce* you have comes from the
grocery store. *Barns* and *vats of wine* may not be your top priority. But
this verse applies. Read these words: *Honor the Lord. . .from the first of all.*

Our God is not a God of leftovers. He wants us to put Him first.
One way to honor God is to give Him our "firstfruits," the best we
have to offer. The truth is that everything we have comes from God.
The Bible calls us to cheerfully give back to the Lord one-tenth of all
we earn.

Giving to God has great reward. You may not have barns you need
God to fill, but you will reap the benefit in other ways. When believers
honor God by giving to Him, we can trust that He will provide for our
needs. In Malachi 3:10, we are challenged to test God in our tithing.
Start with your next paycheck. Make the check that you dedicate to
God's kingdom work the first one you write. See if God is faithful to
provide for you throughout the month.

*Lord, remind me not to separate my finances from my faith.
All that I have comes from Your hand. I will honor You with my firstfruits.
Amen.*

THE LORD'S PLANS

Commit your actions to the LORD, and your plans will succeed.
PROVERBS 16:3 NLT

At an early age, an ambitious woman planned her entire life. She determined she would earn her law degree by age twenty-five, marry by twenty-eight, become a partner in her law firm by thirty-five, and retire at fifty. She was quite disappointed when her plan failed.

Do you have any plans for your life?

The Lord desires that we have plans for our lives. He encourages us to have aspirations, goals, and hopes; however, He provides a framework for developing and implementing those plans. God wants us to develop them in cooperation with His will for us. Those plans should be in line with His plan; His overall purpose for our lives; our spiritual gifts, abilities, interests, and talents; and His perfect timing. God requires us not to hold on too tight to the plan, but rather to commit or entrust it to Him. When we surrender it to the Lord, He will secure, or "make firm," the plan. God's will cannot be thwarted; therefore, God's purpose, plan, and work will be established. There is no need to worry—just commit your plans to the Lord.

Lord, thank You that I don't need to worry about my life, future, or plans. Help me to fully surrender to Your plan, knowing that Your plan cannot be thwarted. Amen.

FEELING THE SQUEEZE

The eye can never say to the hand, "I don't need you."
The head can't say to the feet, "I don't need you."
1 CORINTHIANS 12:21 NLT

*W*e've all heard the term "the sandwich generation," referring to midlifers coping with teenagers on one end and aging parents on the other. Somehow, calling it a sandwich sounds too easy. The in-between filling seems to fit comfortably, like ham and Swiss cheese nestled between two slices of rye bread. Sticking with the sandwich metaphor, a more appropriate term would be the "squeeze generation." Picture peanut butter and jelly oozing out of squished white bread. It is a challenging season of life.

So how do we keep our heads above water when every face we love is looking back at us with genuine, overwhelming needs? By learning to ask for help from family members, friends, the church, and even from resources available in the community.

It's a season in life when we need help. We can't do it alone. And perhaps that is a great blessing to realize. God never meant for us to do it alone! He designed us to live in community—family, friends, and church—helping and serving and meeting one another's needs. "The body is a unit," Paul told the believers at Corinth, "though it is made up of many parts; and though all its parts are many, they form one body. So it is with Christ" (1 Corinthians 12:12 NIV).

There's nothing wrong with asking for help when you need it.

Lord, You promise never to leave us nor forsake us.
Thank You for providing helpers to come along side of me. Amen.

MORE THAN WORDS CAN SAY

"Never will I leave you; never will I forsake you."
HEBREWS 13:5 NIV

Silence—for many people it can be quite uncomfortable. Televisions, stereos, and iPods fill the void. Incessant conversation is the norm. Noise must permeate the air. What is it about silence that agitates us so? Perhaps pondering our own thoughts is frightening. Maybe we need constant reassurance from others that we are not alone.

We may desperately desire to hear from God, yet sometimes He chooses to remain silent. How do we interpret His silence? Do we become fearful, uneasy, or confused? We may feel that He has abandoned us, but this is not true. When God is silent, His love is still present. When God is silent, He is still in control. When God is silent, He is still communicating. Do not miss it. His silence speaks volumes.

Most couples who are deeply in love do not have to exchange words to communicate their love. They can experience contentment and unwavering trust in the midst of silence. The presence of their loved one is enough. That is what God desires in our love relationship with Him. He wants us to abide in His presence. Silence prohibits distraction. As we continue to trust Him amid the silence, we learn that His presence is all we need. God has promised that He will never leave us nor forsake us. Believe Him. Trust Him. His presence is enough.

Dear Lord, help me trust You even when You choose to remain silent.
May I learn how to be content in Your presence alone. Amen.

MUSTARD SEED FAITH

Now faith is being sure of what we hope
for and certain of what we do not see.
HEBREWS 11:1 NIV

$\mathcal{W}$e exercise faith in the unseen on a daily basis. When we step onto an elevator, we can't see the cables that keep us from falling. It is rare to meet the chef face-to-face when dining at a restaurant. Yet we trust him to prepare our food. As we shop, we use debit cards and place faith in the bank across town to back up our payments.

Christians are called to spiritual faith. God is ever-present in our lives, though we cannot see Him with our eyes. Have you found that trusting Him is easier to *talk about* than it is to *live out in daily life*?

The Lord understands the limitations of our humanity. When the disciples asked Jesus to increase their faith, His answer must have been reassuring to them: "If you have faith as small as a mustard seed, you can say to this mulberry tree, 'Be uprooted and planted in the sea,' and it will obey you" (Luke 17:6 NIV). A mustard seed is one of the tiniest of all seeds, yet even mustard seed faith can accomplish great things.

Surely it was not happenstance that Christ chose a seed as His example when teaching about faith. A seed has one purpose—growth. As you trust in Him and find God consistently faithful, your faith will increase.

Father, I cannot see You with my eyes, but I know You are there. I sense that You are at work in my life and all around me. Increase my faith, I pray. Amen.

SMELLING THE ROSES

I know that nothing is better for them than to rejoice,
and to do good in their lives, and also that every man should eat
and drink and enjoy the good of all his labor—it is the gift of God.
ECCLESIASTES 3:12–13 NKJV

*W*omen today work hard—sometimes the labor seems endless. We care for our homes, families, employers, and churches. We cook, sort, haul, clean, and nurture, and that's before we even leave for our jobs outside the home. We run errands at lunch and often eat more meals behind the steering wheel than at the dinner table. Our days start early and end late, and we head for our beds as if sleep were a luxury instead of a necessity.

Yet constant work is not what God intended for our lives. We should work hard, yes, but not to the exclusion of rest and times of renewal for our minds and souls. As the author of Ecclesiastes points out, our work and the results of it—our food, homes, and friendships—are gifts that God meant for us to enjoy and appreciate.

Finding time isn't always easy, but the rewards of a calmer mind and a grateful heart will be well worth the effort.

Lord, thank You for the gifts You've bestowed on me.
Help me find moments to enjoy them and share them with those I love. Amen.

BEYOND THE THORNBUSH

"For this reason I will fence her in with thornbushes. I will block her path with a wall to make her lose her way. . . . But then I will win her back once again. I will lead her into the desert and speak tenderly to her there."
HOSEA 2:6, 14 NLT

*M*aybe, unlike Hosea's unfaithful wife, Gomer, about whom this verse was spoken, you haven't walked away from God. But life has become tough, with challenges outweighing the smooth, peaceful days of easy faith. You feel hedged about with thorns and may frequently ask, "God, what do You want of me?" Frustration becomes your constant companion.

As you wait for God to show you the way, take heart. He hasn't forgotten you. Though He may be redesigning your future, He won't leave you in the dust. Just as the prophet wooed his wife, God will draw you to Himself again. Sin may need to be cleansed from your life or patience learned. But a new, bright future doubtless awaits just beyond that thornbush. Simply obey and wait for God to show you the way beyond its prickly points.

You'll be glad you stayed faithful.

Lord, I must admit I don't relish facing challenging times. Help me to trust that You have a better plan, and all will be well in the end. Amen.

TIMELESS WISDOM

*His wife's name was Abigail. And the woman
was intelligent and beautiful in appearance.*
1 SAMUEL 25:3 NASB

*A*bigail is the only woman in the Bible whose brains are mentioned before her beauty. And how well she used them! She stood before a furious king and his army, calming him with just her words. She returned home at the end of the day but wisely chose just the right time to tell her quarrelsome husband the news. Her wisdom and grace made her so memorable that when her husband died, David sent for her and made her his bride.

With the stress and fast-paced lives we live today, we can easily believe that women in the Bible have little to teach us. After all, they lived thousands of years ago, without the headaches of today's world. Yet our concerns are not that different. We still worry about our families, seek to act responsibly in God's eyes, and strive to do our work with diligence.

And the wisdom to handle those concerns still comes from the same source: God. Just as He granted Abigail the wisdom to soothe a king, the Lord will grant us the wisdom and intelligence to handle whatever today's world throws at us.

All we have to do is ask.

*Lord, thank You for the blessings in my life. Grant me the wisdom
and grace to deal with my family, my home, and my work in
ways that reflect my love and faith in You. Amen.*

A Spiritual Balm

*May the LORD answer you when you are in distress; may the name
of the God of Jacob protect you. May he send you help from the sanctuary
and grant you support from Zion. . . . May he give you the desire of your
heart and make all your plans succeed.*
PSALM 20:1–2, 4 NIV

*T*he psalms of David often speak directly to our hearts. When he writes,
"May the name of the God of Jacob protect you," we are filled with
the assurance that God is defending us. There is a hedge surrounding
us that no demon's arrows can pierce. Nothing can get through God's
shield. Nothing!

David's words of God's support, refreshment, and strength buoy
our flagging spirits. We drink them in, and they quench our thirst for
confidence, enabling us once again to hold our heads up high in God's
power, determined to allow Him to work through us, with us, for us.
We have a faith that can move mountains!

And the words "May he give you the desire of your heart and
make all your plans succeed" give us an optimistic outlook. As we walk
in God's will, He will give us opportunities to help make our plans
successful. We are given the assurance of having our heart's desire. He
provides all that we need and more.

These words are a spiritual balm to be applied daily for sustenance,
growth, confidence, and peace. Apply every few hours if necessary. And
pray them over the lives of others. Share the joy of God's Word!

*God, through Your Word, my heart, soul, and spirit are nourished. Thank You
for the precious gift of Your psalms, a balm to my spirit, a joy in my life! Amen.*

BLOOM WHERE
YOU'RE PLANTED

*The godly will flourish like palm trees. . . . For they are transplanted
to the LORD's own house. They flourish in the courts of our God.*
PSALM 92:12–13 NLT

*H*as your dream job turned into a nightmare? Does your work interfere with your personal life? Are your coworkers uncooperative and rude? Do you feel smothered and stifled?

"Bloom where you're planted," one quip suggests. Not an easy task when our circumstances are less than ideal. But consider the houseplant. Place it near a window and it will stretch toward the sunlight despite its location. Busy women often fail at that kind of flexibility. Whether it involves where we live or work, or the situation we find ourselves in, we struggle to find a more scenic, sunnier place. Yet God has a reason for putting us right where we are.

As a houseplant reaches for the sunlight, it blooms and grows. Likewise, when God sheds his sunlight on our imperfect environments, we, too, flourish and grow. For it matters little where we live or what type of job we have when compared to the plan God has for our lives while we are here.

So if your surroundings look bleak, take a lesson from the flourishing houseplant. Reach toward the *Son*light and bloom.

Heavenly Father, I am wonderfully made to bloom and flourish in the garden of my life. Cause me to grow, not groan, when things don't go my way. Amen.

FEAR NOT

For God has not given us a spirit of fear,
but of power and of love and of a sound mind.
2 TIMOTHY 1:7 NKJV

The writer sat down at her desk, set her coffee cup to the side, and pulled up a blank page on her computer screen. She broke into a sweat as she thought about the writing assignment her editor had just phoned in to her.

What if I can't do it? she thought. *Maybe I've run out of words to write. I could be dried up—an empty well. What if I have nothing more to say to the world?*

Fear is a paralyzing thing, whether it comes when speaking in front of an audience for the first time, accepting a new writing assignment from an editor, or jumping out of a plane with a parachute strapped to your back. The specific thing that frightens is as individual and unique as people, but we all struggle with fear at some time in our lives.

Throughout the Old Testament, God tells His people to "fear not" because He is with them. Remember the battles Israel fought against overwhelming odds. As Christians, we can take the admonition "Fear not," to heart. God knows our fears and encourages us to turn our fear into faith.

The writer sat back in her chair and sipped her coffee, remembering all the times God had calmed her fears and brought writing success. She breathed a prayer of thanksgiving and began typing.

Thank You, Lord, for Your faithfulness and love that casts out fear. Amen.

STEADY AS A ROCK

Jesus Christ is the same yesterday and today and forever.
MATTHEW 24:35 NIV

The world and our lives are constantly changing. Some of this is due to outside circumstances—war, inflation, job loss, death. And some is self-imposed. We change our careers for something more challenging. As our clothes wear out, we buy new ones. When we gain weight, we take an exercise class to lose a few pounds. When gray hair begins to sprout, we may decide to have it colored. Tired of straight hair, we opt for a permanent.

But there is one thing in this world that is more permanent than a permanent. And that is Jesus Christ. No matter what changes are happening in our lives, we can rest assured that He remains the same—yesterday, today, and forever. Minute by minute, we can look to Him for guidance, reassurance, and peace of mind. We can rest in the fact that Jesus, our Rock, is always there, waiting to strengthen us and give us the relief we crave.

No matter how bleak the world looks, no matter what crisis we are going through, we do not have to worry, for although heaven and earth may pass away, God's words—the anchor of our spirit, the bread of our lives, that which gives us peace beyond understanding—will remain forever.

Ah, Lord, what a relief to know that in this ever-changing world, You remain the same. You are always there, waiting for me to come to You, loving me and sheltering me. Thank You for being my Rock, my Refuge, and my Rest. Amen.

THE MASTER'S NEEDS

"If anyone asks you, 'Why are you untying it?' tell him, 'The Lord needs it.'"
LUKE 19:31 NIV

*J*esus gave His disciples strange instructions: "Go to the village ahead of you, and as you enter it, you will find a colt tied there. . . . Untie it and bring it here. If anyone asks you, 'Why are you untying it?' tell him, 'The Lord needs it' " (Luke 19:30–31 NIV). The owners did ask what they were doing, and the disciples repeated what Jesus had said. The owners agreed, and Jesus rode that colt into Jerusalem.

Did the owners recognize the disciples? Had Jesus told them to expect the request? Even if they already followed Christ, giving up the animal took generosity and courage. They offered it willingly because the Master needed it. Jesus' need became their priority.

Today Jesus continues to ask for the unexpected. He may ask us for our things, our time, or our talents. He asks us to align our use of what He has given us with His priorities.

We can't predict when or how Jesus will call on us to serve Him. Maybe He calls us to use our vacation time to go on a mission trip. Perhaps He wants us to give new clothes to the homeless shelter. He may ask us to volunteer in the nursery during the worship service.

What does the Master need? That should become our priority.

Master of all, we invite You to be Master of our hearts, of everything we possess and are. Teach us to make Your priorities our own. Amen.

BUSY WAITING

"Not one of these men, this evil generation,
shall see the good land which I swore to give your fathers."
DEUTERONOMY 1:35 NASB

$\mathscr{F}$or forty years, those woeful Israelites wandered through the desert to reach the Promised Land. How often they must have stared down at a valley or looked to the mountain summits, dreading the thousands of steps required to get to there. Scholars have determined that forty-year journey should have taken only three days—at the very most, two weeks.

Imagine the mechanics of moving more than two million people through the desert. They must have had an organized method for moving so many bodies. Each person probably had duties and responsibilities. Their wandering existence must have become normal, even routine.

But that generation of Israelites had no real purpose to their lives. They were busy people, but faithless. No Bible verses applaud their lives. It's as if they never lived at all. Despite witnessing miracle after miracle, they never saw those tests as opportunities to trust God in a deeper way. What wasted lives!

And what a lesson to the rest of us! Are we trusting and depending on God in deeper ways throughout our full and busy days? Or are we merely moving from one spot to the next, productive, but not purposeful—busy waiting?

Lord, I don't want to wander aimlessly, unaware of how purposeless
my life is. I want my life to count! With single-hearted devotion,
may I look to You in all things. Amen.

CROWN OF SPLENDOR

Gray hair is a crown of splendor; it is attained by a righteous life.
PROVERBS 16:31 NIV

$\mathscr{I}$s there really more fire in the furnace when there's snow on the roof?" Marcie glimpsed more salt than pepper in the mirror's reflection of her sagging curls. She knew she was getting older when she started craving prune juice and sprouting extra chins.

Searching the Bible for comfort, she learned that Queen Esther's beauty routine consisted of twelve months of oil and cosmetics treatments. Marcie shook her head. A year of her life could be much better spent tightening her knowledge of God's Word than her wrinkles.

Proverbs 16:31 is intriguing. How does righteousness elicit gray hair? Perhaps Christians give so much money to missions they can't afford dye. Or maybe avoiding gossip means fewer visits to the hairstylist.

More likely, the verse is referring to maturity and is telling us that as we physically age, our spiritual growth should correspond. The seed of faith planted in our hearts is meant to germinate, bud, and bloom over the natural course of time like a rich, velvety flower. And gray hair—the evidence that God has been cultivating us both physically and spiritually—is the splendid blossom, the crowning touch.

Does that mean we should forsake antiaging strategies? No. It simply means that our focus should be on becoming more like Jesus, not a supermodel.

Counter of the hairs on my head, I give them all to You. As I age,
teach me to wear spiritual maturity as a crown. Physically, help me learn
to rejoice in what is remaining rather than lament what is lost. Amen.

TELLTALE
FINGERPRINTS

"This is the finger of God!" the magicians exclaimed to Pharaoh.
EXODUS 8:19 NLT

*W*ith their two young children in tow, Jessica and her husband left for Kenya, Africa. They had no formal schooling for missionary work but believed God called them to spread the gospel of Jesus Christ after He radically changed their own lives. They sold everything and left to minister in an unfamiliar land and culture.

A year later they remained convinced they were where God wanted them. They had their share of African illnesses and had undergone challenges unlike any they encountered in the United States. But their faithful God provided for them through it all.

When a member of their church planned a trip to Kenya to participate in another ministry, she asked fellow church members for letters or notes to take to Jessica and her family. The subsequent e-mail that Jessica and her husband sent to their church said this:

"We sat on our bed and took turns opening, reading, laughing at, and crying over the wonderful notes you sent us. Though each letter was unique, they all had the fingerprints of God's love all over them."

Accounts of God's fingerprints show up throughout the Old Testament. We see them again when Christ drives out demons in Luke 11:20. Like Jessica, we can look for His fingerprints in our lives today, too.

Father, don't let me miss Your fingerprints in the
little and big things of my life today. Amen.

WANTING MORE

As for man, his days are like grass, he flourishes like a flower of the field; the wind blows over it and it is gone, and its place remembers it no more.
PSALM 103:15–16 NIV

*H*ere lies Jane Doe.

She kept an insanely full schedule.

If we're really honest with ourselves, we would admit that we'd all like to contribute something lasting to this world. But what kind of impact are we making and what kind of legacy are we leaving? Apart from God, no one and nothing else will matter.

Think about past rulers, dictators, and presidents. At one point in time, they were some of the most powerful people in the world. Today we can't name even half of them, let alone remember what they did or didn't do. What they gave their lives for may not have any meaning now.

Our lives begin and end in the blink of an eye. The things that we think are so important may one day be merely trivial. All that will matter is that we told others about Christ. Our mission is to do the will of God, to go where God is working, and to make a difference for Him.

Lord, I am willing to make an eternal difference for You. Amen.

GOD ANSWERS
ALL PRAYERS

I call on you, O God, for you will answer me.
PSALM 17:6 NIV

Connie prayed for twelve years for the salvation of her family members. However, as time continued, her prayers seemed unanswered. Her loved ones still were not saved. Have you ever felt that God did not answer your heartfelt prayers?

Often it is not that God has not answered our prayer, but that we did not like the answer. How often do we think we know best and do not like to hear no from the Lord? We are immersed in a fast-paced society where waiting, especially for a long period of time, is not what we are used to doing. Our society encourages us to have what we want when we want it. Waiting on the Lord is not easy when patience has not been practiced.

God answers all prayers. The answers can come in three forms: "yes," "no," or "wait." God's Word tells us that when we call or cry out to Him, He will answer us. God always hears our requests and responds in accordance with His will.

As a busy woman, what do you have to call on the Lord for today? You can cry out to Him, trusting that He will answer.

Lord, thank You that I can cry out to You for all that is within my heart. I praise You that You are a God who hears and answers. Amen.

EFFECTIVE
BEHAVIOR

*To be discreet, chaste, keepers at home, good, obedient to their own husbands,
that the word of God be not blasphemed.*
TITUS 2:5 KJV

As the luncheon with her coworkers continued, the woman became more uncomfortable. She didn't want to eat alone or seem snobby, so she had agreed to come along. Now she regretted the action. The other women gossiped continually, used language that was embarrassing, and had drinks even though they would be going back to work afterward.

What is important? Having a good time, no matter where or with whom? Is anyone harmed if we seek our happiness at the expense of our godly testimony? This woman realized she shouldn't be at the luncheon. Her desire to be happy put her in a situation where her witness might be compromised.

We have to weigh our options carefully when we mingle with worldly people. On one hand, we want to be a godly inspiration; on the other, we don't want our actions to reflect God in a negative light.

Even when the choice is difficult, we are called to consider God first. Our Christian walk must take priority over our happiness. Sometimes we will find ourselves in situations that are uncomfortable, but we must pray that the light of Christ shines through us so that we reflect God in the situation.

Lord, please help me to glorify You always. Let me consider You first before myself, and help me be the right kind of witness to those around me. Amen.

HELP IN THE MIDST OF TROUBLE

"We do not know what to do, but we are looking to you for help."
2 CHRONICLES 20:12 NLT

*K*ing Jehoshaphat's army was in big trouble. Several of the surrounding nations had declared war on Israel, and a battle was imminent. King Jehoshaphat was a good king, and he immediately called on his people to fast and pray. God answered the prayers of Jehoshaphat and his people by causing the enemy armies to attack each other. As the Israelites marched into battle singing praises to God, they found that not one of the enemy had survived.

So often in this world, we come face-to-face with experiences that are overwhelming to us. We may not be surrounded by enemy armies on all sides, but it sometimes feels that way. Life is full of situations that seem insurmountable. Like Jehoshaphat and the Israelites, God desires that we rely on Him for all our needs, great or small. When we are beset with fear and worry, when we do not know what to do, we must look to God for help.

Trust that God will hear your prayers. Depend on Him to listen and answer. Believe that God will not allow you to be overcome by your trials; instead, He will faithfully and lovingly bring you through to the other side.

Dear Lord, thank You for Your faithfulness. When I am overwhelmed, let me look to You for guidance and help. Help me to trust and depend on You today. Amen.

THE DREAM MAKER

*"No eye has seen, no ear has heard, no mind has conceived
what God has prepared for those who love him."*
1 CORINTHIANS 2:9 NIV

𝒟reams, goals, and expectations are part of our daily lives. We have an idea of what we want and how we're going to achieve it. Disappointment can raise its ugly head when what we wanted—what we expected—doesn't happen like we thought it should or doesn't happen as fast as we planned.

Disappointment can lead to doubt. Perhaps questions tempt you to doubt the direction you felt God urging you to pursue. Don't quit! Don't give up! Press on with your dream. Failure isn't failure until you quit. When it looks like it's over, stand strong. With God's assistance, there is another way, a higher plan, or a better time to achieve your dream.

God knows the dreams He has placed inside of you. He created you and knows what you can do—even better than you know yourself. Maintain your focus—not on the dream but on the Dream Maker—and together you will achieve your dream.

*God, thank You for putting dreams in my heart. I refuse to quit.
I'm looking to You to show me how to reach my dreams. Amen.*

A TALE OF
TWO FAMILIES

*Better is an handful with quietness, than both
the hands full with travail and vexation of spirit.*
ECCLESIASTES 4:6 KJV

A family lived in poverty in a rural community. The husband made less than a thousand dollars per month to care for his wife and five children. Even so, the wife did not work. She stayed home, cared for the children, and spent her days keeping a very frugal home.

Their rental house was old and plain but neat. The children wore hand-me-downs but were clothed and clean.

Despite living in poverty, the family was happy. Love flowed between parents and children. When visitors called, they were welcomed warmly and given the best the family could afford. Although they sometimes wished for nicer, newer, bigger, and better things, the family faithfully lived within their means.

Another family lived in the suburbs, not far from the city. Surrounded by unbridled affluence, they soon found themselves desiring the trappings of the good life—new this, new that, a time-share condo, a boat, and extravagant vacations.

To afford such things, the wife worked opposite shifts from her husband to save on child care. But they rarely saw each other, and their relationship was strained. The children became spoiled and disobedient.

This family had the world's goods, but the price they paid was greater than their credit card debt.

*Father, help me see what is important to You. Remind me constantly
that to be rich in Christ is the greatest blessing of all. Amen.*

OWE LOVE ONLY

*Let no debt remain outstanding,
except the continuing debt to love one another.*
ROMANS 13:8 NIV

$\mathcal{I}$t's easy to get into debt, but how do we get out of it? A recent survey revealed that 87 percent of the respondents admitted they had no emergency fund; 75 percent were at or near their credit card limits, causing them to spend 34 percent more on living expenses than they would if they paid cash; and 71 percent said that debt is causing problems in their home. It's no wonder God admonishes us to stay out of debt.

Christian financial experts offer some suggestions for debt reduction: Make a realistic budget and stick to it. Give to your church and the Lord's work. Start a savings account. Determine what expenses you can eliminate. Pay small debts first. Establish attainable goals. Don't impulse buy. Refrain from buying beyond your means.

Because of God's love, Jesus paid an overwhelming debt He didn't owe through His death on the cross. The apostle Paul admonishes us to incur a debt we can never pay—the debt of continuing love. Love is the only debt God encourages. In that instance, we can never owe enough.

*Dear Lord, thank You for the price You paid for me. Guide me
through the necessary steps to pay off my earthly debts while
increasing the debt of love I owe to others. Amen.*

CONTENTMENT

*I have learned to be content whatever the circumstances. I know what
it is to be in need, and I know what it is to have plenty. I have
learned the secret of being content in any and every situation.*
PHILIPPIANS 4:11–12 NIV

It was her serenity that was so appealing. A peaceful, contented spirit
emanated, quietly expressing itself in her warm smile, easy laughter, and
accepting attitude even in the midst of situations like heavy financial
strain, unknown health problems, and the deaths of multiple children.

Week after week her countenance conveyed a deep genuine joy—
no phony put-on smile or flaky upbeat personality. She was for real!
Tears would sometimes flow as she listened to someone else's struggle
or spoke of her own. She didn't live in denial, but she had an uncanny
way of ending the conversation with rays of hope, faith, and acceptance
of God's plan for her life. Those rays warmed those near her, reflecting
the Source of that strength.

She had indeed learned contentment. She knew God provided all
she needed. She had experienced His giving and His taking away of
life, money, and resources. Because of that, her hand was always open in
giving, knowing that God would provide again if she had need. Material
possessions had no grip on her. Freedom to live life to the fullest was
the result. Refreshment was the result for those around her.

*Gracious Lord, teach me contentment in any circumstance.
Let my heart know, without doubt, that all good gifts come from You.
Help me to accept all Your plans for me. Amen.*

OVERWHELMED IS UNDERPRAYED

Try your best to live quietly, to mind your own business, and to work hard, just as we taught you to do. Then you will be respected by people who are not followers of the Lord, and you won't have to depend on anyone.
I THESSALONIANS 4:11–12 CEV

"Live quietly, mind your own business, work hard, serve on the PTA, chair some committees, sign the kids up for soccer, join an aerobics class. . ." Oops! Is that what it says, or did we add something to the recommendations in the Bible?

None of these things are bad or wrong. However, moving through life as a tornado, leaving destruction in your wake, affects the lives of those around you. To be an effective witness for Christ, you must be in control of your affairs. To be able to attest to the comfort and peace that Jesus provides, you cannot be frantic and out of control.

If your mantra is "I'm overwhelmed," followed by a familiar litany of tasks, duties, and deadlines, perhaps you have not fully sought the will of God regarding your schedule and commitments. His desire is not to overwhelm you. He recommends that you do your very best to lead a quiet, simple life while you work hard at the things you need to do. Find peace as you release yourself from self-imposed requirements and surrender to God's will.

Heavenly Father, please help me to order my life in a way that I bring peace to those around me and gain the respect of those who do not know You. Show me where You would have me place my energy and urgency. Amen.

GIVING GOD
YOUR BURDENS

Cast your burden upon the LORD and He will sustain you;
He will never allow the righteous to be shaken.
PSALM 55:22 NASB

*W*hen we have a problem, our first thought is to contact a friend. In our world today, with so many technological advances, it is easy to communicate even with people who are far away. Just a hundred years ago, people waited days to receive a message from another town!

Certainly God desires that we help to bear one another's burdens and that we seek wise counsel. The trouble is that in doing so, often we fail to take our burdens to the One who can do something about them. We are called to release our cares to our heavenly Father. A cause with an effect is implied in Psalm 55:22—*If* you cast your burden on Him, *then* He will sustain you.

Sustain is defined by Webster as a verb meaning "to strengthen or support physically or mentally" or "to bear the weight of an object." Does it sound inviting to have the sovereign God of the universe strengthen and support you? Would it help if He bore the weight of your current trial? Our sovereign God is there when heartaches are taking their toll. He doesn't have a cell phone or an e-mail address, but He is always just a prayer away.

Lift the worries that weigh on my mind and heart today, Father.
I can't bear them alone any longer. In my weakness, You are strong.
Thank You for Your promise to sustain me. Amen.

SHARPENING FRIENDSHIPS

Iron sharpeneth iron; so a man sharpeneth the countenance of his friend.
PROVERBS 27:17 KJV

One of the first casualties of a busy life is friendship.

Often we don't even realize it is missing, because the more activities we have, the more people that surround us. Yet because we are in a hurry, we don't form real friendships with most of these people.

We all have a need for close friendships. We need others in our lives who will challenge us to make us sharper, bolder, gentler, and more Christlike.

For married women, husbands provide much of this needed intimacy. But no man can meet every need for female interpersonal communication; women need women.

Some may think that a sharpening friendship is characterized by leisurely conversation and prayer over a cup of tea. And sometimes this does happen. But the greater honing comes when abrasives are applied. Days spent helping a needy friend or nights spent beside the bed of a dying one develop patience, strength, and courage.

Friendships like these take time. It's beneficial for our health and countenance—and those of our friends—to make that time.

Dear Jesus, I know You are a friend who sticks closer than a sister,
yet sometimes I need the comfort of friends I can see and touch. Help me
to say no to extra activities so I have time to invest in friends. Amen.

STEADFAST LOVE

Give thanks to the LORD, for he is good;
his love endures forever.
PSALM 107:1 NIV

*W*hen the sea of life batters us, it's easy to forget the Lord's goodness. Caught up in our own storms, tunnel vision afflicts us as we view the troubles before us. We may even doubt the Lord whom we serve. Though we might not consciously separate ourselves from Him, deep inside we fear He won't act to save us—or that He won't act in time.

That's a good time to stop and give thanks to God, who never stops being good or ends His love for us. Our situations change, our love fails, but God never varies. He entirely controls all creation, and His character never changes. The darkest circumstances we face will not last eternally. Life moves on and alters. But God never deserts us.

Even when our troubles seem to be in control, they aren't. God has not changed, and our doubts cannot make alteration in Him. If we allow faith to take control, we will realize that and turn again to Him.

Facing troubles? Give thanks to the Lord. He is good. He hasn't deserted you, no matter what you face, and His goodness will never end. He won't fail us.

Thank You, Lord, that Your love never changes. I can depend on it,
though my life seems to be crashing around me. Nothing is larger than You.
Amen.

COMINGS AND GOINGS

The LORD will protect you now and always wherever you go.
PSALM 121:8 CEV

A local church honored Cathy for thirty-five years of faithful service as church secretary. She began work when her children started school and is still working now that her grandchildren are in high school.

Donna had an entirely different experience. She worked at a dozen different companies before settling into a job that she has had for almost eight years. Sometimes her husband's job relocated; sometimes she lost her job during a corporate takeover. Twice her employer let her go. She thanks God for her current, seemingly stable position, but she has said good-bye to numerous coworkers.

Comings and goings define the American workplace. Our experiences will fall on a continuum between Cathy and Donna's. The loss of a job results in financial hardship and loneliness, away from friends we made on the job. We may want God to shield us from the uncertainties of employment.

God does not guarantee that we will never lose a job. He does promise that He will shield us from our first day on the job to the day we walk out the door for the last time.

God goes behind and before us in all our comings and goings.

Lord, You watch every path that we take. You lead us to and away from our places of employment. We trust You to shield us in the process. Amen.

BE READY!

*Physical training is good, but training for godliness is much better,
promising benefits in this life and in the life to come.*
I TIMOTHY 4:8 NLT

For months Alison trained for her hometown triathlon. She'd been swimming, cycling, and/or running almost daily. Competition would be tough in her age division. When the day of the mini-tri came, she was ready.

Her bicycle wasn't. She went into the garage to find her bicycle had a flat tire. She had no time to buy another tire, inflate it, and be ready. She called a friend to borrow her bike. It wasn't a top-notch road bike, and Alison had never taken a ride on it. But she had no time to quibble over details.

When Alison finished the triathlon in laudable time, people remarked on her great finish.

"You cycled on. . .*that*?"

Alison was glad running was her strong point. Her shoes had been ready when she was.

None of us knows what kind of challenges the day will bring when our alarm clock sounds. An asthma attack, a migraine, or a flat tire may incapacitate us for a competition for which we have trained for months. With consistent, prayerful study of God's Word, and a consistent fellowship with others of "like precious faith" (2 Peter 1:1 KJV), we can be ready for anything. We may not understand how training ourselves in godliness has value for something like a triathlon, but God assures us that such training is of value in every way.

*Strengthen me, Lord, to be diligent to train myself
in the things that matter the most. Amen.*

THE LESSON OF
THE LUGGAGE

*"Bring the whole tithe into the storehouse, so that there may be food in My house,
and test Me now in this," says the LORD of hosts, "if I will not open for you the
windows of heaven and pour out for you a blessing until it overflows."*
MALACHI 3:10 NASB

*E*ven though finances would be tight, Sharon finally decided to give
her tithe to the church, beginning the first of the month. A few days
preceding the first, she visited the mall and noticed a set of luggage
at 25 percent off. The luggage was perfect for her business trips. The
price was exactly the amount that she would be tithing. *Perhaps I can
wait one more month.*

She picked up the luggage and carried it to the cashier. As Sharon
waited in line, she envisioned herself at the airport looking savvy.
Finally, no more embarrassment with tattered luggage. However, as the
line shortened, she remembered her promise. With a pang of guilt, she
stepped out of line and returned the luggage to the shelf.

On Sunday, Sharon placed her tithe in the offering plate. It felt
good to be obedient to the Lord. Nevertheless, she still dreaded using
her old luggage on business trips.

Driving home, Sharon spotted a garage sale. Out of curiosity, she
pulled over. She couldn't believe her eyes. There was a set of luggage
almost identical to what she had seen at the mall.

"How much are you asking for that luggage?" she queried.

"For you, five dollars," came the reply.

*Lord, help me to faithfully tithe and never to doubt Your abundant provision.
Amen.*

STAND IN THE GAP

"I looked for a man among them who would build up the
wall and stand before me in the gap on behalf of the land
so I would not have to destroy it, but I found none."
EZEKIEL 22:30 NIV

*E*ach prayer request you offer up to God is important to you, and when you ask others to pray, you're counting on them to help carry you through the tough times.

Do you give the same consideration to those who ask you for prayer? It's easy in the busyness of life to overlook a request someone else has made. Maybe you don't know the person very well or you don't really have an understanding of what he or she is going through. Perhaps the request came in an e-mail that you quickly glanced at and then deleted. Yet even with e-mailed prayer requests, others trust you to stand in the gap for them during difficult times in their lives.

Don't delay. Take time right when you receive a request to talk to the Lord on the requester's behalf. Be the bridge that carries that person through the valley of darkness back to the mountaintop of joy.

Heavenly Father, help me to have a heart of compassion for those I
know and even for those I don't know who need Your comfort and love.
Help me never to be too busy to pray for them. Amen.

SAY YOU'RE SORRY

*"Don't tear your clothing in your grief but tear your hearts instead.
Return to the LORD your God."*
JOEL 2:13 NLT

Tell your sister you're sorry," Lynn instructed her younger daughter.

Blue eyes glaring, the four-year-old mumbled the ordered command. "Sorry."

How many times in a week do moms tell their children, "Say you're sorry"? And how many times does the "sorry" come out sounding like anything but an apology? There's sorrow for sin, and then there's sorrow for getting caught in sin. There's begrudging contrition, and then there's genuine repentance.

Pastor and Bible teacher David Jeremiah tells of unintentionally cutting off a woman in traffic. He could see she was angry. When he pulled into a fast-food drive-through, she was still behind him. So he did something she probably never expected. He paid for her order.

When God commands us to repent, He doesn't want a mumbled apology. He doesn't even want demonstrative tears—unless they come from a repentant heart. The scripture above from Joel shows true repentance. Repentance for sinning against God involves a willful action, a changing of direction. It's doing it God's way, going in God's direction. We can't always undo or fix all our wrong actions. But when it's in our power to do so, the Lord gives us specific guidelines. When we do our part, He does His because "he is merciful and compassionate" (Joel 2:13 NLT).

*Forgive me, Lord, for my sin against You and others. Help me to right those
things I can right and not to repeat the same errors. Amen.*

TOO BUSY
FOR GOD?

*"You are my witnesses," declares the LORD, "and my servant whom I have
chosen, so that you may know and believe me and understand that I am he."*
ISAIAH 43:10 NIV

*H*ave you had thoughts like the following? *I am way too busy to spend
time with the Lord today. I could have thirty more minutes today if I just skip my
quiet time and get to work early.* Many of us feel uncomfortable admitting
this, but how often do we skip our quiet time? How often do we think
we are too busy to partake in fellowship with other believers one day
a week? How often do we fail to participate in a Bible study because
there is "homework" to complete?

When we are not engaging in the activities that draw us closer to
the Lord, we are hindering ourselves from our true calling. God tells us
that our purpose in life is to be His witnesses. We have been chosen to
serve Him alone. God intends for us to be witnesses and to serve Him
so that we may know and believe Him. God draws us into that intimate
relationship of knowing Him through these Christian activities of quiet
time, Bible study, and church attendance. As we deepen our relationship
with the Lord, we will understand that we can trust and believe Him
and then reflect Him to others through the many responsibilities He
gives us.

*Lord, thank You that I am chosen to serve as Your witness in
order to know and believe You. Particularly during busy days,
draw me into Your constant fellowship. Amen.*

PACE YOUR RACE

Let us strip off every weight that slows us down, especially the sin that so easily trips us up. And let us run with endurance the race God has set before us.
HEBREWS 12:1 NLT

$\mathcal{N}$ervously, the young woman approached the starting line. It was her first footrace since she began jogging a few months before. At the sound of the gun, she bolted forward in stride with the advanced runners. And then it hit: Exhaustion. Shuffling and gasping for breath, she realized she had not paced herself.

The apostle Paul likened our spiritual journey to an endurance run. The race begins with faith in Christ. As we allow God to lift the weight of sin, we become swifter and more efficient with each step.

Often, though, we fight to stay ahead of those who appear more "spiritually mature" than we are. Meanwhile, God desires to train us at a pace developed exclusively for us.

Those who train at their own level of ability and maintain realistic expectations are the true winners. The key to finishing the course takes a balance of patience, perseverance, and an unfaltering dependence on our heavenly trainer. God promises an eternal prize for those who persevere, at their own pace, to the end.

So run the race at your own pace!

Heavenly Father, help me to run this spiritual race balanced with patience, perseverance, and faith. I rely on You to strengthen me on the road of life toward my heavenly reward. Amen.

TROUBLED BONES

Have compassion on me, LORD, for I am weak. Heal me, LORD, for my bones
are in agony. I am sick at heart. How long, O LORD, until you restore me?
The LORD has heard my plea; the LORD will answer my prayer.
PSALM 6:2–3, 9 NLT

$\mathcal{W}$e associate creaking, aching bones with aging, but they can strike
at any age. Even children may suffer from rheumatoid arthritis; and
sports injuries, cancer, and accidents do not spare the young.

We have not all broken a bone. But we do all know the deep-down
pain of troubled bones. Illness and exhaustion carry physical pain.
Broken relationships or the death of someone close to us weighs down
our souls. Debts loom over us. Whatever the cause, we ache with a pain
beyond words. Rest that refreshes the spirit as well as the body seems
out of reach.

In the midst of that trouble, we wonder if God knows and hears
us. With David, we cry, "How long? We can't take any more."

That cry is the starting point. God loves us, and the Holy Spirit
carries our prayers to Him "with groans that words cannot express"
(Romans 8:26 NIV). God will answer every prayer at the right time
according to His will.

The next time troubled bones keep us awake at night, we can take
them to God in prayer.

Lord, our bones are troubled. We cry "How long?" We know You have heard our
prayers. We ask that You will give us peaceful rest in that assurance. Amen.

Suffering in Silence

*Confess your sins to each other and pray for each other so that
you may be healed. The earnest prayer of a righteous person
has great power and produces wonderful results.*
JAMES 5:16 NLT

*Y*ears ago, Ruth decided the best way to maneuver through life was
to plaster on a smile and go about her day. Inside her heart, however,
she is dying. She has struggles—addictions. One day it's overeating;
the next it's gossip. Next week it'll be those trashy romance novels she
swore off months ago. She promises herself that next time will be the
last time. But that's what she always says. She wishes she could tell
someone—another woman—who would listen, but what if she is the
only one struggling?

So she remains silent—mostly because she thinks people will
judge her, but also because everyone seems to be in such a hurry. Sure,
her friends mean well, but with life's busyness, few have time to stop
to listen to a friend's deepest hurts.

Ruth's story is a painful but common one—one that many women
experience alone. Too embarrassed or ashamed, they suffer in silence
without receiving the support and prayer they need. How can we help
them receive care and support? We can make an effort to slow down
and look past the plastered-on smiles. We can ask questions and
actually listen to the answers. We can be willing to help and pray for
someone.

Who knows? A day may come when we are the ones who need to
express the truth and be set free.

Lord, break through our silence and give us compassion for one other. Amen.

THE ULTIMATE PRIZE

The LORD will not reject his people;
he will not abandon his special possession.
PSALM 94:14 NLT

*D*iplomas and certificates cover Deidre's office walls. Her master's degree in business administration hangs there, as well as many awards presented by her company: employee of the month—three times—and a plaque commemorating her two-year anniversary of employment. Birthday cards from coworkers sit on the windowsill behind her desk.

Sally collects ribbons for her mouth-watering pies. She also has earned a brown belt in karate alongside her children. She still has the perfect attendance pins she earned in Sunday school as a child and collects certificates for completed Bible studies in a scrapbook.

Prizes. We long to be the best at something, and we keep mementos of our achievements.

The psalmist says we are the prizes on display in God's office. He won us in the battle at Calvary. Much as He pointed out Job to Satan long ago (Job 2:3), God holds us up for the unseen world to see. Of everything on display in heaven, His favorite showcase features the people He has redeemed.

God the heavenly curator takes immense pride in us. He showers His love and care on us. He polishes us, putting us through the refiner's fire until we gleam. He will never forsake us or cast us out.

Father, You cherish us as Your special possession. What an awesome thought.
The God who made the universe takes most pride in—His people!
Teach us to live in such a way that we bring glory to You. Amen.

THE BLESSING OF FRIENDSHIP

Two are better than one, because they have a good return for their work:
If one falls down, his friend can help him up. But pity the man
who falls and has no one to help him up!
ECCLESIASTES 4:9–10 NIV

*T*wo friends sat in a doctor's office waiting for one of the ladies' test results. The doctor entered the room in a white lab coat, carrying a clipboard. On the clipboard were papers filled with numbers representing hormone levels and blood cell counts that could only be deciphered by a trained eye. Before the doctor spoke, she asked her patient if it was okay to deliver the news in front of the woman waiting with her. "Yes, of course, Doctor," the patient replied, "This is my *friend*."

Life is filled with surprises, some wonderful but others horrifying. A loved one dies. A spouse leaves. An employer treats us unjustly. We face breakups and breakdowns, full schedules and empty nests. Life is much easier with a friend.

Do you have a friend that is, as Proverbs 18:24 states, closer than a brother? If you have not cultivated this type of friendship, pray that God might lead you as you seek to do so. If you have a close friend, thank the Lord for her today.

All of us stumble in life. Occasionally we even fall down. What a blessing it is to have a friend to help us up!

Father, thank You for my friends. Help me to be
a friend that is always ready to help others. Amen.

MOUNTAINS OUT OF MOLEHILLS

"I will make a pathway through the wilderness.
I will create rivers in the dry wasteland."
ISAIAH 43:19 NLT

*S*ome days mountains of work are piled in front of us. Whether they consist of schoolwork, diapers, dirty laundry, business reports, or all of the above, the height of such tasks can sometimes seem overwhelming. We don't even know where to begin. Immediately the enemy begins whispering in our ears, "Good luck trying to get all that done. You don't have a chance. And if you try to rush through it, no one will be happy with the results. Especially not you."

These are the times when we need to take stock of the situation. First things first. Don't panic! Take a deep breath. Tell yourself that you can do all things with Christ's strength (see Philippians 4:13). You have God's word on it. Send up a prayer for strength. Then just do the next thing. Take the first step.

Although situations sometimes seem impossible, we have a God— a great big, mighty God—who makes a way in the wilderness for us. He can *move* mountains. Nothing will stop Him from helping us— except maybe ourselves and a negative mind-set. Do not doubt. But take that first step forward, knowing He will make a way where there seems to be no way.

God, I have so many to-dos in front of me. I don't even know where
to begin. But I know You are with me. Help me to feel Your presence,
to know that I can do whatever You set before me, and to rest
in the promise that You will make a way. Amen.

How About Some Fun?

A twinkle in the eye means joy in the heart,
and good news makes you feel fit as a fiddle.
PROVERBS 15:30 THE MESSAGE

*H*ave you had any fun this week?"

This query, in and of itself, might sound odd, but two friends agreed to ask each other this question periodically because both had the tendency to plow through an entire week of school, work, church, and community commitments forgetting—or neglecting—to plan an activity or two for the sole purpose of recharging their own burnt-out batteries. Both women realized they would have to make an effort to carve out time for activities that brought them joy. For one, it was kayaking and hiking; for the other, it was settling into her favorite reading chair with a mystery novel.

God does not want His kids to be worn out and stressed out. He did not design us to be like little Energizer Bunnies that keep on going and going and going. We need time to *recreate*—to revive and refresh our bodies and minds. A little relaxation, recreation—and yes—*fun* are essential components of a balanced life. Even Jesus and His disciples found it necessary to get away from the crowds and pressures of ministry to rest.

There's a lot of fun to be had out there—playing tennis or golf, jogging, swimming, painting, knitting, playing a musical instrument, visiting an art gallery, playing a board game, or going to a movie, a play, or a football game. Have you had any fun this week?

Lord, You are the One who gives balance to my life. Help me to
find time today for a little relaxation, recreation, and even fun. Amen.

TUNING OUT DISTRACTIONS

*We must pay more careful attention, therefore,
to what we have heard, so that we do not drift away.*
HEBREWS 2:1 NIV

*H*ollie and Noelle sat in a canoe with their well-earned lunch spread over their knees. They had been paddling down the river all morning, and as the sun blazed overhead, they decided to take a break for lunch. The girls laughed and talked through mouths full of warm apples and smooshy peanut butter and jelly sandwiches.

After the last snack cake was eaten and the lunch bags were packed away, Hollie and Noelle picked up their oars. Suddenly, they realized that as they had been eating lunch, the canoe had drifted into a mass of logs where the current was much stronger. The struggle to free themselves from the logs required a great deal of strength, and they lost valuable daylight as a result of their inattention.

Drifting away from the Word of God can be unnervingly easy. We think we are just taking a break—having a little fun—and suddenly we find ourselves entangled in a mass of sin, fighting to free ourselves and struggling to get back to where we started. Distractions from and inattention to God's Word cause us to drift further and further from the truth. Instead, we must constantly be focused on the Word, heading purposefully toward our goal.

Dear Lord, keep me from distractions. Help me to pay attention to Your Word, and let me grow ever closer to You. Amen.

BRIDEZILLA

A righteous man is cautious in friendship.
PROVERBS 12:26 NIV

College days had ended. Jackie began paying off all her student loans by joining the workforce of corporate America. Sometime later one of her college sorority sisters asked Jackie to be her maid of honor. Jackie happily consented. But things soured quickly.

The bride chose high-priced bridesmaids dresses. Then she instructed her bridesmaids to wear flat shoes (the bride wanted to be the tallest woman in the wedding party) and not get suntans because *she* would have a suntan.

The bride thought her bridesmaids should host her bachelorette party in Vegas. As their gift to her, they could all buy her plane ticket—in addition to their own. When her friends balked at the seventeen-hundred-mile (one way) flight, she got another idea. They could all go for a fun day at a luxurious spa—at five hundred dollars per person. And again, the bride thought her bridesmaids should pay for her day there.

This bride had crossed the line. Jackie told Bridezilla to find herself another maid of honor.

Most value their friendships with other women. But selfishness can rend those friendships more quickly than a distant move. When thoughtfulness doesn't go both ways, a friendship's sinking is certain. People do sometimes change—just like the bride into Bridezilla. But usually, if we choose our friends carefully, we will have fewer fractured relationships.

Father, I thank You for the friends I have. I pray I won't be guilty of taking advantage of them and that I won't take them for granted. Amen.

LEADERSHIP'S
RESPONSIBILITY

Because of the transgression of a land, many are its princes; but by
a man of understanding and knowledge right will be prolonged. A poor
man who oppresses the poor is like a driving rain which leaves no food.
PROVERBS 28:2–3 NKJV

$\mathcal{G}$od raises up individuals in families, at work, at church, and in government to become leaders. The decisions they make and the instructions they give have an impact on people's lives.

Everyone has been placed in some kind of leadership role. The president of the United States and a homemaker certainly have different responsibilities, but in God's eyes, each has important and specific tasks that have an influence on others. When we think about our jobs, our thoughts might center on weariness, lack of time, or day-to-day boredom. Rarely might we recognize that our job was specifically given to us for this specific time. No one else does exactly what we do the way we do it.

Whatever our jobs are, we are responsible. How we behave and what we believe not only influence us but those we come into contact with. What influences a good leader is a person who, like Christ, is willing to humble herself rather than oppress.

Lord, give me seeing eyes and hearing ears to guide others. Amen.

HEALING WORDS,
HURTING WORDS

May the words of my mouth and the meditation of my heart
be pleasing in your sight, O LORD, my Rock and my Redeemer.
PSALM 19:14 NIV

*C*onsider this scene at a swim meet where parents cheered their young athletes to victory. One mother leaned over the edge of the pool, screaming at her nine-year-old daughter as she backstroked to the finish, "Touch the wall! Touch the wall!" When the exhausted little girl finally touched the wall, her mother screeched, "How do you expect to win if you don't touch the wall?" The girl was crestfallen, revealing her broken heart as she heaved herself over the pool's edge.

In sharp contrast, another mom gave her daughter the thumbs-up sign and a wide smile just as her daughter dived into the pool. As her child struggled toward the finish, the mother yelled, "Pull, pull—you can do it!" The eager woman looked as if she might dive into the pool herself to help her daughter swim the last ten yards. When the girl reached the wall, her mother bent down to give her a hand out of the water. "Great race, honey," she said, giving her a quick hug.

Whether they won or lost was unimportant compared to how each girl responded to her mother's words. One looked dejected and disappointed that she'd failed to meet her mother's expectations, while the other looked as if she'd won an Olympic gold medal. What a contrast! What a difference the right words can make.

Lord, help us to offer words of life and encouragement
to someone who needs them today. Amen.

REACH OUT
AND TOUCH

She thought, "If I just touch his clothes, I will be healed."
MARK 5:28 NIV

*W*e should never underestimate the power of touch. In our busy lives, as we rush from one appointment to another, skimping on affection with our families and loved ones can become routine. We wave good-bye to our children without stopping for a hug. Husbands head off to work with the barest brush of a kiss.

We do our loved ones a disservice, however, when we skip touching them. Touching communicates our affection but also our affirmation and sympathy. You can encourage people—or comfort them—with a simple touch. The Bible records Jesus touching many people, comforting and healing them. He also let people touch Him, such as the sinful woman who touched and kissed His feet (Luke 7:38).

In Mark 5, however, the true power of a simple touch is beautifully portrayed. This woman who had suffered for so long believed so strongly in Jesus that she knew the quickest touch of His hem would heal her. She reached out, and her faith made her well.

So hold those you love close. Hug them, and let them see a bit of Jesus' love in you every day.

Lord, I turn to You when I need comfort. Let me also
offer those around me the comfort of a loving touch. Amen.

FINDING
REAL REST

And I said, Oh that I had wings like a dove!
for then would I fly away, and be at rest.
PSALM 55:6 KJV

There are days. . .
    when the family gets sick and the dog disappears,
    when the phone doesn't stop ringing,
    when your favorite sweater ends up in the dryer,
    when your boss takes his frustration out on you,
    when you think things can't get any worse, but they do.
    There are days.

On such days, it's tempting to wish for an easy way out. If only you could get away from phones and responsibilities and people who want more of you than you have to give.

If only you could fly away! Then you could be at rest.

Really?

It takes more than a quiet place or a time away to bring true rest. Often, even if we go away from the noise and demands of family, we find ourselves thinking of the very ones we wanted to leave. Instead of being at peace, we're full of guilt and regret.

Instead of flying away, we must jump into God's everlasting arms and dive into His Word. Rest is found in knowing Christ and understanding that through His sacrifice, we are at peace.

As we allow God's peace to fill us, we will find real rest.

Father God, there are many days when I don't have time to sit. And too often my house is Crisis Central. In all these times, remind me that peace comes from knowing You and resting in the work You have done. Amen.

QUIET SPACE

Thou art my hiding place.
PSALM 32:7 KJV

An afternoon walk in the fig orchards near Herndon revealed to Janice dusty remnants of formerly lush environments. Sadly, green orchards died as housing developments transformed the rural charm of agricultural land into bustling neighborhoods and high-rise buildings.

Later, perched on her bed, Janice rests from her walk and listens to the city sounds—trains, cars, sirens, power tools on construction sites, airplanes overhead, a TV blaring in the next apartment. These manmade sounds assault her soul.

The serenity of the countryside calls to her: rolling hills, clean air, flocks of birds, trees teeming with life, ground squirrels busy at play and work, the soft rustle of leaves fluttering in the breezes, unencumbered by humanity's monstrous steel creations.

Janice's soul longs for regular quiet space. She closes the windows to block the city noise. She plays soft praise music with nature sounds to mask the outside noise and to draw her soul into quietness. In these times of solitude, God's voice speaks to her, sometimes in soft whispers, sometimes in loud proclamations. She cannot miss His voice when she is quietly resting in a posture of listening. Every fiber of her being resonates with His presence. She hears His voice. She hears His directions. She knows His plans for her.

Oh Lord, help me keep a quiet space in my daily living. Help me stop to rest, to pray, to listen, to hear Your voice, to come to You—my hiding place. Amen.

OH, RUBBISH!

*I consider everything a loss compared to the surpassing greatness of
knowing Christ Jesus my Lord, for whose sake I have lost all things.
I consider them rubbish, that I may gain Christ.*
PHILIPPIANS 3:8 NIV

*S*ue, the church secretary, had been working really hard and felt she
deserved a vacation. As proven by her empty savings account, she had
also recently "deserved" new clothes and some other expensive things.
But despite her lack of funds and the spiritual conviction that begged
her not to, she wanted that vacation so badly that she used several
nearly maxed-out credit cards to pay for it.

A vacation can be a glorious and rewarding rest from hard work.
But it is also one of the most fleeting acquisitions imaginable. When
Sue's trip ended, her tan quickly faded, as did many of the memories.
But the debt will remain for years, while minimum monthly payments
cripple an already limping budget. Sue realized, too late, that every
earthly thing is rubbish compared to Christ.

Far greater than anything the world offers are the rewards of being
a good steward of your finances. Ask the Lord to help you control your
spending by leading you into wise decisions. He wants you to enjoy the
beautiful things He created, but only after you have learned that they
mean nothing compared to the treasure found in knowing Christ.

*Father, thank You for all of the wonderful blessings You have given me.
Help me to remember that the greatest prizes are eternal, and that
nothing I can acquire on earth has lasting value. Amen.*

GOD'S MOUNTAIN SANCTUARY

"And seeing the multitudes, he went up into a mountain. . .and. . .
his disciples came unto him: and he opened his mouth and taught them."
MATTHEW 5:1–2 KJV

*M*elissa felt crushed beneath work, home, and church responsibilities. So much so, she could no longer give or listen, let alone hear from God. So she decided to take a day trip to the mountains to unwind.

There the forest hummed with a symphony of sound as beams of sunlight filtered through the vast timberland. As she strolled a wooded path, she noticed how God's creation kept perfect cadence with its Creator. No one directed the wildflowers to bloom, no one commanded the trees to reach upward, and no one forced the creek to flow downstream. No one but God, and nature simply complied.

Jesus often retreated to a mountain to pray. There He called His disciples to depart from the multitudes so that He could teach them valuable truths—the lessons we learn from nature. Don't fret; obey God's gentle promptings and simply flow in the path He clears.

Do you yearn for a place where problems evaporate like the morning dew? Do you need a place of solace? God is wherever you are—behind a bedroom door, nestled alongside you in your favorite chair, or even standing at a sink full of dirty dishes. Come apart and enter God's mountain sanctuary.

Heavenly Father, I long to hear Your voice and to flow in the path You clear
before me. Help me to find sanctuary in Your abiding presence. Amen.

EYE CARE

*For thus says the LORD of hosts. . ."he who
touches you touches the apple of His eye."*
ZECHARIAH 2:8 NKJV

*T*he apple of the eye refers to the pupil—the very center, or heart, of
the eye. Consider the lengths we go to in order to protect our eyes. We
wear protective glasses in some workplaces. We close our eyes or squint
in windstorms or bright light. When dust blows, we turn our heads or
put up our hands to keep the dirt from ending up in our eyes.

When we do get something in an eye, the ache and discomfort are
instant. Tears form, and we seek to get the particle out as quickly as
possible to stop the pain. If we are unable to remove the offending bit,
we often become unable to do anything but focus on the discomfort.

To think that we are the apple of God's eye is incredible. Consider
the care He must take for us. He will go to great lengths to protect
us from harm. When something or someone does attack us, God feels
our pain. He is instantly aware of our discomfort, for it is His own.
When the storms of life come, we must remember how God feels each
twinge of suffering. Despite the adversity, we can praise God for He is
sheltering us.

*Thank You, God, that You are so aware of what is happening to me.
Thank You for Your protection. Amen.*

CAN GOD INTERRUPT YOU?

In his heart a man plans his course, but the LORD determines his steps.
PROVERBS 16:9 NIV

*B*efore rushing out of the house each morning, we grab calendars or PalmPilots. Our day is efficiently planned. We are eager to check off our to-do list. But wait! The phone suddenly rings. There is an unexpected knock at the door. The car tire is flat.

How do we react when our plans are interrupted? Do frustration, resentment, and anger quickly surface? We have places to go and people to meet. We do not have time for interruptions!

Have you ever considered that perhaps God has ordained our interruptions? A friend could be calling in need of encouragement. God knew you'd be just the right person to lift her spirits. Maybe the knock on the door is a lost child seeking help. Perhaps, just perhaps, God may be trying to get your attention.

There is nothing wrong with planning your day. However, we have such limited vision. God sees the big picture. Be open. Be flexible. Allow God to change your plans in order to accomplish His divine purposes. Instead of becoming frustrated, look for ways the Lord might be working. Be willing to join Him. When you do, interruptions will become blessings.

Dear Lord, forgive me when I am so rigidly locked into my own agenda that I miss Yours. Give me Your eternal perspective so that I may be open to divine interruptions. Amen.

THE GRAND OBSESSION

I will instruct you and teach you in the way you should go;
I will counsel you and watch over you.
PSALM 32:8 NIV

In his book *Prayer*, Richard Foster wrote that he had become obsessed with his work. "Before writing my first book, *Celebration of Discipline*, I did nothing but talk about it for a solid year. Carolynn [his wife] grew tired of hearing me rattle on. It was my grand obsession."

Foster happened to attend a writing conference in which the speaker shared how destructive his writing career had been to his marriage. "It was a casual comment," Foster wrote, "not pertinent to the topic of the conference, but I heard nothing else the entire week. Echoing in my ears was the query: 'Are you willing to relinquish this book in favor of Carolynn and the boys?' "

Foster said he went home from the conference and told his wife she was more important than the book project, and that he would give up writing if it damaged their relationship.

Foster's book was eventually published, but more important, he heard God's warning and acted on it, reprioritizing his marriage.

Even good things, like enjoying your work, can crowd out the best things, like loving your family. When God rings a warning bell that we are neglecting areas of importance, we need to listen, gratefully, and hasten to make changes before it's too late.

Fix my attention today, Lord! Help me to identify my imbalances and areas of neglect. Lead me to spend my energy in lasting treasures that You value. Amen.

SNAZZY
SNAPDRAGONS

We have different gifts, according to the grace given us. . .
if it is leadership. . .govern diligently.
ROMANS 12:6, 8 NIV

*O*ne fine spring day, Deborah stepped out into her front yard and observed the most magnificent snapdragons she had ever seen—brilliant reds, oranges, yellows, whites, and pinks. She'd never seen such gorgeous snapdragons before.

Curious, she asked her neighbor and gardening partner, "I can't believe how *big* these snapdragons are. Did *you* plant them or did *I*?"

"I did."

"Oh. . .what's your secret?"

"I dug big holes and I prepared the soil with *lots of good fertilizer.*"

Deborah felt a pang of guilt, recalling how she often dug shallow holes and skimped on fertilizing the soil, just so she could see fast results.

While gazing at the magnificent snapdragons, Deborah couldn't help but consider how similar her gardening habits were to other projects she had undertaken at home, at church, and at the office. Because she was impatient and wanted fast results, she often jumped in and acted too quickly. She often didn't take the time to "prepare the soil" by thinking through all of the much-needed early steps of a project that could potentially lay a stronger foundation for a successful venture. In her leadership roles at church, home, and work, she suddenly realized she had skimped on soil preparation.

Dear Lord, in my leadership roles at home, church, and work, help me to be
diligent in preparation, prayerfully preparing the soil for each new project.
Amen.

LOST AND FOUND

"And the one who sent me is with me—he has not deserted me.
For I always do what pleases him."
JOHN 8:29 NLT

$\mathcal{W}$e lose things on a daily basis. Each year we probably spend hours looking for things—keys, sunglasses, lipstick, or even the saltshaker that normally rests next to the stove. We know these items don't sprout wings and walk off but have been set somewhere and forgotten by you or someone you know.

You are God's most prized possession, and while He'll never forget where you are, sometimes we walk off from Him. We lose ourselves in the things we need to do, the places we need to go, and the people we need to see. Our calendars fill up with commitments we're obligated to keep. We often commit to too many things and exhaust ourselves trying to stay ahead of our schedules.

The further we displace ourselves from God—not necessarily on purpose—the more we become lost in our own space While we're doing life on our own, we can forget that He is standing there waiting to do life every day with us. If you feel distant from Him today, look up. He's waiting for you to find your rightful place with Him.

God, I never want to become so busy that I lose sight of You. Show me what things I should commit to and what things are for someone else to do, so that I am available to You and ready to serve in the capacity You've prepared me for.
Amen.

TRUE BLUE

And we, who with unveiled faces all reflect the Lord's glory,
are being transformed into his likeness with ever-increasing glory,
which comes from the Lord, who is the Spirit.
2 CORINTHIANS 3:18 NIV

*I*t's called *Morpho rhetenor*.

This South American butterfly has something in common with a genus of beetles unique to France. It also shares some similarity with the male peacock. What peculiarity connects a French beetle to a South American butterfly and the colorful peacock? It's their amazing iridescent blue coloring. The wings of *Morpho rhetenor* are constructed of tiny scales. The blue beetle of France has a complex network of airspaces and polysaccharide rods in its "shell." And the peacock has variations in color at the nanoscale level.

Given all that scientific mumbo jumbo, here's the startling thing: As brilliant as the iridescent blue shimmers in each of these creatures, not one of them has anything blue in or on them! There's no blue in those butterfly scales, none in the beetle rods, and no blue feathers on the peacock. Their blue coloring comes only from the reflection or absorption of certain light frequencies. What makes those butterflies, beetles, and peacocks look iridescent blue is an outside source of light—the sun.

That's just how we reflect the Lord's glory. There is no "blue" in us, because of sin. But our transformation—or glory—comes from an outside light source, the Son of God. As we daily look to Him and live in His light, so we increasingly reflect His glory.

Lord, I want to look more like my Savior every day.
Help me to walk in Your light. Amen.

WALK IN THE LIGHT

Then Jesus spoke to them again, saying, "I am the light of the world.
He who follows Me shall not walk in darkness, but have the light of life."
JOHN 8:12 NKJV

A woman and her family regularly vacationed on an island off the
Florida coast. They loved this speck of sand because it was secluded
and could be reached only by boat. There were no roads—only dirt
paths for walking or golf carts—and few people.

One night the woman went out for a walk without thinking to
take along a flashlight. She found her way easily along the paths where
porch lights were on, but the farther she walked, the less light there was,
until finally, the path was so black she was forced to stop. She stood
listening to the sounds around her—rustling leaves, snapping twigs.
She wondered about the creatures that might be watching her as she
stood, frozen, afraid to take a single step.

Before her imagination got the better of her, however; she heard
her daughter's voice and saw the light bobbing down the sandy trail
toward her. "Mom, you forgot your flashlight; I was worried." How
thankful she was for the light that illuminated their way back to the
cottage.

We can be thankful for the light that illuminates our paths—the
Word of God. Without it we would stumble along through life not
knowing which paths to take in a world that sometimes looks dark and
scary.

Heavenly Father, thank You for Your Word that is a
lamp unto my feet and a light to my path. Amen.

NOTHING TO LOSE

Saul replied, "You are not able to go out against this Philistine and fight him;
you are only a boy, and he has been a fighting man from his youth."
1 SAMUEL 17:33 NIV

Goliath, a pagan Philistine, defied Israel's army and challenged it to send a single man to fight him to decide who would rule the land. As the Israelites observed his giant body and fearsome war equipment, they quaked in their sandals. How could they win?

Victory lay in the hands of a visionary shepherd, David, who recognized that the battle was not his, but God's. The intrepid shepherd stepped forward to accept the challenge.

"Wiser" heads warned the youth of danger. King Saul counseled against fighting the Philistine warrior, then tried to deck the shepherd out in his own armor. But David had a better armor—the Lord God.

Sometimes we clearly hear the call of God to move ahead into spiritual battle. Others warn us against it, and their counsel seems wise. But God's call pulls at our hearts. Who are we listening to? Are these counselors godly people or discouraging, worldly wise Sauls, with at best a tenuous connection to God?

If God is fighting your battle for you, trust in Him, seek godly counsel, and follow His call implicitly. You have nothing to lose.

If You lead me, Lord, I cannot lose. Show me Your path and give me courage.
Amen.

IN THE LIGHT

*[Jesus] said, "I am the light of the world. Whoever follows
me will never walk in darkness, but will have the light of life."*
JOHN 8:12 NIV

The hurricane forced the family to huddle inside without electricity
for a second consecutive day. If days were dreary, nights seemed eternal.
Not knowing how long they would be without electricity, they conserved
flashlight batteries, candles, and oil for the lamp. Even walking posed a
challenge without tripping over the dog or whacking a chair leg. Games
and conversation by candlelight soon lost their appeal. Reading strained
the eyes. By eight o'clock there was nothing else to do but go to bed and
sweat for hours on end, praying for sunshine the next morning.

The basics of life were difficult and burdensome. When the dark
clouds finally lifted, sunlight streamed in and power was restored.
Despite the mess outside, their spirits were revived.

Jesus said followers will never have to walk in darkness again but
will have a life in the light. No more stumbling—we have His guidance.
No more dreariness—we have His joy. No more heaviness—we have
freedom to bask in the warmth of His forgiveness! His light of life is
a vibrant life lived confidently because we can see the path before us
through eyes of faith.

*Light of Life, thank You that we do not hover in darkness any longer.
In You we walk boldly in the light of life, forgiven, free and vibrant. Amen.*

COMFORT FOOD

For whatever things were written before were written for our learning,
that we through the patience and comfort of the Scriptures might have hope.
ROMANS 15:4 NKJV

A big mound of ice cream topped with hot fudge; a full bowl of salty, buttery popcorn; grilled cheese sandwiches and warm chicken noodle soup fixed by Mom—comfort food. There is nothing like a generous helping of things that bring the sensation of comfort to a worn body at the end of a long day or to a bruised mind after a disappointment. Those comfort foods soothe the body and mind because, through the senses, they remind us of happier and more secure times.

Romans 15:4 tells us that the scriptures are comfort food for the soul. They were written and given so that, through our learning, we would be comforted with the truths of God. Worldly pleasures bring a temporary comfort, but the problem still remains when the pleasure or comfort fades. However, the words of God are soothing and provide permanent hope and peace. Through God's Word, you will be changed, and your troubles will dim in the bright light of Christ. So the next time you are sad, lonely, or disappointed, before you turn to pizza, turn to the Word of God as your source of comfort.

Thank You, Father, for the rich comfort Your Word provides.
Help me to remember to find my comfort in scripture rather
than through earthly things that will ultimately fail me. Amen.

POWER UP

The Spirit of God, who raised Jesus from the dead, lives in you.
ROMANS 8:11 NLT

$\mathcal{G}$od is the same yesterday, today, and forever. His strength does not diminish over time. That same mountain-moving power you read about in the lives of people from the Old and New Testaments still exists today. The same power that caused the walls of Jericho to fall, an ax to float, and a dead girl to live again is still available today. The force of God that formed the world, brought the dry land above the waters of the sea, and raised Jesus from the dead is available to work out the details of your life.

It's natural to want to do things on our own. We all want to be independent and strong. When faced with a challenge, the first thing we do is try to work it out in our own skill and ability—within our own power. But there's another way.

We don't have to go it alone. Our heavenly Father wants to help. All we have to do is ask. He has already made His power available to His children. Whatever we face—wherever we go—whatever dreams we have for our lives, take courage and know that anything is possible when we draw on the power of God.

Father, help me to remember that You are always with me,
ready to help me do all things. Amen.

THE REWARDS OF SACRIFICE

And the young men that were spies went in, and brought out Rahab,
and her father, and her mother, and her brethren, and all that she had.
JOSHUA 6:23 KJV

Rahab, one of the most dynamic women in the Bible, took risks that would make most of us shudder today. She believed in the majesty and truth of the God of the Israelites when everyone around her worshipped pagan idols. Every citizen of Jericho knew the power the Lord held, yet they chose to rely on the safety of the city's infamous walls. Rahab saw that God not only destroyed His enemies but safeguarded those who followed Him.

Because of her beliefs, Rahab opened her home to the two spies, an act that easily could have gotten her and her entire family executed. She risked everything to protect the spies from the king, asking in exchange that the Israelites spare her family in the destruction to come (Joshua 2:12–13). They did, and the ultimate reward for her faithfulness was a place in the lineage of Christ.

We are not always called to take the chances Rahab had to take. Yet, as mothers, sisters, and daughters, we are called upon every day to stand up for our beliefs. Rahab is a reminder that God does, indeed, provide for those who love and believe in Him.

Lord, I love You. Let my eyes always turn to
You for protection and hope in the days to come. Amen.

OUT OF EGYPT

"When Israel was a child, I loved him, and out of Egypt I called my son."
HOSEA 11:1 NIV

*W*hen we think of these words, it is usually in connection to Jesus, as God called Him out of Egypt after Herod's death. But read the verse after it, and you will discover God's condemnation of His wandering people. Though God called Israel with love, they turned aside from Him to pagan worship.

Scripture often holds similar surprises. An uplifting verse is followed by one that speaks of deep sin. God's promises and humanity's sin run together in entwined messages.

Isn't that just the way the Christian life is? God's merciful thread runs through our pain-filled, erroneous lives. Like a bright, gold line, it brightens our existence and begins to turn us from sin-filled ore to bright, pure gold.

For not only did God call His Son from Egypt; He calls us, too, to leave behind the darkness of sin and live in His holiness. His love strips evil from us and brings us into close relationship to Him.

God has called you out of Egypt because He loves you. Love Him in return.

Lord, thank You for calling me out of sin and into Yourself. Cleanse me from sin and let Your golden love shine through my life. I want to glorify You. Amen.

GUARD YOUR
HEART

Guard your heart, for it is the wellspring of life.
PROVERBS 4:23 NIV

$\mathcal{D}$o the words of Proverbs 4:23 instruct us to isolate ourselves, building walls around our hearts like fortresses to keep others out? Should we avoid letting others touch our lives and get close to us? Certainly this is not what God would want! We are designed for fellowship with other believers and even for an intimate loving relationship with a spouse. Guarding our hearts, however, is an important command that women in the twenty-first century often fail to heed.

When we fall into relationships or activities that are unhealthy or that consume us, our hearts lose their focus and get wounded along the way. Even good things can become idols in our lives. An idol is anything that we allow to come before God. The Lord is always there to take us back and to help us heal, but He would much prefer to help us make wise decisions on the front end. If we seek God first in all things, He can protect us from pitfalls.

Christians are meant for a close walk with God, talking with Him daily, reading and applying His Word. This walk suffers when our hearts are given carelessly to other things or people in our lives. We must, therefore, *guard our hearts* in order that we may live the abundant lives God desires for us.

Father, help me to love freely but also to guard my heart.
Walk and talk with me today. Guide the steps that I take. Amen.

A DIFFERENT CUP TO FILL

O God, thou art my God; early will I seek thee.
PSALM 63:1 KJV

$\mathcal{I}$t is early morning and we stumble from our beds to take a shower, apply makeup, and blow-dry our hair. Meanwhile, coffee brews in the kitchen, and with a yawn we fill our cups. Busy women have limited time to relax, reflect, and pray. Yet a different and more significant type of cup longs to be filled—our spirit.

King David resided over the nation of Israel and all that that entailed. Yet he found time to seek the counsel, mercy, and direction of God daily. The more responsibilities he assumed, the more he prayed and meditated on God's precepts. Well before David was inundated with worldly concerns, nagging obligations, and his administrative duties, the Bible suggests that he sought the Lord in the early morning hours.

If the king of Israel recognized his need to spend time with God, how much more should we? When we seek our heavenly Father before daily activities demand our attention, the Holy Spirit regenerates our spirits, and our cups overflow.

Dear Lord, I take this time to pray and spend time with You before I attend to daily responsibilities. Fill my cup with the presence and power of Your Spirit. Give me the wisdom and direction I need today. Amen.

AMBASSADORS

We are therefore Christ's ambassadors,
as though God were making his appeal through us.
2 CORINTHIANS 5:20 NIV

An American flag gently flapped in the balmy air. The sight appeared quite patriotic at first glance, yet upon closer inspection it was obvious something was not right. The flag was flying upside down! The stars appeared at the bottom instead of the top. Although any American would quickly realize this misrepresentation, a foreigner might incorrectly conclude that this is how the American flag should be displayed.

As Christians, we represent Christ to others. Our lives wave the Christian flag for the world to see. Do we honor Christ with our lives or are we flying His flag upside down? We must choose either to look like the world or to look like Christ. The two are complete opposites. If we become a friend of the world, it's as if we have chosen to fly Christ's flag upside down.

We are called to be Christ's representatives, His ambassadors. Humility, not arrogance, should be observed in our lives. Forgiveness and love should be readily displayed. Peace should shine forth. When nonbelievers observe your life, do they receive an accurate picture of Jesus?

Dear Lord, help me realize the responsibility I have as Your ambassador.
May I correctly represent You to others so that they will be drawn to You. Amen.

FREE INDEED

*For you have been called to live in freedom. . .
freedom to serve one another in love.*
GALATIANS 5:13 NLT

*C*heri felt joy, pride, and strangely, trepidation battling within her for precedence as she watched her son Mark's high school graduation ceremony. She was thrilled for Mark, as he crossed this threshold into manhood with his faith strong, body firm and healthy, and future bright. But somewhere deep inside, her happiness dimmed, knowing Mark would be leaving for Marine boot camp within four short weeks.

She'd been surprised by his decision to enlist, even though she'd known he had been praying about it for months. "It's what God is calling me to do, Mom," he said, looking down at her from his new adult height while laying a firm hand on her shoulder. "I want to serve my country and protect the freedom of those I love."

Freedom, Cheri mused as her eyes misted, *is such a costly blessing.* How often she'd taken it for granted—until the price became pieces of her heart.

Jesus, too, paid an enormous price to ensure our spiritual freedom. "So Christ has truly set us free" (Galatians 5:1 NLT). Because of His sacrifice on the cross, we are no longer slaves to sin and death but can enjoy new lives in Christ—free of guilt, condemnation, and oppression. Freedom is a costly blessing, indeed.

*Liberator of our souls, on this day our country celebrates freedom from oppression, we pray for protection for those willingly paying the precious cost of our liberty. And we thank You for Your ultimate sacrifice for our freedom.
Amen.*

TIME WITH THE MASTER

Elisha said, "Please let a double portion of your spirit be upon me."
So [Elijah] said, "You have asked a hard thing."
2 KINGS 2:9–10 NKJV

*W*hen Kelley was a little girl, she learned from observation and participation how to create beautiful things for the home. From her mother she learned how to sew, how to arrange flowers, and how to "pull a room together" with fabrics, colors, and patterns. Though she had no formal education in interior decorating, today Kelley is a successful interior decorator.

Many things in life can be learned only by spending time with an expert. An Internet search or a study of a technical manual seldom matches a hands-on learning experience. Elisha learned how to conduct himself as a prophet under the tutelage of his predecessor, Elijah. The disciples of the Lord Jesus spent every day for three years or more in the company of their Master. All these men learned firsthand the lessons they needed to learn. They did their part, and God did His.

Elisha saw his teacher and master taken up into heaven. Then he continued the ministry Elijah had begun. The disciples saw their teacher and master ascend to heaven, too. Then they stopped gaping and went to work, showing the world that the empowering gospel was unstoppable in its spread and influence (Acts 5:38–39).

If we want to do God's work in God's world, we too must spend time with the Master. We learn our lessons best in His presence.

Lord, teach me to be more like You. Amen.

DEBORAH:
WISDOM IN ACTION

Deborah said unto Barak, Up; for this is the day in which the LORD hath delivered Sisera into thine hand: is not the LORD gone out before thee? So Barak went down from mount Tabor, and ten thousand men after him.
JUDGES 4:14 KJV

*D*eborah, the only female judge in the Old Testament, kept a demanding schedule. She was married to Lapidoth and referred to herself as "a mother in Israel," so she no doubt carried the typical, heavy-home responsibilities of the era. Deborah also spent much of her time holding court under a palm tree that bore her name. Whenever her countrymen could not agree on land boundaries, animal possession, or family grievances, they argued their cases while she listened, prayed, and often made difficult decisions.

God also spoke His messages to Deborah. Through her, He had called Barak, a soldier, to deliver Israel from Sisera, the captain of the cruel Canaanites who had overrun their land. Barak obeyed, but no way was he going to battle without Deborah beside him! So she left her family and her courtroom under the palm tree and traveled many miles with Barak and his men to do God's will. Deborah made her own safety and comfort secondary as she urged Barak on with God's truth and encouragement.

Lord, when my schedule seems impossible, please give me the grace and patience to help others who inconvenience me. May we grow into all You want us to be.
Amen.

DONE IN BY DELILAH

*She sent and called for the lords of the Philistines, saying, Come up this once,
for he hath shewed me all his heart. Then the lords of the Philistines
came up unto her, and brought money in their hand.*
JUDGES 16:18 KJV

As a girl, Delilah discovered her smile could get whatever she
wanted.

As a beautiful woman, Delilah wanted Samson. Although seven
braids of hair hung to his knees, no one dared call Samson feminine.
His rippling muscles won every contest with ease. Samson's tendency
to worship his God annoyed Delilah, but he amused her. Delilah knew
she fascinated him. For a while, it was enough.

One day Philistine leaders offered her a huge sum of money. She
only had to learn the secret of Samson's enormous strength. Delilah
used every word, look, and movement to torture him into telling her
the truth. Finally, Samson told her that if his hair was cut, his strength
would disappear. Delilah lulled him to sleep then called for a barber—
and for the Philistine lords who blinded Samson and chained him to a
treadmill like a beast.

What a sad ending to romance. What if Delilah had used her great
gifts of beauty and persuasion to inspire Samson to serve God?

*Father, You have given me, as a woman, special influence in many arenas.
Help me bless others and point them to You. Amen.*

LOCATION, LOCATION, LOCATION

Those who live in the shelter of the Most High will find rest in the shadow of the Almighty. This I declare about the LORD: He alone is my refuge, my place of safety; he is my God, and I trust him.
PSALM 91:1–2 NLT

*W*here do you live? Where are you living right now, this instant?

If you are abiding in Christ, moment by moment, you are constantly safe under His protection. In that secret place, that hidden place in Him, you can maintain a holy serenity, a peace of mind that surpasses all understanding. If you are trusting in God, nothing can move you or harm you.

If money problems, physical illness, time pressures, job woes, the state of the world, or something else is getting you down, check your location. Where are you? Where is your mind? Where are your thoughts?

Let what the world has conditioned you to think go in one ear and out the other. Stand on the truth, the promises of God's Word. Say of the Lord, "God is my refuge! I am hidden in Christ! Nothing can harm me. In Him I trust!" Say it loud. Say it often. Say it over and over until it becomes your reality. And you will find yourself dwelling in that secret place every moment of the day.

God, You are my refuge. When I abide in You, nothing can harm me. Your Word is the truth on which I rely. Fill me with Your light and the peace of Your love. It's You and me, Lord, all the way! Amen.

A Good Decision

*Therefore, whether you eat or drink, or whatever you do,
do all to the glory of God.*
1 CORINTHIANS 10:31 NKJV

The decision should have been a simple one to make, but Karen had struggled with it for days, ever since her supervisor had brought her the option of working through the weekend on a rush job. She'd almost accepted right away, since the money would take care of a debt that had been hanging over the family for weeks.

Then the church festival came to mind, where she'd been asked to run a booth on Sunday afternoon. And the Saturday morning soccer tryouts. She had not promised to be at either, but she loved helping out with church events, and the very idea of missing her daughters' attempts to make one of the local teams tore her heart. On the other hand, alleviating the debt would give them more freedom.

As she weighed the pros and cons, Karen remembered three letters and three questions her pastor had used in a sermon a few weeks before. He'd said that when making a hard decision, "spell" it out—SPL— **S**tudy the Bible; **P**ray for God's will; **L**isten for the guidance of the Holy Spirit. The three questions were (1) Will it cause anyone to stumble? (2) Will it strengthen and encourage you? (3) Will it glorify God?

With those as her guidelines, Karen found the decision easy. Loyalty to her family and faith had to take precedence.

*Lord, whenever I have a hard decision to make, help me
remember the right priorities for my life and faith. Amen.*

BREAD IN THE WILDERNESS

*"I will rain down bread from heaven for you. The people
are to go out each day and gather enough for that day."*
EXODUS 16:4 NIV

*O*ur faith is a living, breathing organism that needs to be fed every
day. Christ, His Word, and His presence, are our daily manna. He has
been rained down upon us, given to us by God. All we have to do is *take*
Him into our lives, gathering a day's portion every day.

Jesus Himself knows that we need a daily portion of Him to renew
ourselves. When He faced the hungry crowds in the wilderness, He
showed His concern for their welfare. In Matthew 15:32 (NKJV), Jesus
says, "I have compassion on the multitude, because they have now
continued with Me three days and have nothing to eat. And I do not
want to send them away hungry, lest they faint on the way."

Christ is so gracious to us. He gives us "each day our daily bread,"
nourishment that shields us against our mood swings, unrelenting problems,
and the influence of unbelievers surrounding us. This miraculous,
daily intake of Christ keeps us from fainting along the way!

God has provided you with the manna you need to feed your faith.
Don't go away hungry. Take your daily portion each morning, just what
you need, to live the victorious life.

*Christ, I come to You hungry, needing Your nourishment, Your power, to renew
my faith. I stand before You, ready to ingest Your presence, to feed upon Your
Word, to gain the strength to survive the wilderness of this world. Amen.*

AMBITION

A heart at peace gives life to the body, but envy rots the bones.
PROVERBS 14:30 NIV

Sarah always did her best. But one day, when she heard a colleague being praised, she bristled. Sarah admitted that Karen was really good at what she did, but Sarah wished she were that good, too. Then Karen became Sarah's supervisor.

Karen was a fair supervisor, and Sarah knew it. But Sarah couldn't stand it. Karen was *too* good. Plus, Sarah had been hoping for the promotion. Instead of supporting Karen, Sarah challenged her authority in meetings. Then she began to gossip about Karen, stretching the truth to make her look bad, even though Karen hadn't done anything unfair. Sarah felt bad about what she was doing, but she was so riveted on the unfairness of Karen's promotion that she was blind to her own ambitions.

Envy plays out in several ways but most often through ambition. If ambition means wanting to do well at your job, then ambition is good. But, if ambition means you want to compete against your neighbor, destroy her reputation, and rejoice when you do better than your colleague does, then ambition is destructive.

Oh Lord, forgive me for my jealous heart. Help me be content in who You made me and how You made me. Help my only ambition to be to do my best and to become like You. Amen.

A WOMAN AROUND TOWN

*Fear not; I will do to thee all that thou requirest: for all the
city of my people doth know that thou art a virtuous woman.*
RUTH 3:11 KJV

*A*nna felt like an outsider in the small town. Most of the inhabitants
seemed to trace their local ancestors back to the 1800s. She had moved
here only three years before when her ailing parents needed a helping
hand.

Anna found a job—not as profitable as her former one in a larger
city—and settled down to assist her mother and dad. She drove them
to medical appointments and stayed with them during hospitalizations.
Anna made their church congregation her own. She reinforced their
close ties with the church family, especially during their last days.

Anna had connected with many community organizations during
this difficult time in order to maximize care for her parents. After
both passed away, she remained in town and volunteered at the local
senior center to help other elderly people and their families. Because
she demonstrated a caring spirit and personal integrity, most agencies
were glad to grant her requests.

To Anna's surprise, community leaders asked her to head up the
center, then to run for town council.

"Surely there are other people more qualified than I am!" she
objected.

"Nobody I can think of," the mayor answered. "We're glad you live
in our town!"

*Father, Please help me represent You well wherever and however I serve.
Thank You for opportunities to impact my world. Amen.*

HIS SCHEDULE

Love and faithfulness meet together;
righteousness and peace kiss each other.
PSALM 85:10 NIV

Cathy dropped the kids off at school and headed straight to the gym for a much-needed workout. She had a full day's schedule laid out on her car's passenger seat, and there wasn't a moment to lose. After the gym, there would be grocery shopping, a parent meeting at school, mountain-high laundry, and an overdue haircut appointment. She would have just enough time to make it back to the school for the children's three o'clock pickup.

Sweating and spent after her workout, Cathy jumped back into the car, cranked up the air conditioner, and checked the voice mail on her cell phone before pulling out of the parking lot. "Oh no," she sighed, as she shut off the car engine and listened to her friend's voice, near tears, telling Cathy about having to put her terminally ill mother back into the hospital for the fourth time in as many months.

All of a sudden, Cathy's to-do list seemed unimportant. The parent meeting would have to go on without her, the laundry and the groceries could wait, and nobody but she would care what her hair looked like. Cathy crumpled up her list and dialed her friend. "I'm on my way. What do you need?"

I yield my daily schedule to You, O Lord. Help me not to miss important opportunities to make an eternal difference in another's life. Amen.

OUR POWER
SOURCE

"Do not be afraid or discouraged because of the king of Assyria...
for there is a greater power with us than with him. With him is
only the arm of flesh, but with us is the LORD our God to help
us and to fight our battles." And the people gained confidence.
2 CHRONICLES 32:7–8 NIV

$\mathcal{S}$ometimes when the battle lines are drawn, we begin to panic. We don't think we can accomplish what God has called us to do—whether that is to run a household, hold down a full-time job, take college courses, head up a committee at church, or all four! Sometimes there are days when it seems like everything is against us. But the amazing thing—the wonder of it all—is that whatever we attempt *in God's power* will be accomplished. We won't burn out if we are relying on Him instead of our flesh.

As David said before defeating Goliath, "The battle is the LORD's" (1 Samuel 17:47 NIV). With that kind of mind-set, we are sure to be victorious in all that we do—not stressed out by trying to accomplish everything under our own steam. Whew! What a relief!

Whenever your energy is lagging, whenever you are discouraged or afraid, look to your Source of power. Call on Jesus to give you strength. And you will have confidence and victory, for He will do—through you—more than you can ever ask or imagine.

Jesus, help! I'm stressed out, burned out, tapped out. Fill me with
Your power. Provide me with confidence, strength, and fearlessness
as I go throughout my day, walking in Your will. Amen.

JUST HALF A CUP

*"I am coming to you now, but I say these things while I am still in the world,
so that they may have the full measure of my joy within them."*
JOHN 17:13 NIV

"Just half a cup, please." A friend is offered a cup of piping hot coffee,
but she declines a full cup, accepting only a small amount. Perhaps she
is trying to be polite, or maybe she feels as though she's had enough
coffee already that day. But it is difficult and unnatural for her friend
to stop pouring at half a cup, so she pours just a bit more than what
was requested. She wants to give her friend the fullest possible measure
of enjoyment that she can in that one cup of coffee.

That's how our Father feels when He longs to bestow His richest
blessings and wisdom on us. He loves us, so He desires to fill our cup
to overflowing with the things that He knows will bring us pleasure
and growth. Do you tell Him to stop pouring when your cup is only
half full? You may not even realize it, but perhaps your actions dictate
that your cup remain half empty. Seek a full cup and enjoy the full
measure of the joy of the Lord.

*Dear Jesus, forgive me for not accepting the fullness of Your blessings and
Your joy. Help me to see the ways that I prevent my cup from being filled to
overflowing. Thank You for wanting me to have the fullness of Your joy. Amen.*

Reflecting God in Our Work

Whatever you do, work at it with all your heart,
as working for the Lord, not for men.
COLOSSIANS 3:23 NIV

Parents often tell their children to do their best in school or to behave well when they visit friends' homes. Children are a reflection of their parents. When a mom and dad send their offspring out into the world, they can only hope that the reflection will be a positive one.

As believers, we are God's children. No one is perfect, and for this there is grace. However, we may be the only reflection of our heavenly Father that some will ever see. Our attitudes and actions on the job speak volumes to those around us. Although it may be tempting to do just enough to get by, we put forth our best effort when we remember we represent God to the world. A Christian's character on the job should be a positive reflection of the Lord.

This is true of our work at home as well. No one would disagree that daily chores are often monotonous, but we are called to face them with a cheerful spirit. God will give us the ability to do so when we ask Him.

Father, help me today to represent You well through my work.
I want to reflect Your love in all I do. Amen.

TAKE A LOAD OFF

Give all your worries and cares to God, for he cares about you.
1 PETER 5:7 NLT

*O*f the ten million Americans afflicted with osteoporosis, 80 percent of them are women. Over the years, this disease can lead to loss of height or curving of the spine, giving people what is commonly referred to as a "dowager hump." To help prevent osteoporosis, medical experts advise getting regular exercise and taking supplements, such as calcium and vitamin D.

When we encounter older women afflicted with a dowager hump, our hearts go out to them as we see them bowed down beneath what seems to be an invisible weight. Yet sometimes we ourselves are bowed down within, weighed down by the cares of this world—cares we should have given up to God that morning or perhaps years before.

Daily exercising your faith and digesting God's Word can help prevent the development of an inner dowager hump. Give Christ your concerns, worries, what-ifs. Put all those cares on Him, for His shoulders are broad enough to carry them. And the amazing thing is that He actually *wants* them!

Don't become bowed down by the weight of this world, but stand straight and tall in your faith, moment by moment, walking in the newness of the day (see Isaiah 43:18–19) and in the power of His strength.

God, I come to You today with all my burdens, worries, and "what ifs."
They are rolling right off my shoulders and onto Yours. Whew! That's
a load off. Thank You for taking my burdens. I arise lighter and ready
to begin anew, walking in the strength of Your awesome power! Amen.

FAULTLESS

*To him who is able to keep you from falling and to present you
before his glorious presence without fault and with great joy.*
JUDE 1:24 NIV

*W*ho is at fault? Who is to blame? When something goes wrong at
work, at home, or at church, someone is held accountable. People want
to know who is responsible, who made a mistake. The ones pointing
fingers of accusation don't always care about the truth as much as they
do about making sure they aren't blamed for the transgression.

Ever since God confronted Adam and Eve in the Garden of Eden,
we have been pointing fingers at someone else instead of taking responsibility for our own actions. Shame and fear make us want to deny we
have done any wrong even when we have done so accidentally or by
mistake. We value what God and other people think of us. When we
are at odds with God or others over a transgression, we often become
depressed.

Jesus loves us so much despite our shortcomings. He is the One
who can keep us from falling—who can present us faultless before the
Father. Because of this we can have our joy restored no matter what.
Whether we have done wrong and denied it or have been falsely accused,
we can come into His presence to be restored and lifted up. Let us keep
our eyes on Him instead of on our need to justify ourselves to God or
others.

*Thank You, Jesus, for Your cleansing love and
for the joy we can find in Your presence. Amen.*

An Unexpected Turn

"He makes my way perfect."
2 Samuel 22:33 nkjv

We always want to be in the right place at the right time. Life moves in a hurry, and with it, we thrust ourselves forward into each appointment or commitment. We get frustrated when we miss a turn or mistakenly veer down a wrong road.

What if you were to choose to put a different spin on the frustration of going out of your way? You can get bent out of shape and become frustrated because of the time you feel you have lost, or you can choose to believe that God makes your way perfect and He has kept you from harm's way. What if that wrong turn that you thought cost you ten extra minutes in traffic actually kept you from a fender-bender or something worse?

Instead of feeling lost and undone, consider that perhaps this was the path you were destined to take. A series of unfortunate events or a trip down an unexpected path can lead to a positive spin on your day. Be open to taking a different route today. It could open new doors of opportunity in unexpected ways.

*Father, help me to relax, trusting that You order
my steps and make my way perfect every day. Amen.*

WATER'S COST

*"To him who is thirsty I will give to drink without
cost from the spring of the water of life."*
REVELATION 21:6 NIV

Drinking an ice-cold glass of water on a hot summer day is a wonderful experience. It seems that the thirstier we are, the better water tastes and the more of it we can drink.

Imagine attending a sporting event in the heat of the day. The sun beats down on you, you sweat like crazy, your senses become dull, and an overwhelming desire for a cold bottle of water gradually becomes the only thing you can think about. The players disappear, and the hard bleachers cease to matter; you would pay any amount of money for one sip of water.

Jesus, well aware of basic human needs, likens His message to water, "the spring of the water of life." Just as we cannot live without water, we cannot live without the Word of God. We are shocked to learn that this life-giving message, one we must have at any price, and one to which we cannot assign value, costs us nothing. Jesus loves us so much that He gave up His life that we might partake of these invigorating waters. So drink up, and leave your money at home; the water of life is free.

*Dear Lord, thank You for letting me drink for free from the spring of the water of
life. Help me to remember Your sacrifice and Your love for me. Amen.*

TWENTY QUESTIONS

"Thus, by their fruit you will recognize them."
MATTHEW 7:20 NIV

*S*everal friends laughed the night away as they enjoyed playing with a tiny electronic "Twenty Questions" game. The group would think of a common noun, such as a piano, mop, eyelash, or spoon, and then the gadget would begin asking questions:

"Animal, mineral, or vegetable?"
"Is it lighter than a duck?"
"Smaller than a microwave?"
"Can you put it in an envelope?"
"Can you hold it?"
"Would you find it at a school?"

Amazingly, the game could figure out what they were thinking of in almost every instance by asking fewer than twenty questions—simply by finding out characteristics of the object.

People are similar to this tiny computer. They don't have to be told who is a Christian. Every action answers their every curiosity: how people spend their time and money and set their priorities, how much they help the needy, whether they are patient when wronged, how generous they are, how they treat children, whether they gossip, how they show or fail to show love for people. Every action bears fruit, revealing whether individuals are true disciples of Jesus Christ. "A good tree cannot bear bad fruit, and a bad tree cannot bear good fruit" (Matthew 7:18 NIV). The lives we lead *shout* whether Christ is front and center in our lives.

Lord, may my every action bear witness of Your Holy Spirit's work,
leading people to a direct knowledge of the truth. Amen.

My Way or God's Way?

Good and upright is the LORD; therefore He instructs sinners in the way. He leads the humble in justice, and He teaches the humble His way. . . . He will instruct him in the way he should choose.
PSALM 25:8–9, 12 NASB

*J*n today's culture, it is easy to follow "my way." We are bombarded with advertisements from TV, magazines, billboards, and the Internet that tell us "It is all about me" and "We can have it all." We have access to people, information, and products 24/7. We have the Internet, e-mail, telephone, cell phone, fax, and pager that provide us with availability and resources. In buying anything, there is an overwhelming number of options to choose from. With all these distractions, it is not surprising that we have difficulty surrendering daily to God's way.

Nevertheless, God wants us to live life His way. Our good and upright God tells us that when we come before Him as humble, meek, needy, or afflicted, He will teach us what is right and just. God will teach us His way of living. If it is a decision that needs to be made, a course of action that needs to be taken, or a word that needs to be spoken, God will instruct us in a manner consistent with who He is. Therefore, it is of the utmost importance that we intentionally fall before the throne of God seeking His way, not our own. What way will you choose today?

Good and upright God, please allow me not to be distracted in this world but to focus on You. Teach me Your way, I humbly pray. Amen.

A HEALTHY FEAR

To fear the LORD is to hate evil;
I hate pride and arrogance, evil behavior and perverse speech.
PROVERBS 8:13 NIV

*W*hen we think about our fears, our minds and bodies almost always tense. Whether it's a fear of heights, spiders, public speaking, failure, or being alone, everyone has fears. In fact, it's considered perfectly natural to avoid what we fear.

Why does the Bible say we should "fear" God? In reality, to fear God is not the same as fearing the creepy-crawly spider inching up the living room wall. Instead, we fear God when we have a deep respect and reverence for Him.

Imagine that the president of the United States was paying your home a visit. The house would be extra clean, the laundry would be washed and put away, and the children would be instructed to be on their best behavior. Why? Because the visitor deserves respect.

Our lives should reflect a similar reverence for our heavenly Father every day—our souls scrubbed extra clean, sin eliminated, and love for our Creator bursting forth in joy. God wants speech and actions to match. Take time today to stand in awe of the One who deserves our greatest respect and love.

Lord, help my daily actions and speech to reflect my respect for You. Amen.

SAY AGAIN. . . ?

Do not think of yourself more highly than you ought, but rather think of yourself with sober judgment, in accordance with the measure of faith God has given you.
ROMANS 12:3 NIV

*L*indsay and her husband, both public school teachers, send all three of their children to public school. They understand education as both parents and teachers. One afternoon their son, Josh, came home with an unusual assignment. Lindsay looked it over.

"This is dumb," she remarked. "This is really dumb." Just the same, she gave Josh the help he needed to start the assignment. She thought no more about it.

Not long after that assignment, Lindsay and her husband went to the school's open house. When they had opportunity to introduce themselves to Josh's teacher privately, Lindsay assured her of their full support.

"We're teachers, too," she told her. "You can count on us to back you up on everything."

The teacher gave Lindsay a tight smile. "Would that include 'dumb' assignments?"

After that, Lindsay was more careful of teacher criticism in front of her kids.

How important to keep a balanced perspective of ourselves! And how much more important it is to resist bragging—even in small ways—to gain the respect of others. Some of our most embarrassing moments follow on the heels of something we've said about ourselves. Mortifying moments can bring us back to reality—and humility. Embarrassing lessons serve as painful reminders that humility doesn't come easy.

Lord, help me to be careful in what I say. Amen.

St—Stuttering

*"For if you forgive men when they sin against you, your heavenly
Father will also forgive you. But if you do not forgive men their sins,
your Father will not forgive your sins."*
MATTHEW 6:14–15 NIV

*M*ary's young son stuttered when he talked. Most likely he would
grow out of it, the doctor advised. Still, Mary worried about it and
started him in speech therapy.

"I think I know why he stutters," volunteered Mary's highly opinion-
ated mother-in-law. "You talk too fast."

The nerve of that remark! How guilt provoking! How very un-
helpful! Mary explained to her that the part of the brain that controls
speech was complicated, and she was doing everything she could to
help her son. But she felt accused by her mother-in-law, as if she were
to blame. That remark felt like an arrow that hit a bull's-eye on a
target: her insecurity at being a good mother.

Mary had a hard time forgiving her mother-in-law. She knew she
shouldn't let that remark fester within her, but she couldn't let it go.
Why was forgiveness so hard? Especially when the person who needed
to be forgiven didn't seem to care?

We've all been in Mary's shoes—struggling to forgive a careless
or hurtful remark. In the Sermon on the Mount, Jesus encouraged
His listeners to forgive offenders, but He didn't mention whether the
offenders sought forgiveness. Jesus was only concerned about believers'
obligations. We forgive because we are forgiven!

*Lord, how often I ask You for forgiveness—and how readily You give it.
May I never take for granted the gift of Your forgiveness. Amen.*

FAITH,
THE EMOTIONAL BALANCER

No man is justified by the law in the sight of God,
it is evident: for, The just shall live by faith.
GALATIANS 3:11 KJV

*O*ur moods often dictate our actions. For instance, we schedule lunch with a friend for Saturday afternoon, but on Saturday morning we regret having made plans. Or we strategize what to accomplish on our day off but suffer from mental anemia and physical fatigue when the day arrives. So we fail to do what we had intended to do in a more enthusiastic moment.

Emotions mislead us. One day shines with promise as we bounce out of bed in song, while the next day dims in despair and we'd prefer to hide under the bedcovers. One moment we forgive, the next we harbor resentment.

The emotional roller coaster thrusts us into mood changes and affects what we do, what we say, and the attitudes that define us.

It has been said that faith is the bird that feels the light and sings to greet the dawn while it is still dark. The Bible instructs us to live by faith—not by feelings. Faith assures us that daylight will dawn in our darkest moments, affirming God's presence so that even when we fail to pray and positive feelings fade, our moods surrender to song.

Heavenly Father, I desire for my faith, not my emotions, to dictate my life.
I pray for balance in my hide-under-the-cover days, so that I
might surrender to You in song. Amen.

SIBLING RIVALRY

"Let's not have fighting between us. . . . After all, we're family. . . .
Let's separate. If you go left, I'll go right; if you go right, I'll go left."
GENESIS 13:8–9 THE MESSAGE

God led Abram (later Abraham) to the land of Canaan. Abram responded by giving half of the land away

Faithful, responsible Abram brought his nephew Lot with him to Canaan. Problems arose because the land couldn't support both men's herds. Abraham let Lot choose where he wanted to settle. Lot, unlike his uncle, thought first of himself. He chose the well-watered plain by the Jordan River.

Abram recognized the problem. Their employees were arguing over the land. He proposed a radical solution. He gave away what was rightfully his, and he let Lot choose first. Even though he ran the risk of getting the less desirable land, he did it anyhow.

Abram exemplifies the kind of love that should exist among Christians. Jesus said we would be known by our love. But loving others doesn't mean that disagreements will not arise. From the Greek widows in the Jerusalem church to the quarrelsome women at Philippi, early Christians had to learn how to get along.

When faced with disagreements, do we dig our feet into the ground and refuse to budge? Or do we put our desires second? Much bitterness among Christians could be avoided if we said, "You choose first. I will accept your decision."

Heavenly Father, You have adopted us into Your family.
Teach us to live together as brothers and sisters, united in Your love. Amen.

HOLD ON

"Hold tight to GOD, your God, just as you've done up to now."
JOSHUA 23:8 THE MESSAGE

*L*ife is the moment—the here and now—yet we spend much of our time outside of that moment worried about, focused on, and trying to figure out the next hour, the next day, week, or month. *Where will the money for this come from? Where will I be next year? How will my children turn out?*

Life comes at us fast—and we have to take each challenge as it comes. Sometimes there are so many variables to juggle that we just want to give up. Don't let go—but hold on. The enemy of your soul *wants* you to quit. You've gotten this far in your faith believing that God will keep His promises and help you reach your destiny.

When you don't think you can take another step—don't! Just hold on. Tomorrow will give you a fresh start with the strength you need to go a little further and hold on a little longer. Take a deep breath, get a fresh grasp on your faith, and don't let go. God will help you get to your dream.

Lord, help me to hold fast to You. With You by my side, I can make it through all the circumstances of life no matter how tough they seem. I trust You to help me hold on. Amen.

SLEEP WELL!

It is vain for you to rise up early, to sit up late,
to eat the bread of sorrows: for so he giveth his beloved sleep.
PSALM 127:2 KJV

$\mathcal{W}$e women are funny creatures.

If we are asked if we want God's blessings, we passionately say, "Of course we do!"

Why then do we reject His gifts?

Psalm 127 says, for example, that children are a heritage and reward. Yet we say, "Two rewards are enough, God."

That same psalm also says that sleep is a gift. Of all God's gifts for health and prosperity that He wants to bestow on us, it's the one modern women reject without a thought.

Thanks to the lightbulb, we have options. We don't have to go to bed when the sun goes down. We can now sit up late doing anything we want.

Ignoring sleep is faithlessness. Long nights of work show that we don't trust God to provide our needs. He says, "Sleep, and I will take care of you."

Not only will God take care of us when we sleep, but He also promises new mercies each morning (Lamentations 3:23). Waking renewed is one such mercy.

Instead of vainly burning the midnight oil, be blessed: Go to bed.

Thank You, Father, for giving me sleep. Let me rest in You each night,
knowing You will provide for my needs according to Your
exceedingly abundant riches in Jesus. Amen.

PERSISTENTLY
PRESENTED PETITIONS

"O woman, great is your faith! Let it be to you as you desire."
MATTHEW 15:28 NKJV

When our loved ones are troubled—emotionally, spiritually, financially, physically, mentally—our hearts are heavy and we feel helpless. But with Christ's ear within reach of our voice, we are anything but powerless. We have an interceder, someone to whom we can continually go and present our petitions.

In Matthew 15:21–28, a Canaanite woman asked Jesus for mercy and to heal her demon-possessed daughter. At first Christ seemed not to hear her pleas. The disciples, irritated with her persistence, told Jesus to send her away.

Yet this woman had dogged determination. She *knew* that the Son of God could heal her daughter. She continued to plead, driven by love for her child and faith in Christ's power.

Her insistence was met by a reproach from Christ, who told her He did not come to help the Gentiles but the Jews. This had to have crushed her expectations. Yet even then she persisted. She did not despair but continued running after Him, worshipping Him, pleading with Him, begging for mercy.

Jesus reproached her again. But still she was undeterred. Finally, Jesus said the words we all long to hear: "Woman, great is your faith! Let it be to you as you desire."

May we live our lives as persistent in our petitions as the Canaanite woman. And may God see our faith and honor our requests as we boldly bring the needs of others before His throne!

God, I come to You, bringing the concerns of others. Lord, have mercy!
Help these people in their hour of need. Amen.

ABIGAIL:
GOD'S PEACEMAKER

Blessed be thy advice, and blessed be thou, which hast kept me this day from coming to shed blood, and from avenging myself with mine own hand.
1 SAMUEL 25:33 KJV

*W*omen often play the role of diplomat with spouses, in-laws, bosses, customers, and kids. Although Abigail enjoyed wealth and privilege, she faced special challenges. Her husband, Nabal, radiated all the friendly tact of a charging rhino. David's six hundred men had protected Nabal's livestock, so David asked for a contribution, a reasonable request during that era. But Nabal's name literally meant "fool." He sneered, "Who is David?"

A furious David and his army set out to inform him.

Fortunately, Nabal's servants told Abigail, who took immediate action. She knew what would stop hungry, angry men in their tracks: food. Lots of it. She sent servants ahead with donkeys loaded with provisions. When David and his soldiers surrounded them, she offered one of the most persuasive apologies in the Bible. Abigail took responsibility for her husband's actions yet pointed out she knew nothing of his rudeness. Abigail gently reminded David of God's plan to make him king and that taking vengeance, especially on the innocent, would hurt his future reign.

David, mesmerized by her food-and-faith approach—and probably by her fair face—thanked Abigail for keeping him from unnecessary bloodshed. Later, after Nabal's death, she became David's wife.

Father, when someone attacks me or those I love, I want to hurt that person! By Your Spirit, help me extend wisdom and grace instead. Amen.

DOG BREATH

*"These people are a stench in my nostrils,
an acrid smell that never goes away."*
ISAIAH 65:5 NLT

*T*here is nothing like the sense of smell to give information that needs no explanation. Mothers learned a long time ago that smells like cigarette smoke can easily give away an experimenting preteen who was out "doing nothing" with friends. It only takes a few minutes of talking with someone to know if she ate Italian, Greek, or Chinese food for lunch. For decades doctors have known that certain breath odors are associated with diseases like diabetes. Some think dog breath surpasses morning mouth in repugnance, but dogs may have something to say about that.

Dogs can detect cancer by smelling people's breath. For some years researchers have been studying how dogs can sniff out cancer. People who have used canines in human cancer detection postulate that it is the waste products produced by cancer cells that dogs can readily identify.

In the Bible neither cancer nor spicy food stinks to God. Disobedience to His way and resting in our own self-righteousness repel Him. The cancer of sin is a stench to our gracious God. If we want to please Him, we must live lives of submissive love as Christ did—that's a pleasing fragrance to the divine sense of smell (Ephesians 5:2).

I pray, Lord, that my life will be a sweet aroma to You. Amen.

THE END IN MIND

*And the people said unto Joshua, The LORD our God will we serve,
and his voice will we obey. So Joshua made a covenant with the
people that day, and set them a statute and an ordinance in Shechem.*
JOSHUA 24:24–25 KJV

The college chaplain stood at the podium and looked out across the seated students and faculty. It was the first day of classes and everyone was assembled together. Excitement mixed with nervousness was on the students' faces—especially the incoming freshmen. The chaplain glanced at his notes, cleared his throat, and then introduced his talk in six simple words: "Begin with the end in mind."

He went on to speak about the school's history and the beliefs they professed, but then he quickly went back to his introduction.

"Knowledge is good," he stated. "You'll be challenged and learn while you're here. But even if you have all the knowledge in the world, at the end of the day, what is the point of having it? Your job is to be a student, but your *first* job is to serve God—now."

As we go about our day, doing whatever exciting or mundane activities we do, it is easy to lose focus and forget that our first priority is to serve God. In each action, our service and attitudes can reflect Christ—the Beginning and the End.

God, help me to reflect You in all I do. Amen.

STOP AND CONSIDER

*"Listen to this, Job; stop and consider God's wonders. Do you know how
God controls the cloud and makes his lightning flash? Do you know how the
clouds hang poised, those wonders of him who is perfect in knowledge?"*
JOB 37:14–16 NIV

$\mathcal{O}$n a late summer morning, as the sun streamed through the window,
Charlotte sat at her desk and stopped for a moment. She heard a
radio blasting a popular song through the hallway, muffled sounds of
her daughter talking on her cell phone in her bedroom, the washing
machine rumbling in the laundry room.

Today the sounds of an ordinary morning caught at her heart.
Charlotte knew it wouldn't last. Change was coming. Her daughter
would be leaving for college soon, and those noises would move with
her. It wasn't that Charlotte couldn't accept change. It was just that
for one moment she stopped, paused, and really soaked up the sweet
ordinariness of family life. *Too rare, too rare.*

"Stop and consider my wonders," God told Job. Then He pointed
to ordinary observations of the natural world surrounding Job—the
clouds that hung poised in the sky, the flashes of lightning. "Not so
very ordinary" was God's lesson. Maybe He was trying to remind us
that there is no such thing as ordinary. Let's open our eyes and see the
wonders around us.

*O Father, teach me to stop and consider the ordinary moments of
my life as reminders of You. Help me not to overlook Your
daily care and provisions that surround my day. Amen.*

BUILD FOR TODAY

*"Build homes, and plan to stay.
Plant gardens, and eat the food they produce."*
JEREMIAH 29:5 NLT

Skeptics sometimes accuse Christians of being so heavenly minded that they are no earthly good. Today few of us would sell all our earthly possessions and camp out on a hilltop, waiting for the Lord's return. However, we still often live in "Tomorrowland."

Tomorrow, we think, we will serve God more fully, after our children are grown and we have more time. Tomorrow we will give more, after we have paid off the car and saved enough for a down payment on a house. Tomorrow we will study the Bible more, after we no longer work full-time.

Jeremiah's audience, Jews deported from their homeland to Babylon, knew all about Tomorrowland. They said, "Soon God will return us to our homes. As soon as that happens, we will serve God." They lived with their suitcases packed, ready to return.

God sent a stern message through His prophet Jeremiah. "You're going to be there a long time. Put down roots where I have sent you."

God sends the same message to us. He wants us to live for today. We can't allow dreams for tomorrow to paralyze our lives today.

God's presence enables us to live in the present.

Dear heavenly Father, You have given us the gift of today. You want us to plant gardens and make homes. Show us joy and fulfillment in the present. Amen.

DON'T BE ANXIOUS?

Do not be anxious about anything, but in everything, by prayer and petition, with thanksgiving, present your requests to God.
PHILIPPIANS 4:6 NIV

*T*oday's world does not make worry-free living easy. With all of our commitments and responsibilities, stress tends to overwhelm us. Instead of putting things into perspective, we let our anxieties spiral out of control. Often we rely on our own means to solve problems, accomplish interminable to-do lists, and balance overfull lives. When we trust in ourselves to deal with life's pressures, we become bogged down, weary, and disheartened.

In this verse, Paul urges his readers not to be anxious about anything. Instead, he writes that we should present all of our requests—with expressions of gratitude—to God. We find these words extremely challenging to integrate into our daily lives. *Don't be anxious? Be thankful instead?*

Paul was certainly familiar with trials. His words to the Philippians are actually written from jail. Undoubtedly, he could have succumbed to anxiety and worry. Yet he writes to the Philippians with thanksgiving and joy. Paul knows that we will experience hardship and adversity. However, he has experienced the solace that comes from trusting God with every aspect of life. While this way of life is admittedly a challenge, Paul assures us that relying on God for all of our concerns—and giving thanks all the while—is both comforting and rewarding.

Dear Lord, thank You for Your Word. Teach me to look to You in times of trouble. Let me always give thanks for my experiences. Amen.

What Riches Do You Possess?

*Command those who are rich. . .not to be arrogant nor to put their
hope in wealth, which is so uncertain, but to put their hope in God
who richly provides us with everything for our enjoyment.*
1 Timothy 6:17 niv

Brick facades and sprawling landscapes adorned every house in
the community. The neighborhood was known for its lavish living,
and the neighbors socialized in the craft of one-upmanship. If one
neighbor installed an in-ground pool, it wasn't long before the other
neighbors did, too. If one erected an elaborate gazebo, others were sure
to follow.

A quote from Benjamin Franklin reads, "He does not possess wealth
that allows wealth to possess him." The more we labor for "things," the
more "things" take priority and govern our lifestyles.

God desires to bless us with possessions we can enjoy. But it displeases Him when His children strain to attain riches in a worldly
manner out of pride or a compulsion to flaunt. Riches are uncertain,
but faith in God to meet our provisions is indicative of the pure in
heart.

Pride diminishes the capacity for humility and trust in God. We
are rich indeed when our hope and faith are not in what we have but in
Whom we trust.

*Heavenly Father, my hope is in You for my needs and my desires.
I surrender any compulsion to attain earthly wealth; rather,
may I be rich in godliness and righteousness. Amen.*

WISE UP

*When the queen of Sheba heard of the fame of Solomon concerning
the name of the LORD, she came to prove him with hard questions.*
1 KINGS 10:1 KJV

*A*llison had prayed about starting a Bible study among women in
her apartment complex, but she couldn't bring herself to invite her
neighbors. First, Allison feared rejection. What if people avoided her
at the pool or tennis courts? Then she struggled with the possibility
of success. "What if they actually come?"

"Oh, *no*! That would be awful!" Her husband, Josh, grinned.

"I mean, what if they ask me lots of tough questions?" Allison's
hands turned cold and clammy at the thought. "I'm no Bible scholar. I
sure don't know all the answers!"

Unlike Allison, King Solomon fielded all the questions asked him
by the inquisitive queen of Sheba. But years before, knowing he lacked
experience in his role, Solomon asked God for help. In answer, God
gave Solomon the gift of wisdom (1 Kings 3:9-11).

God *wants* to guide us in the right direction. If we pray for enlighten-
ment as we study His Word; ask advice from trusted Christian leaders; and use available resources; including bookstores, libraries,
and the Internet, God will provide abundant spiritual food for those
we nurture in His name. Like the queen of Sheba, they will carry God's
wisdom back to their spheres of influence—perhaps where people
know nothing of Jesus and His love.

*Lord, please help me get past my own inadequacies
to care about those around me. Amen.*

THE MARTHA SYNDROME

But the Lord said to her, "My dear Martha, you are worried and upset over all these details! There is only one thing worth being concerned about. Mary has discovered it, and it will not be taken away from her."
LUKE 10:41–42 NLT

*M*ary and Martha perfectly depict the inner battle that most women fight daily. Martha busied herself with tasks in her desire to serve people. Mary, on the other hand, ignored the tasks, choosing fellowship with her Master over service to others. Martha surely felt as though she had no choice, because the people needed to be fed and someone had to do it. And, as scripture reports, she resented the lack of help that she got from Mary.

What Martha was doing was not wrong; she just had her priorities out of order. Jesus teaches her that relationship with her Lord is the highest priority. Mary was not about to give up precious moments with her Lord while she labored in a kitchen.

It's very easy to create a life jam-packed with responsibilities and commitments with no time to enjoy any of it or seek fellowship with the Father. If you find yourself worried and upset about many things, like Martha, take some time out to sort through the priorities and decide what is really important.

Jesus, I want to be like Mary, patiently and expectantly sitting at Your feet in relationship with You. Help me to sort out my duties and commitments in such a way that proves that I have discovered the one thing worthy of my concern.
Amen.

WHERE DO YOU WALK?

I have no greater joy than to hear that my children are walking in the truth.
3 JOHN 1:4 NIV

$\mathcal{I}$f the apostle Paul delighted in seeing his spiritual children walk in truth, how much more must God appreciate those who devotedly follow Him! He, too, wants those who love Him to walk in His ways.

Wouldn't all Christians naturally follow close on Jesus' heels? After all, doesn't the same salvation affect them all? Would anyone want to be a hair's breadth farther from Jesus than she need be?

In an ideal Christian world, that would be true—and it will be so in eternity. But while we remain on earth, sin easily tempts us. Our hearts are more prone to wander than we'd like to admit. Unfortunately, sin often sticks to us and holds us back from God.

That's just why believers must continually resist sin's hold and draw near to Jesus. He has opened the doors of forgiveness for every believer who habitually confesses the sticky sin that pulls her or him away from God. Again and again, we can turn to our Lord for a new lease on the new life.

As we habitually turn to God, sin's grip loosens. The goop sticks less, and God sticks more.

Cleanse me, Lord, from the goop of sin,
and help me stick to You alone. Amen.

YOU'RE LOOKING GOOD

You yourselves are our letter, written on our hearts, known and
read by everybody. You show that you are a letter from Christ,
the result of our ministry, written not with ink but with the Spirit
of the living God, not on tablets of stone but on tablets of human hearts.
2 CORINTHIANS 3:2–3 NIV

*R*ebecca checked her face in the mirror one more time. Her makeup
was perfect, her hair smooth and styled just the way she liked it. She
turned her head—the right side. . .great. The left side?

She sighed. The scar that ran from her hairline to her jaw still
flared out like neon, red and angry. It made her feel ugly and unwanted.
Since the accident, she'd stayed in the house, but Rebecca couldn't
stand it one day longer. She had to get out, even if the world stared and
condemned her. She'd start with church and see what happened. "Lord,
help me," she whispered.

In a world where an unachievable standard of physical beauty is in
front of us almost every day, Rebecca's hesitation is understandable. At
times like these, remembering that God sees within, that we are called
to be beautiful from within because of Him, is never easy.

Worldly standards of beauty change; God's standards never do.
It is not our *makeup* but what we are *made of* that lets our true beauty
shine.

Lord, help me remember that I may be the only "scripture" some people ever see.
Let my heart and manner represent You as best I can. Amen.

A WOMAN'S WORK

Well reported of for good works; if she have brought up children, if she have lodged strangers, if she have washed the saints' feet, if she have relieved the afflicted, if she have diligently followed every good work.
1 TIMOTHY 5:10 KJV

With so many choices in today's world, what's a woman to do?

What's she to do with her time and her talents?

That's a tough question, especially in this me-centered, career-driven world. Women have so many opportunities that we can get ourselves quite confused as we look at all the options.

This confusion persists in our service to God. What does *He* want me to do? Wouldn't it be better to be working with orphans in Zambia than washing dishes in suburbia?

Who knows?

God does. His Word clearly explains a woman's work. This work includes keeping house, ministering to the poor, helping those in the church, and practicing hospitality. A widow who was worthy of church support had to have done all these things.

Such work is not very glamorous. It's not worthy of headlines or large paychecks. It is disdained by the world and even by some in the church.

But this is the humble work God honors, the work that will one day be praised.

Dear Lord, Your Word is so clear on what You expect of me. How can I miss it? And why do I so easily reject it? Teach me contentment in my calling as a woman, knowing that You will reward the humble labor of homemaking. Amen.

MIRROR IMAGE

Behold, thou art fair, my love; behold, thou art fair; thou hast doves' eyes.
SONG OF SOLOMON 1:15 KJV

Getting up in the morning and looking in the mirror can be tough. The glass reflects back our exact image with all the blemishes in plain sight. In our eyes, the flaws stand out. Instead of seeing any beauty, we focus on the imperfections. The longer we consider them, the more pronounced they become. Before long, we see only ugliness in ourselves.

No matter how hard we try, when the focus is on self, we see shortcomings. Beauty treatments, plastic surgery, makeup, beautiful clothing—nothing helps. There is no way to cover the flaws we see. Our outlook even affects how others view us.

Our only hope is to see ourselves through a different mirror. We must remember that as we grow as Christians we take on the characteristics of Christ. The more we become like Him, the more beautiful we are in our own eyes and to those around us.

When God looks at us as Christians, He sees the reflection of Christ. He sees us as very beautiful. God loves to behold us when we are covered in Christ. The mirror image He sees has none of the blemishes or imperfections, only the beauty.

Oh God, thank You for beholding me as being fair and valuable.
Help me to see myself through Your eyes. Amen.

LADY WISDOM
GIVES DIRECTIONS

Does not wisdom cry out, and understanding lift up her voice? She takes her stand on the top of the high hill, beside the way, where the paths meet.
PROVERBS 8:1–2 NKJV

*W*isdom. The very term sounds outdated, a concept hiding in musty, dusty caverns of the past. Has it anything to do with real life?

Many answer, "No, especially in a new millennium!"

But biblical wisdom, crafted by God before the earth existed, remains as fresh and powerful as its Creator. In the book of Proverbs, God personifies wisdom as a godly woman who does not hesitate to let her voice be heard. She stands atop a high hill "where the paths meet," at busy intersections, trying to help travelers find their way. But they rush past Wisdom, most talking into cell phones glued to their ears. Business meetings must start on time. Carpools must follow schedules. Bills must be paid. The travelers hardly notice Wisdom as they scurry past her. Focused on themselves, they make their deadlines and achieve their goals. Most do not realize they are completely lost.

Wisdom longs to make a difference in their stressful existence that leads to destruction. She never stops sharing her vital message: Whoever heeds God's instruction gains more than silver, gold, or rubies. His truth, His directions lead listeners to life.

Father, help us shake off the hypnotizing effects of our culture's values and listen to Your wisdom. Give us courage to share with others who desperately need Your truth. Amen.

WOMEN DISCIPLES

He went throughout every city and village, preaching and shewing the glad
tidings of the kingdom of God: and the twelve were with him, and certain
women, which had been healed of evil spirits and infirmities.
LUKE 8:1–2 KJV

*W*omen, along with the twelve disciples, accompanied Jesus as He
built the kingdom of God. Luke lists Mary Magdalene, from whom Jesus
exorcised seven evil spirits; Joanna, the wife of Chuza, King Herod's
household manager; and Susanna, as well as many others. Jesus healed
these women and met their needs, and they supported His ministry
with their own money—a risky business, as women could not generate
much income at that time.

The women also endured the inconvenience and outright danger
shared by His other disciples. Perhaps rumors about the women's
relationships with Jesus or the men in their party generated criticism,
threatening their reputations and even their marriages. Still they
chose to sit directly under His teaching. And despite the political
implications, these brave women stayed with Jesus while He died on
the cross. Some, including Mary Magdalene and Joanna, were among
the first to see Jesus after His resurrection.

What an encouragement these verses gives to women everywhere!
Jesus loved and honored His women disciples. When we choose to
devote our lives to Him today, He welcomes our love with all His
heart.

Lord Jesus, I am thankful You died for all people.
Please help other women understand the truth about Your love for them. Amen.

Peace through Prayer

*Be anxious for nothing, but in everything by prayer and supplication,
with thanksgiving, let your requests be made known to God; and the
peace of God, which surpasses all understanding, will guard
your hearts and minds through Christ Jesus.*
PHILIPPIANS 4:6–7 NKJV

Some days it is easy to be thankful. We nearly bubble over with thanksgiving. These are mountaintop days—a graduation day, a wedding, or a reunion with old friends. The day comes to a close, and we whisper a prayer. It flows easily off the tongue. "Thank You, God," we say, "for a perfect day."

There are days when thankfulness is not as natural, not as easy. These are valley days—in the hospital room, at the graveside, or when we are distraught about a relationship or work issue. It is in these times that the Father wants us to give Him our burdens through prayer. It seems impossible to be thankful for the pain, the confusion, or the longings in our lives. We can be thankful, though, that we have a loving heavenly Father who stands ready to help.

The peace of God cannot be explained. It cannot be bought. The world cannot give it to us. But when we release our cares to the Lord in prayer, His peace washes over us and fills our hearts and minds. What a comfort is the peace of God when we find ourselves in the valley.

*Sovereign God, You are the same yesterday, today, and tomorrow.
You are with me through the good and the bad. Draw near to me
and replace my worry with Your peace. Amen.*

A WOMAN'S ROLE

A certain woman from the crowd raised her voice and said to Him, "Blessed is the womb that bore You, and the breasts which nursed You!" But He said, "More than that, blessed are those who hear the word of God and keep it!"
LUKE 11:27–28 NKJV

Every Jewish woman wanted to be the mother of the Messiah. Perhaps other women congratulated Mary on her Son, God's Chosen One. Once Jesus heard a woman bless His mother for giving Him life—certainly appropriate. God had called Mary to offer her body for His special purpose.

But Jesus gave a radical answer to the woman in the crowd that must have wrinkled the foreheads of religious leaders. This rabbi objected to such a limited view of women. He advocated spiritual pursuits in women the same way He did in men! Trashing centuries of tradition, Jesus taught women, single and married. They accompanied Him on His travels. He claimed Mary and Martha, as well as their brother Lazarus, as His close friends. He even told Martha to worry less about fixing dinner and focus more on His teaching. (One wonders how the hungry apostles reacted to *that!*)

Jesus does not diminish women's roles at home. But He came that we might know Him for ourselves by studying His Word, listening to His voice, and obeying Him.

Lord Jesus, thank You for the part I play in my family.
Help me to know You better so I can impact my world for You. Amen.

PHONE HOME

"I called, but you did not answer, I spoke, but you did not listen.
You did evil in my sight and chose what displeases me."
ISAIAH 65:12 NIV

Cindy and her husband packed up their son for his first year away at college. The university their son chose was several states and over a thousand miles from home. They would not be seeing their firstborn for several months.

Cindy called her son, Matt, a day or so after he arrived on campus. She didn't hear back from him. She called again a day later. Still no response. By the third day with no word from the freshman, she left her final message.

"This is your mother. If you don't call back within the hour, your phone will be turned off."

Cindy got a call back within minutes.

Does God have to threaten shutting heaven to our prayers because we refuse to listen when He calls us? Do we turn on the television when we sense a need to pray for a missionary overseas? Do we continue loading the dishwasher when our daughter says, "Watch me, Mom"? Do we pick up a magazine when we should call a lonely friend or elderly aunt? Are we sometimes guilty of choosing what God doesn't delight in?

Tasks must be done and recreation does rest us, but prioritizing the important over the urgent shows our Father that we are listening for Him and to Him.

Father, give me the hearing and the heart to recognize Your call to me. Amen.

HOLD ON!

*Let us not become weary in doing good, for at the
proper time we will reap a harvest if we do not give up.*
GALATIANS 6:9 NIV

*H*ave you ever felt that God abandoned you? Have the difficulties in your life pressed you to physical and mental exhaustion? Do you feel your labor is in vain and no one appreciates the sacrifices you have made?

When Elijah fled for his life in fear of Jezebel's wrath, depression and discouragement tormented him. Exhausted, he prayed for God to take his life, and then he fell asleep. When he awoke, God sent an angel with provisions to strengthen his weakened body. Only then was he able to hear God's revelation that provided the direction and assistance he needed.

God hears our pleas even when He seems silent. The problem is that we cannot hear Him because of physical and mental exhaustion. Rest is key to our restoration.

Just when the prophet thought he could go on no longer, God provided the strength, peace, and encouragement to continue. He does the same for us today. When we come to the end of our rope, God ties a knot. And like Elijah, God will do great things in and through us, if we will just hold on.

*Dear Lord, help me when I can no longer help myself. Banish my discouragement
and give me the rest and restoration I need so that I might hear Your voice.
Amen.*

SHARPER THAN
A SCALPEL

For the word of God is living and active. Sharper than any double-edged sword,
it penetrates even to dividing soul and spirit, joints and marrow;
it judges the thoughts and attitudes of the heart.
HEBREWS 4:12 NIV

A Southeast Asian missionary translated Hebrews 4:12 as "the
Word of God is living and active and sharper than any bush knife."
His Indonesian colleague read the verse and wept, not because the
translation was inaccurate, but because he was moved by the power of
the metaphor. A bush knife was used to clear weeds from a field so that
a farmer could plant and reap a harvest for his family. The bush knife
needed to be sharp to cut away intrusive growth. He copied down the
translation and quickly ran home to share the passage with his family.

Geoffrey, a member of a U.S. congregation, was asked how he would
translate Hebrews 4:12 for today's culture. He replied, "The Word of
God is sharper than a scalpel." What a perfect metaphor. The scalpel, used
by doctors to remove harmful tissues and cancers, cuts with precision,
just as the Word of God cuts with precision, removing damaging aspects
of our interior spiritual life and allowing space for holy habits to replace
ungodly ones.

Heavenly Father, use Your Word like a scalpel to perform surgery on my heart.
Cut away the cancerous sin and make me holy within. Amen.

A Better Offer

"So in everything, do to others what you would have them do to you."
Matthew 7:12 NIV

$\mathcal{I}$ need to cancel plans on Friday because I have the opportunity to go out of town with friends," Anne said. Marsha felt rejected, unloved, and inconsequential again as Anne canceled their weekly prayer and Bible study time because a better offer came along.

"At least," Marsha thought, "she didn't cancel on me this time because she needed to get her nails done."

How do you treat friends, colleagues, and acquaintances? Do you remain committed to your responsibilities? What are your priorities? Do you take on more than you can handle? Do you not give 100 percent to a task or relationship?

Jesus took responsibilities, commitments, and obligations seriously. In fact, Jesus said, "Simply let your 'Yes' be 'Yes,' and your 'No,' 'No'; anything beyond this comes from the evil one" (Matthew 5:37 NIV). Satan desires for us to be stressed out, overcommitted, and not able to do anything well. Satan delights when we treat others in an unkind, offensive manner. However, God, upon request, will help us prioritize our commitments so that our "yes" is "yes" and our "no" is "no." Then in everything we do, we are liberated to do to others as we would have them do to us.

*Lord, please prioritize my commitments to enable me in everything
to do to others as I would desire for them to do to me. Amen.*

To Your Health

"'I will restore you to health and heal your wounds,' declares the LORD."
JEREMIAH 30:17 NIV

*T*he woman mastered the art of multitasking. It was customary for her to jog several miles, clean the house, plant flowers, cook dinner for a needy friend, and squeeze in several hours of office work. She worked, ministered, and mentored until an undetected medical problem changed everything.

She once had the stamina of a racehorse, and now she moved slower than a garden slug despite her best efforts. Poor health forced her to slow down, to do less, and to rely fully on God.

"We don't know the worth of water until the well runs dry," reads one axiom. So it is with the gift of good health. Most of us take our health for granted and push beyond our limits, caring for everyone except ourselves. . .until a health hazard strikes.

Good stewardship includes good health practices. When we take time for regular doctor's visits, daily exercise, and good nutrition, and avoid the temptation to overschedule, we develop the art of caring for ourselves.

Sometimes, however, even when we do all the right things, illness occurs. Life holds no guarantees except one. Namely, God loves us enough to care for us when we cannot care for ourselves. And He will restore us to health.

Heavenly Father, thank You for caring for me in sickness and in health. Remind me to care for myself as I care for others. I trust You to bring forth the healing and restoration I need today. Amen.

WELL WATERED

*"The LORD will guide you always; he will satisfy your needs in a
sun-scorched land and will strengthen your frame. You will be like
a well-watered garden, like a spring whose waters never fail."*
ISAIAH 58:11 NIV

The county restrictions allowed for watering only twice a week. It just wasn't enough. Her carefully tended acre—once lush, green, and profuse with color and variety—was now brown and crunchy underfoot. The blooms hung limp, pale, and dehydrated. She couldn't ignore the living word picture this was to her own spiritual life. For months now, she'd actually only watered her spirit with Sunday morning sermons. She, too, felt lifeless and dried up from the stresses that weighed on her—too many demands, the urgent bumping out the important, a frenzied sprint from place to place, poor nutrition from grabbing unhealthy foods on the run, no margin to properly rest or enjoy life.

She needed a downpour of God's Word and the Holy Spirit's presence in her parched spirit. Not an occasional sprinkle but a soul soaking to replenish her frazzled body and weary mind. She knew this soaking came from consistent Bible study, the necessary pruning of confessed sin, and prayer time. These produce a well-watered garden, fruitful and lush, mirroring God's beauty, creating a life to which others are drawn to come and linger in His refreshing presence.

*Eternal Father, strengthen my frame, guide my paths, and satisfy
my needs as only You can. Make my life a well-watered garden,
fruitful for You and Your purposes. Amen.*

NO MORE STING

Day 235

O death, where is thy sting? O grave, where is thy victory?
1 CORINTHIANS 15:55 KJV

Two female golfers were driving from one hole to the next when a huge bumblebee flew into the cart. The passenger panicked. Attempting to avoid the bee, she overreacted, lost her balance, and fell out of the cart. Later she sheepishly remarked to friends, "I was frightened for nothing. That kind of bee doesn't even sting!"

We have so many fears that names have been given to identify our phobias. Arachnophobia: the fear of spiders. Claustrophobia: the fear of being in closed spaces. Acrophobia: the fear of heights. What are you afraid of? Do we make situations even worse by overreacting? Perhaps our fears are unfounded in the first place.

We have a choice to make. We can either live life in fear or live life by faith. Fear and faith cannot coexist. Jesus Christ has conquered our greatest fear—death. He rose victorious and has given us eternal life through faith. Knowing this truth enables us to courageously face our fears. There is no fear that cannot be conquered by faith. Let's not panic but trust the Lord instead. Let's live by faith and experience the victory that has been given to us through Jesus Christ, our Lord.

Lord, You alone know my fears. Help me to trust You more.
May I walk in the victory that You have purchased for me. Amen.

CONFIDENT
PERSISTENCE

*"Don't be afraid. Just stand still and watch the LORD rescue you today.
The Egyptians you see today will never be seen again."*
EXODUS 14:13 NLT

*S*haron was confused. Doubts and fears assailed her mind. *Lord, I think
I've bitten off more than I can chew. Now I'm out here, in the middle of nowhere,
ready to give up.*

Her confidence waning, Sharon cried out to God. Then, reaching
for her Bible, she opened to where she'd last left off reading in Exodus,
where the Israelites were running from Pharaoh.

The hard-hearted pharaoh thought he had a good chance to bring
his slaves back to him. He figured that the Israelites, hemmed in by the
desert, would be wandering around the land in confusion.

Indeed, the Israelites had gone out of Egypt with boldness. Yet
when trapped by the sea, they became discouraged and frightened. But
while at a literal standstill, they called out to God and He became a
shield for them, using a cloud in front and behind them and the walls
of the sea on either side. And after going through the sea on dry land,
God's people never saw those Egyptians again.

When you become bewildered and petrified with fear, "don't be
afraid. Just stand still and watch the LORD rescue you *today*," because
the problems, frustrations, and barriers you see today will never be seen
again (emphasis added). Be persistent, and God will see you through.

*Lord, be my shield. Surround me with Your presence.
Help me to keep still in this situation and watch You see me through it.
And I will praise You forever and ever, in Jesus' name. Amen.*

LISTENING TO GOD'S VOICE

"You have today declared the LORD to be your God, and that you would walk in His ways and keep His statutes, His commandments and His ordinances, and listen to His voice."
DEUTERONOMY 26:17 NASB

*W*hat would have happened had Moses been less than an excellent listener? Would Israel's tabernacle have ended up a cubit short on one side? Would Israel's burnt offerings have turned out medium-rare? Would Moses have written down only nine of God's Ten Commandments?

While Moses was on Mount Sinai, God gave him detailed instructions on how the children of Israel were to live and to worship. God gave Moses the law, including the Ten Commandments, a blueprint for the tabernacle, and the method by which He would receive Israel's sacrifices. Listening carefully was of utmost importance, for God told Moses to tell Israel: "Now if you obey me fully and keep my covenant, then out of all nations you will be my treasured possession" (Exodus 19:5 NIV).

Developing good listening habits is as important for Christians today as it was for Moses and all the other biblical patriarchs. It takes practice and time alone with God to hear His unique voice. God has much to say to us if we will listen carefully.

Dear Lord, teach me to listen well so that I may learn obedience and not miss Your blessings in my life. Amen.

YET PRAISE HIM

Why are you downcast, O my soul? Why so disturbed within me? Put your
hope in God, for I will yet praise him, my Savior and my God.
PSALM 42:11 NIV

$\mathcal{M}$any individuals and prayer groups use the acronym ACTS to guide their prayers. The letters stand for **A**doration, **C**onfession, **T**hanksgiving, and **S**upplication. Note that adoration comes first, before the believer confesses sin, thanks God, or asks anything of Him. God delights in His children's praise and adoration.

If you have cared for a child, you have probably received genuine adoration at times as well as times of appreciation in response to something you have done for her or him. Which warms your heart more? Certainly it means more to be held in high esteem simply because of who you are in the child's life than to be told "I love you" when you hand out dollar bills or promise a trip to the zoo!

Imagine how God feels when one of His children praises Him simply for who He is, even when her circumstances are far from perfect. Don't you suppose it feels like a tight hug around His neck? A "just because" sort of hug, not the "I got something from you" sort.

Praise God regardless. Praise Him *yet*, as the psalmist did. Adore Him today, for He is God.

Father, You are the great I Am, faithful and good. I adore You.
I choose to praise You whether You alter my circumstances or not. Amen.

DON'T BITE THE APPLE!

*"But seek first his kingdom and his righteousness,
and all these things will be given to you as well."*
MATTHEW 6:33 NIV

$\mathcal{S}$atan vehemently opposes God's will. As we desire to draw close to the Lord, Satan pulls in the opposite direction. He attempts to dissuade us from seeking the Lord at the beginning of each day. He whispers subtle lies, hoping that we will take the bite.

Temptingly, he says, "You can have a quiet time after you fold the laundry" or "You can read your Bible tonight after work." If we choose to embrace those lies, we know how the scenario usually plays itself out. The quiet time or Bible reading never happens. Satan has deceived us once again. We have taken one step in his direction instead of the Lord's.

We must be on guard against Satan's covert tactics. Each morning upon rising, we must purpose to put the Lord first. When we do, the Lord prioritizes our day and stretches our time. He helps us accomplish what we must and let go of what we should. Satan is defeated. We experience victory. The Lord is glorified.

The Lord desires to walk close by our side throughout the day. In order for that to happen, we must seek Him first in the morning. Refuse to give credence to other options. Believe God's truth and don't bite the apple!

*Dear Lord, help me seek You at the beginning of each day.
Protect me from Satan's lies that would tempt me to do otherwise.
May I bring glory to You today. Amen.*

Basic Math

*Jesus answered and said to him, "If anyone loves Me,
he will keep My word; and My Father will love him,
and We will come to him and make Our home with him."*
JOHN 14:23 NKJV

If you disliked math in school, perhaps at some point you asked, *How will I ever use it in real life?*

A certain kind of relational math is fundamental to your daily life. The words and actions exchanged throughout your day add to or take away from your life and the lives of those around you. Are you a positive or negative force? Are those around you positive or negative influences in your life?

God's nature is to give—to add—to every life He encounters. As Christians, we are created in His image and should be positive influences on those around us each day. Look around you and determine who adds to your life and who takes away. You will probably find that you prefer to spend time with pleasant communicators. Words of anger, frustration, confusion, and jealousy take away from the spirit of a man, but words of affirmation and gestures of kindness add to every heart.

Think before you act. Consider your words before you speak. Will you be adding to that person or taking away with what you are about to say or do? Share the love God shows you with others.

*God, help me to think before I speak so that
I can be a positive influence on others. Amen.*

JUDGED!

*A woman who had lived a sinful life. . .brought an alabaster jar
of perfume, and as she stood behind him at his feet weeping, she began
to wet his feet with her tears. Then she wiped them with her hair,
kissed them and poured perfume on them.*
LUKE 7:37–38 NIV

*W*hat a beautiful story of repentance. Though we don't know her
name, we relate to this woman's loving testimony. How we would like
to be able to anoint Jesus with our love.

Had it been up to the Pharisee who shares the story with her,
we probably wouldn't know about the sinful woman. This man who
had invited Jesus to dinner missed the point of her actions and began
judging her and the Master who accepted her loving gift. *Surely*,
assumed the Pharisee, *a prophet would know this woman is a sinner.*

This first-century Jew isn't alone in leaping to judgment. Many
churchgoers fall into the same trap. A new person comes to our church
and doesn't follow the rules. Maybe she doesn't dress like everyone else
or doesn't use the right spiritual jargon. In an instant, we doubt her
salvation.

But if she doesn't know Jesus, isn't this the right place for her
to be? Standing near Him, an unbeliever may come to faith—if the
people in God's congregation are loving and nurturing.

We need not judge a casual acquaintance's spiritual life—God can
do that. All we need to do is love, and He will bring blessings.

*Thank You, Lord, that Your first reaction to me was love, not condemnation.
Turn my heart in love to all who don't yet know You. Amen.*

WISDOM IN ACTION

*God who takes care of me will supply all your needs from his
glorious riches, which have been given to us in Christ Jesus.*
PHILIPPIANS 4:19 NLT

*M*oney. You could always use more no matter how hard you work
or how much money you make. It is one of the biggest stresses in the
world today. People worry about job security, growing debt, gas and
food prices, and how to get ahead.

Sometimes when Christians express financial concerns, they hear
well-meaning believers say, "Oh, Jesus is all you need." Really? When
you truly have a need and you're doing all you know to do, is that really
what you need to hear? What about a little wisdom, a little knowledge,
a little understanding of how to find and experience a great place of
peace in the middle of your need?

God has promised to supply all your needs, but it takes action on
your part. Searching for wisdom for your situation and asking God to
direct you in the right decisions will lead you down a path of financial
success. It may be as simple as skipping dinners in nice restaurants so
you can save money to purchase living room furniture with cash. We
can all make better decisions if we put wisdom into action.

*Lord, show me the wisdom of making good decisions financially.
Help me to choose wisely when and where to spend or save. Amen.*

WORK AS UNTO THE LORD

And whatever you do, whether in word or deed, do it all in the name of the Lord Jesus, giving thanks to God the Father through him.
COLOSSIANS 3:17 NIV

*S*helly thought to herself, *There is no way I can get everything done. I am exhausted from working around the clock. Even my weekends are filled with hustle and bustle.*

Have you ever thought that twenty-four hours in a day are not enough time to get everything done? Has life ever left you feeling worn out? Do you feel all you do is work? You are not alone.

Nevertheless, this is not what God intends for our lives. Often when we feel fatigue, we are working not for God, but for someone or something else. Could it be for our own self-recognition? How about our own sense of worthiness? Perhaps we have a supervisor we desire to please.

God tells us that whatever our task, we are to do it in the name of the Lord Jesus. We are to set our minds on things above, not on earthly things (Colossians 3:2). We are to work as though Jesus were our supervisor, glorifying Him in thought, word, and deed.

Also, we are to give thanks to God for the work He has commissioned us to do. How often do we stop, in the menial and mundane or challenging and taxing tasks and thank God for the work He is accomplishing through us?

Lord, please help me to do everything in Your name and with thanksgiving to God the Father. Amen.

THE BAR IS
TOO HIGH!

She gets up while it is still dark; she provides food for her family. . . .
Her lamp does not go out at night.
PROVERBS 31:15, 18 NIV

The Proverbs 31 woman puts Wonder Woman to shame. Up before dawn, late to bed, caring for her household, negotiating business contracts down at the city gate. She gives to the poor, plans for her household to run smoothly, anticipates future needs, such as snowy weather. Even her arms are buff! "She sets about her work vigorously; her arms are strong for her tasks" (Proverbs 31:17 NIV).

She is highly energetic, an efficiency expert, *and* gifted in relationships. "Her children arise and call her blessed; her husband also, and he praises her" (v. 28). This woman is downright intimidating!

So how do we benefit by reading about the Proverbs 31 woman? Reading about her day makes us feel overwhelmed, discouraged by our inadequacies. That bar is too high!

God doesn't place the bar so high that we live in its shadow. He wired each of us with different gifts, different energy levels, different responsibilities. Proverbs 31 casts a floodlight on *all* women—those gifted in business, in home life, as caregivers. This chapter displays how women undergird their families and their communities.

Remember, the book of Proverbs was written in the tenth century BC, when women were considered chattel. But not in God's eyes. He has always esteemed women and the many roles we fulfill in society.

Father, thank You for the important women in my life. You made each
one of us with gifts and abilities. May we be used to glorify You. Amen.

PRICKLY LOVE

*"A new command I give you: Love one another.
As I have loved you, so you must love one another."*
JOHN 13:34 NIV

Tumbleweeds have a reputation of being an annoyance. They grow with little water. When they are mature, they break free of their roots in a wind and blow whichever direction the breeze takes them. They are full of little stickers that can poke into you or your car's radiator. If you walk too close to them, you can also get small, painful barbs in your skin.

One woman riding her bike had an accident and landed in the middle of a large tumbleweed. The plant was still a bit green, and she'd never seen one so close. To her amazement, in the midst of all the prickly parts were tiny, beautiful flowers. After she extricated herself, she bent close to examine the beauty she couldn't have noticed without getting close to the irascible plant.

Oftentimes people we meet in the workplace, at the store, or even in church have prickly exteriors. They grumble, complain, or are disagreeable in a number of ways. Jesus commanded us to love one another. When we take the time to get close to a person who is difficult, we can often see some small piece of beauty amid the orneriness. The willingness to love as Jesus loves is worth the risk of getting pierced by a word or an attitude.

*Jesus, show me how to love the unlovable. Help me to understand
their attitude and to emulate You, not those around me. Amen.*

LOOKING FOR HIM

*O my Strength, I watch for you; you, O God,
are my fortress, my loving God.*
PSALM 59:9–10 NIV

*I*t was in the quietest of ways that God revealed Himself to her. . .gentle reminders to reassure her, "I am here. I am your strength. I love you." Others may discount these as circumstantial, insignificant, or just plain wacko. But she knew.

She saw His glory in the explosion of pink blooms that donned the ancient tree along her work commute, bringing a smile. *"I know you love beauty. I created this for you to enjoy."*

She saw His goodness reflected in the Christian dry cleaner who provided above-and-beyond service: "I mended the rip in your shirt— no charge, ma'am." As small as that seemed, it was a gift to her. She had intended to mend it herself for months, just wearing a sweater over it instead.

God's providence was revealed in the timing of the call from a dear, long-distance friend who could always cheer her up. His provision appeared in the good-as-new garage sale rug. It was the exact hard-to-find oval size; dark enough to hide kid and animal traffic, and adorned with fruit to match her decor! These were no coincidences—just a loving God revealing Himself to those who watch for Him.

*Loving God, remind me to watch for You in daily life.
Help me to see You in people, nature, and circumstances. Amen.*

Pass It On

"You must be very careful not to forget the things you have seen God do for you. Keep reminding yourselves, and tell your children and grandchildren as well."
DEUTERONOMY 4:9 CEV

*W*hy don't we throw this old thing away?" nine-year-old Crystal asked, gingerly fingering the worn wood of the rustic three-legged stool. "It must be fifty years old."

"Actually, it's almost eighty years old," Dina told her daughter. "And I wouldn't dream of throwing it away. In fact, I've taken special care of it my entire life, as my mother did, and her father before her."

"Why would you want to keep an old stool?"

"It's more than just an old stool. It's a symbol of God's grace to our family. That was the first piece of furniture your great-grandfather owned when he arrived in our country after fleeing the Nazi occupation of Poland. That stool represents the answered prayers and provision of God for our family through the years, even down to you, Crystal. It helps us remember to thank God for the blessings He's given us."

"Oh, I see. It's kind of like wearing a cross pendant to remember Jesus dying for us." Crystal tenderly ran her hand over the rough wood with new respect. "I'll keep it for my children, too."

God created families, and it was His plan that we share His workings in our lives with generations yet to come.

Rock of Ages, help us always to remember Your loving kindnesses and pass the word on to those who share our genes, blood, and even our knobby knees. Amen.

LAVISH LIVING

Practice hospitality.
ROMANS 12:13 NIV

*B*ecause of its large foreign-student population, Ohio's University of Toledo offers international students a home-away-from-home connection. The university connects interested students with volunteer families who invite their "adopted" students to share meals, holidays, or special events with them. These students are provided a sampling of family fun and intimacy—a sprinkling of normalcy in a repetitive environment of dorm life, classes, and studies. Severed from all that's been normal and routine for them in the past, the students' connection with an American family gives them a sampling of home life, often complete with younger "siblings," family pets, and old-fashioned home cooking.

The first time one family had their adopted students to their home for a meal, the two collegians were intrigued by the couple's detached garage.

"Who lives there?" they asked.

"That's our garage," Susan replied. "That's where we keep our cars."

The two students exchanged shocked looks.

"You have a house for your *cars*?"

Living lavishly doesn't mean the same thing to everyone. But in most cultures—maybe every culture—lavish living best translates as hospitality. Welcoming next-door neighbors (or students from a third world country), gives Christians the God-ordained privilege to live lavishly by extending genuine hospitality.

Father, thank You for all that You've given me. Thank You for the privilege of encouraging others with something as simple as a genuine welcome. Amen.

EQUIPPED FOR GOOD WORK

All Scripture is inspired by God and profitable for teaching, for reproof,
for correction, for training in righteousness; so that the man of
God may be adequate, equipped for every good work.
2 TIMOTHY 3:16–17 NASB

Have you thought, "How am I to accomplish this work?" Have you ever felt inadequate for the task set before you?

God gives us the aptitude and ability to do the work He leads us to. However, we may find it challenging at times because God is using the tasks to draw us in a closer relationship to Him through His Word. We are told that all of God's Word, the Bible, has the purpose of teaching, admonishing, correcting or modifying our behavior, and instructing us to be right with the Lord. Regardless of the type of work, God is enabling us to do the work He has purposed for us.

Therefore, it is important that we spend time in God's Word. We are to participate in Bible studies, worship God with fellow believers, and have a daily time of prayer and devotions. It is through these activities that we will become proficient, equipped for the good work God has planned for us. God's Word tells us we can trust Him to make us capable, adequate, prepared to do the good work we are destined to do for His kingdom.

Lord, I praise You that Your Word can mold me into a being capable of carrying out Your good works. Help me to consistently study Your Word. Amen.

THE FATHER'S VOICE

*What use is it, my brethren, if someone says he has
faith but he has no works? Can that faith save him?*
JAMES 2:14 NASB

A young family set out on a three-day hike. The mother and father
were avid hikers and were excited to share the experience of the mountain
trails and campsites with their young son and daughter. The children
marveled at the sights and sounds of the wilderness. At nightfall they
sat around the fire after their meal. The young son explored the edges
of the campsite, and his father warned him not to step outside of the
light.

Curious, the boy traced the shadows on the trees and followed a
night crawler to its hiding place under a rock. Suddenly, the son had
lost sight of the campfire and of his family. He cried out in panic,
"Daddy, I'm lost!" The father responded calmly, "As long as you can
hear me, you're not lost." The father called out to him over and over
again until the son had followed the sound of his voice safely back to
the campsite.

Perhaps you've felt like that small boy, lost with darkness all
around you. Your heavenly Father is always listening, and as long as
you follow His voice, He will guide you back to safety and into His
loving arms.

God, help me to listen for Your voice and follow Your direction. Amen.

Changeable?

Beloved. . .I found it necessary to write to you exhorting you to contend
earnestly for the faith which was once for all delivered to the saints.
JUDE 1:3 NKJV

*G*od delivered your faith to you once and for all, and He'll never back out on His covenant. But that isn't all there is to faith. You have a part, too, as you contend earnestly to work out your salvation in a sin-filled world.

On the one hand, God is unchanging—His Word does not alter, and His character never changes. Once you are His child, He will never let go of you.

The changeable part of the equation is the human variable. Each of us tries to follow Jesus, some with great success, while others barely seem to know His name. Could it be that some of us are more aware of our need to "contend earnestly" than others? Do some of us keep our eyes on the prize more successfully?

If we depend on our own power to follow Jesus, we'll soon get worn out and slip away. We're changeable by nature. But if we put all our trust in Him, we latch on to the One who never changes. In Him our earnest contention finds success.

Are you contending in your own power or the power of Jesus? With the first, you'll only fail; with the other, you'll never lose.

Lord Jesus, help me contend simply in Your power. Amen.

THE SECRET OF
SERENDIPITY

A happy heart makes the face cheerful.
PROVERBS 15:13 NIV

*C*an you remember the last time you laughed in wild abandon? Better yet, when was the last time you did something fun, outrageous, or out of the ordinary? Perhaps it is an activity you haven't done since you were a child, like slip down a waterslide, strap on a pair of ice skates, or pitch a tent and camp overnight.

Women often become trapped in the cycle of routine, and soon we lose our spontaneity. Children, on the other hand, are innately spontaneous. Giggling, they splash barefoot in rain puddles. Wide-eyed, they watch a kite soar toward the treetops. They make silly faces without inhibition; they see animal shapes in rock formations. In essence, they possess the secret of serendipity.

A happy heart turns life's situations into opportunities for fun. For instance, if a storm snuffs out the electricity, light a candle and play games, tell stories, or just enjoy the quiet. When we seek innocent pleasures, we glean the benefits of a happy heart.

Jesus said, "I am come that they might have life, and that they might have it more abundantly" (John 10:10 KJV). God wants us to enjoy life, and when we do, it lightens our load and changes our countenance.

So try a bit of whimsy just for fun. And rediscover the secret of serendipity.

Dear Lord, because of You, I have a happy heart.
Lead me to do something fun and spontaneous today! Amen.

FINDING YOUR FIRST LOVE

Nevertheless I have somewhat against thee,
because thou hast left thy first love.
REVELATION 2:4 KJV

*I*f any church was zealous for Christ, it was the church at Ephesus.

Here was a church that was planted by the apostle Paul and pastored by Timothy. It was a church that did not faint from the work of the gospel. The people of Ephesus *labored* for the Lord. But they became consumed by their labor and forgot that they were ultimately working for the Lord.

We are in danger of falling into the same trap today. As we pour ourselves into living a godly life, we can easily get consumed with the task. Soon we can forget the very One we want to model.

Why God would want to fellowship with us is a great mystery, but He does. He has gone to great lengths to do so. He sent His Son to the cross to make it possible. How can we neglect so great a love?

Today, put aside life's never-ending demands. Open your Bible and return to your first love.

"Out of myself to dwell in thy love, out of despair into raptures above. . .
Jesus, I come to thee." Amen.

THE WAVES
OF LIFE

"In quietness and confidence shall be your strength."
ISAIAH 30:15 NKJV

*O*pportunities abound, but do we have the confidence to meet the challenges that arise when the going gets tough?

Many times we begin in confidence as we rest in the Lord, leaning on His strength. But we begin to falter when the waters rise or the wind picks up. We take our eyes off Christ, and the waves begin to take us wherever they will.

But God tells us that when we return to Him, when we focus on and rest in Him, our quietness and confidence will keep us strong. We can be like Esther, who, although facing a dire situation, put her confidence in God and garnered the courage to go before the king for the sake of her people, saying, "If I perish, I perish!" (Esther 4:16 NKJV). This lone woman had more faith in her God than the disciples in the boat who, in the midst of a terrible storm, woke Jesus and said, "Teacher, do You not care that we are perishing?" (Mark 4:38 NKJV).

These men were filled with fear because they didn't know who Jesus was. Do you? If not, learn about Him, and garner your confidence by reading, believing, and storing God's Word in your heart. (Start with Isaiah 30:15!) Do it today, and you'll find yourself confidently riding on the waves of life, making the most of every opportunity!

*God, I believe in You, that You can help me take on any new challenge,
any opportunity You put before me. Thank You, Lord. I sail
through this life, keeping my eyes on You! Amen.*

LOOK UP,
NOT AROUND

We're not, understand, putting ourselves in a league with those who boast that they're our superiors. We wouldn't dare do that. But in all this comparing and grading and competing, they quite miss the point.
2 CORINTHIANS 10:12 THE MESSAGE

*H*umans tend to be competitive. It's a part of our nature that shows up at work, on the ball field, even at church. Human competition is also seen throughout the Bible, from Cain and Abel, Jacob and Esau, David and Saul, all the way through to the apostles (Luke 22:24). Women are not immune to the pull of competition either (Luke 10:41–42), and often the busier we are, the harder we compete with those around us, as if the very act of winning will make our lives easier.

Nowhere does scripture condemn the drive to achieve a worthy goal. Ambition, in itself, is not a problem. It is how ambition manifests itself that Paul warns the Corinthians about. Are we striving to better ourselves for God, for our families, for our employers? Or has the goal become winning, looking better than others? Are we looking for worldly admiration only?

If we strive toward our goals in a way that causes other believers to stumble or violates the values God has set forth for us, then perhaps we should take a step back. After all, our final victory has little to do with what the world thinks about us.

Father God, Your standards are what I need to hold before me. Grant me the wisdom to keep Your values in mind as I aim for any higher goal. Amen.

MEAT OR MUSH?

Anyone who runs ahead and does not continue in the teaching of Christ does not have God; whoever continues in the teaching has both the Father and the Son.
2 JOHN 1:9 NIV

*H*ave you had to contend with "smorgasbord Christianity"? Suddenly, your minister leaves, and as your congregation seeks a new leader, a succession of preachers fills the pulpit week after week. And every week you're being fed a different kind of spiritual food.

Don't relax and figure you're on a spiritual vacation. This is the time to listen very carefully. You have no idea where these people come from theologically, and it might be easy to be led astray by a deep, mellow voice or empty but high-sounding words.

Spiritual ideas abound, but not all are sound. Sometimes it's easy to assume you're getting good meat when you're actually being served mushy, rotten vegetables.

How can you tell meat from mush? Compare the message to Christ's words. Is the preacher avoiding the Bible's tough commands, preaching ideas that are not biblical, or appealing to non-Christian ideas? Better beware.

Jesus gave us strong doctrines and good teaching to lead us into His truth. Faithful expositors cling to His Word. They offer meat and milk but no rotten teachings.

Eat well!

Keep me aware of Your truth, Lord.
I want to live on it, not on mush. Amen.

HINDSIGHT

Now we see but a poor reflection as in a mirror; then we shall see face to face.
Now I know in part; then I shall know fully, even as I am fully known.
1 CORINTHIANS 13:12 NIV

Hindsight is 20/20. From the vantage point of experience, we can reflect on former days with wisdom. With each passing twenty-four-hour period, time turns the page and today becomes yesterday. We cannot rewind the clock and relive the past. We are given but one opportunity to experience today.

One day our physical clock will stop ticking and we will be ushered into eternity. Discarding the physical world, we will embrace the spiritual realm. We will see clearly and understand completely. No more confusion. No more questions. No more excuses. What will we know then that we wished we had known now? Based on that wisdom, how will we wish we had lived our life on earth?

Perhaps we would have spent more time developing our relationships with the Lord and others rather than being consumed by our homes or careers. Maybe we would have emphasized inner beauty instead of obsessing over calories, wrinkles, or hair. Possibly we would have served others rather than demanding that they serve us.

We don't have to look back with regret. We can live today with tomorrow in mind. We can gain spiritual wisdom by keeping our eyes on the Lord today. Let today count for eternity!

Dear Lord, help me live today in light of eternity
Give me spiritual wisdom so that Your priorities become my priorities.
May Your will be done in my life today. Amen.

ACTIONS SPEAK
LOUDER THAN INTENTIONS

*"What good will it be for a man if he gains
the whole world, yet forfeits his soul?"*
MATTHEW 16:26 NIV

*F*orfeiting isn't just losing; it is willingly and voluntarily surrendering to an opponent and admitting defeat. No Christian woman actually believes that she would ever knowingly forfeit her faith—much like Peter believed he wouldn't deny Christ. The best of intentions are always outweighed by actions.

While it is not impossible for a woman to have it all and keep her soul, the Bible tells us that it is easier for a rich person to fit through a needle's eye than to find heaven. Rich people aren't excluded from heaven. But rich, busy, or ambitious people are often so focused on material things that they can't maneuver through the mire of worldly pursuits. They lose sight of the eternal prize and risk handing the victory to the enemy by forfeit.

When a woman spends most of her time and money on worldly pursuits and selfish ambition rather than on the things of God, she is being disobedient. Willful disobedience—ignoring the will of God— leads to a spiritual forfeiture. What do your actions prove about you? Do they show you to be faithful to the calling you have received, or do they prove that you still value the world more than the eternal prize and high calling of Jesus?

*Father, please help me to keep my life balanced. Let my primary
desire always be to remain in the center of Your will, that I
never forfeit the prize and surrender in defeat. Amen.*

NATURE REJOICES

*"You will go out in joy and be led forth in peace; the mountains and hills will
burst into song before you, and all the trees of the field will clap their hands."*
ISAIAH 55:12 NIV

The bumblebee-yellow float plane dropped off the young couple and
their guide near a remote lake in the wilds of Alaska. It was the couple's
first Alaskan adventure vacation, and they expected to catch a lot of
fish, but they hadn't realized how awestruck they would be as they
drank in the majestic views that surrounded them. Standing in thigh-
deep glacial waters, they cast their lines. A snowcapped volcano rose
up on their left, and an ancient glacier reflected the sun on their right.
The only sounds were those of nature itself—the rushing river, the
wind in the trees, and an occasional whoop from the woman when she
got a fish on her hook. They marveled at the pair of bald eagles that
soared above them most of the day and the young bear that came out
of the bush to investigate the strangers who had usurped his fishing
rights.

We don't have to be outdoorsmen like our Alaska vacationers to
appreciate and be inspired by the wonders of God's creation wherever
we find ourselves. Wildflowers that grow alongside highways, a shed
snakeskin—a found treasure that a boy brings to his mother—or the
unusual cloud formations that dance in the sky before a storm inspire
us to praise God, the Creator of all things. Nature declares the glory
of the Lord.

*Lord, the beauty in Your creation inspires me to sing Your praises.
Praise be to God. Amen.*

JUST SAY NO

"You're going to wear yourself out—and the people, too.
This job is too heavy a burden for you to handle all by yourself."
EXODUS 18:18 NLT

Jennifer, a pediatrician and mother of two preschoolers, had to learn how to "just say no."

When she was finally able to conceive after years of frustration, she knew she had to make a choice. It was motherhood or doctorhood. Jennifer knew her limits. She chose motherhood.

When she got pregnant with her second son, her pregnancy was a repeat of the first. As she puts it, "I spend most of my pregnancies on the bathroom floor." Jennifer's pregnancies were also spent in the hospital. Special intravenous lines kept her alive through her difficult pregnancies.

Jennifer loves to lead women's Bible studies. And she's good at it. Now that she has two sons, however, she's had to say no. Jennifer knows her limits.

Unlike Jennifer and like Moses, many of us try to do it all. We want to fix what is not fixable. Important things need to be done, and if we do them, we're certain they will be done right. But we can't do it all. We, too, have to learn to say no sometimes—without guilt and without apology.

What God gives us grace and strength to do, let's do wholeheartedly. But let's learn to "just say no," too.

Lord, give me the wisdom I need to say yes and the discernment I need to say no.
Amen.

MOUNTAIN-MOVING COMPANY

*"If you have faith as small as a mustard seed, you can say to this mountain,
'Move from here to there,' and it will move. Nothing will be impossible for you."*
MATTHEW 17:20 NIV

$\mathcal{W}$e've all made the lament at some point, "If only I had enough faith. . ."

". . .my parent/child/friend/husband wouldn't have died."

". . .I would have received that job offer."

". . .I would have enough money for everything in my budget and more besides."

Any of those laments for greater faith pale when compared to faith to move a mountain. After all, doesn't Jesus say that all we need is faith the size of a tiny seed?

The problem with that line of thought is that we put the emphasis on ourselves. If *we* have faith, our problems will go away.

Jesus isn't prodding us to show more faith. He is pointing us to the object of our faith—God. However small our faith, God can move mountains. When we drop the seed of our faith into the ground of His will, He will move the mountains out of our way. He will show us the direction He wants us to take. He may move the mountain; or He may carry us over, around, or through it.

The next time a mountain looms ahead, God wants us to apply to His moving company. He will take us to the right destination.

*Lord God, You are the God of the impossible. We trust You to move
the mountains of our lives and to move us through them. Amen.*

PATHWAY TO GOD'S HEART

*The LORD is my rock and my fortress and my deliverer,
my God, my rock, in whom I take refuge.*
PSALM 18:2 NASB

*D*espite being blessed by God, Hezekiah's life was anything but smooth. In 2 Kings 18, Rabshakeh speaks out against Hezekiah's leadership, telling the people not to listen to Hezekiah's teachings that the Lord will save them. Hezekiah understandably reacts strongly to Rabshakeh's speech. He tears his clothes and puts on sackcloth. But instead of wallowing in self-pity, Hezekiah goes straight to the house of the Lord and sends a message to God's prophet Isaiah.

Isaiah's response to Hezekiah regarding this threatening situation is "Do not be afraid because of the words you have heard" (2 Kings 19:6 NASB). The prophet then tells Hezekiah how the Lord will take care of the situation. Hezekiah seeks the Lord in prayer *again*. And the response he receives is that the Lord has heard his prayers, and deliverance does come, just as the Lord promised.

Hezekiah, with the kingdom at stake, sought the one, true, holy God on bended knee. He knew prayer was the pathway to the heart of God, and God blessed him.

*Oh Lord, help me to seek You first in every situation,
placing my confidence in You alone. Amen.*

REALITY CHECK

Instead, you must worship Christ as Lord of your life. And if someone asks about your Christian hope, always be ready to explain it. But do this in a gentle and respectful way. Keep your conscience clear. Then if people speak against you, they will be ashamed when they see what a good life you live because you belong to Christ.
1 PETER 3:15–16 NLT

$\mathcal{R}$esearchers sometimes conduct behavioral studies on groups of people. The hope is often to observe the similarities and differences in individuals' character, attitude, and behavior and learn from them.

To make the study effective, subjects are not always told they are being watched but instead think they are simply in a holding room, waiting for the study to begin. The study's conductors often are watching and listening from behind mirrors or walls.

Findings show that people's speech and attitudes often are different in public than they are in private. When in public, people seem to put on faces and attitudes that don't reflect their real selves.

Every day we are being watched—both by the Father and by the people around us. Our attitudes and speech often are weighed against beliefs we profess and the hope we claim. Take time to search your heart and your motivations. If your speech and attitude aren't Christ-centered, re-aim your heart to hit the mark.

Lord, help me to be a good representative for You. Amen.

BOARD GOD'S BOAT

*Then, because so many people were coming and going that they
did not even have a chance to eat, he said to them, "Come with
me by yourselves to a quiet place and get some rest."*
MARK 6:31–32 NIV

*A*re you "missing the boat" to a quieter place of rest with God? You
mean to slow down, but your church, work, and family responsibilities
pile higher than a stack of recyclable newspapers. Just when you think
a free moment is yours, the phone rings, a needy friend stops by, or
your child announces she needs you to bake cookies for tomorrow's
school fund-raiser.

The apostles ministered tirelessly—so much so, they had little
time to eat. As they gathered around Jesus to report their activities,
the Lord noticed that they had neglected to take time for themselves.
Sensitive to their needs, the Savior instructed them to retreat by boat
with Him to a solitary place of rest where He was able to minister to
them.

Often we allow the hectic pace of daily life to drain us physically
and spiritually, and in the process, we deny ourselves time alone to pray
and read God's Word. Meanwhile, God patiently waits.

So perhaps it's time to board God's boat to a quieter place and
not jump ship!

*Heavenly Father, in my hectic life I've neglected time apart with You.
Help me to board Your boat and stay afloat through spending
time in Your Word and in prayer. Amen.*

CHOOSING WHAT YOUR LIFE LOOKS LIKE

For as many as are led by the Spirit of God, these are sons of God.
ROMANS 8:14 NKJV

*H*e's Got the Whole World in His Hands" is a song that generations of children have sung. The lyrics of this song say that God is in control, and that whatever is going to happen in our lives will happen no matter what.

The truth is, you were created in God's image with a will, and that means you have the right to choose your own life, whether it's what God desires most for you or not.

Jesus said, "Not my will, but Yours, Father!" He chose to live God's dream for His life over His own. Each day you also decide what your life looks like. The Spirit of God stands ready to lead and guide you, but you must choose to follow His lead to reach the destiny He planned for you.

He has the whole world in His hands, but daily choices belong to you. Choose to live in His will, making decisions based on His direction. Knowing His will comes from a personal relationship and from time spent with Him in prayer and in the Word. Jesus knew the path laid before Him, and you can, too. Choose today.

Heavenly Father, thank You for making a way to form me to be your daughter. I choose Your dream, Your destiny for my life. Help me to make the right choices for my life as I follow You. Amen.

QUICK AND SLOW

My dear brothers, take note of this: Everyone should be quick to listen,
slow to speak and slow to become angry, for man's anger does
not bring about the righteous life that God desires.
JAMES 1:19–20 NIV

$\mathcal{K}$indergartners learning traffic signals know that yellow means "slow down." James 1:19–20 also is a yellow light!

Have you wished, after a conversation with a friend, that you had not given that unsolicited advice? Your friend needed a listening ear, but you attempted to fix her problem instead.

Have you raced through a hectic day, only to end it by taking out your frustrations on family members or friends? Or perhaps you have borne the brunt of someone else's anger and reacted in the same manner, thus escalating the situation. Later, when tempers calmed, you found yourself regretting the angry outburst.

Too often words escape before we know what we are saying. Like toothpaste that cannot be put back in the tube, once words are spoken it is impossible to take them back. Words, whether positive or negative, have a lasting impact.

Practice being quick and slow today—quick to listen, slow to speak, slow to become angry.

God, grant me the patience, wisdom, and grace I need to be a good listener.
Remind me also, Father, to use my words today to lift others
up rather than to tear them down. Amen.

YOU ARE WHAT YOU CLING TO

Hate what is evil; cling to what is good.
ROMANS 12:9 NIV

The invention of superglue was revolutionary, because the glue has the ability to bond immediately with a variety of materials. That is wonderful news if your grandmother's porcelain vase breaks in half. But superglue must be used with extreme caution. Accidents can happen in a split second. If the tiniest drop falls in the wrong place, two items will unintentionally and permanently bond.

What are we cemented to? Bonding takes place as we draw close to something. Choose to cling to what is good and avoid evil at all costs. We should not even flirt with sin, because it can quickly get a foothold in our lives. Like superglue in the wrong place, we could unintentionally find ourselves in bondage by embracing temptation. What may seem innocent at the time could destroy us.

Beware of your temptations. Know your areas of vulnerability and avoid them. If you struggle with unhealthy eating habits, do not buy tempting foods. If gossip is a temptation, avoid the company of friends who enjoy passing on tidbits about others. If overspending is an issue, stay away from the mall. Instead, draw close to the Lord. Allow Him to satisfy your deepest longings. When we cling to good, evil loses its grip.

Dear Lord, help me avoid temptation. May I draw close to You so I can cling to good and avoid evil in my life. Amen.

SLIPPED MOORINGS

But Jonah ran away from the LORD. . . . He went down to Joppa,
where he found a ship bound for [Tarshish]. After paying the fare,
he went aboard and sailed for Tarshish to flee from the LORD.
JONAH 1:3 NIV

*H*as God ever made it clear that He wants you to head in a certain direction—one you just balk at? Maybe fear fills your heart as you think of a move, or doubts weigh heavily on you as you consider your future prospects.

You may not run down to Joppa and find a ship, but you do find yourself slipping away from the center of His will. Maybe Bible study becomes harder or you think of things to do that don't involve the church. New, unbelieving friends may begin to attract you.

Though you have never gone aboard ship, you are heading for Tarshish. As your spiritual ship slips its moorings, you are sailing in a dangerous direction.

Before you leave port, consider your course and head back to shore. For, like Jonah, you can't evade God. Wherever you go, He'll be there already, calling you back to Himself. But the adventure you face first may be no more pleasant than Jonah's visit in a whale's belly.

You can walk away from God, but you can't escape Him. Even if you did, you would find yourself in a very lonely spot. A huge piece of your heart, God's piece, would be missing.

Turn my heart always to You, Lord. I never want to leave You. Amen.

Attitude Is Everything

A cheerful disposition is good for your health;
gloom and doom leave you bone-tired.
PROVERBS 17:22 THE MESSAGE

A large banner hung in the classroom where Andrea was substitute teaching. In bold red letters, the banner read: ATTITUDE IS A LITTLE THING THAT MAKES A BIG DIFFERENCE! Andrea stood in the doorway as the middle school students filed into the English class. Just before the bell rang, the last student entered the classroom. She was in a motorized wheelchair, and Andrea could not help but notice that the girl had no legs.

"Good morning," the teenager said with a broad smile across her face. "I'm Jenny. Are you subbing for Mrs. Browning today?" She was the only student who had greeted Andrea.

Have you ever noticed that many people with serious hardships in life choose to make lemonade from the lemons life has dealt them? Scientific studies of terminal patients indicate that a positive attitude influences the quantity and quality of their final days. Many books have been written on the power of positive thinking. The Bible was around long before any of these books, and this proverb still rings true today.

Sometimes we have to fake it till we feel it. Experiment with this strategy today. Put a smile on your face when you feel discouraged over a setback or frustrated about an inconvenience. A cheerful heart is good medicine.

Father, thank You for this day You have given me.
Create in me a happy heart. Amen.

CHARM BRACELET

But the fruit of the Spirit is love, joy, peace, patience, kindness, goodness,
faithfulness, gentleness, self-control; against such things there is no law.
GALATIANS 5:22–23 NASB

$\mathcal{A}$ charm bracelet is a beautiful way to commemorate milestones or special events. A dangling baby bootie, a tiny graduation cap, a pair of wedding bells, or a palm tree from Cancun are all commonly treasured trinkets. Each tiny charm signifies a huge achievement.

We are told in Galatians that the marks of the Holy Spirit are love, joy, peace, patience, kindness, goodness, faithfulness, gentleness, and self-control. It takes constant growth, through a consistent pursuit of godliness, to acquire these character traits. It is a struggle to walk consistently in patience, always showing love and kindness to people. Self-control is another struggle all its own. These things do not come easily to most of us, and they require concentrated effort.

Consider your spiritual charm bracelet. If you had a charm to represent your growth in each of those traits, how many would you feel comfortable attaching to your bracelet in representation of that achievement? Ask your Father which areas in your Christian walk need the most growth. Do you need to develop those traits more strongly before you feel comfortable donning your bracelet?

Lord, please show me which milestones of Christian living I need to
focus on in order to have the full markings of the Holy Spirit in my life.
Please help me to grow into the Christian woman You call me to be. Amen.

So That You May Know

These things I have written to you who believe in the name of the Son of God, that you may know that you have eternal life, and that you may continue to believe in the name of the Son of God.
1 JOHN 5:13 NKJV

*W*hat are "these things" to which the author of 1 John refers? The verse preceding this one says: "He who has the Son has life; he who does not have the Son of God does not have life." In other words, *Jesus equals life.* Accept Jesus, and receive life. Reject Jesus, and pay the price for your own sins, which is death. These are heavy statements. They address our eternity.

Have you placed your faith in Christ as your personal Savior? If so, you do not have to question where you will spend eternity. If not, pray right now and ask Him to save you from your sins. Accept the free gift of salvation He offers.

There are many unknowns in life. As a Christian, there is one thing that you can know. Although your earthly body will wear out one day, you will live forever in heaven with God. This verse does not say "that you may *think* that you have eternal life" or "that you may *wonder.*" It says that you may *know.*

Pray earnestly for unbelievers that they, too, may choose life!

God, I claim the promise from Your Word that I will live forever with You. As I lift their names to You, I ask that You touch the hearts of my lost friends and family members. Amen.

A Clear
Conscience

*Paul looked straight at the Sanhedrin and said, "My brothers,
I have fulfilled my duty to God in all good conscience to this day."*
ACTS 23:1 NIV

$\mathcal{A}$cts 23:1 is not part of a social conversation over tea. The day
before, a violent Jewish mob had beaten Paul and tried to kill him.
He had been arrested and bound. Yet he had the composure—or
audacity—to speak to these angry people, telling them his testimony
of meeting Christ. Now, squaring off with the Sanhedrin, he made the
bold statement that his conscience was clear before God. Then, when
the high priest ordered him struck, he proceeded to blast him for his
self-righteousness. Recognizing that the Sanhedrin was split between
opposing factions of Sadducees and Pharisees, he called for support
from the Pharisees. Again violence broke out.

So intense were these confrontations that the following night the
Lord Himself came to stand near Paul to encourage him.

Paul's example shows the effect a clear conscience can have in the
life of a believer. The effect is boldness! Boldness to live for Christ,
courage to speak truth when it is not popular, and strength—not
arrogance—in the face of opposition are the result when one lives in
obedience to God. Obedience, readily confessing sin, and total reliance
on God to replace that sin with righteous living help create a clear
conscience. Paul practiced these godly habits, causing him to truthfully
say he acted in good conscience.

*Holy Spirit, reveal to me my sin, cleanse me, and empower
me to walk obediently with a clear conscience that I might
live boldly and courageously for You. Amen.*

MARITAL GOALS

"But those who are considered worthy of taking part in that age and in the resurrection from the dead will neither marry nor be given in marriage."
LUKE 20:35 NIV

Scripture teaches that marriage can be a wonderful thing, reflecting God's relationship with His people, and it should be treated with honor. Marriage has delighted many believers, and it's wonderful when God joins two people and they serve Him together.

But as a goal, marriage has serious limitations. Singles may defer happiness until they're wed, and churches may even imply that those who remain single into their later twenties or beyond are missing out on God's will. But Jesus pointed out that marriage is limited to this age, not eternity. In heaven, we will doubtless have special relationships with others, but marriage won't be one of them. So marriage shouldn't be our major life goal.

On earth, if our marriages reflect our love for Jesus, they achieve their goal. Loving families are part of God's earthly plan. That is why He created the institution. But whether we are single or wed, our ultimate goal remains the same: to serve our Lord, not just a spouse.

Married or single, you can do God's will. Just love Him best. That's all He asks.

Lord, You love me just as I am. Make my life a witness to Your love no matter what my marital status happens to be. Amen.

HERD BALL

For the time will come when men will not put up with sound doctrine.
Instead. . .they will gather around them a great number of
teachers to say what their itching ears want to hear.
2 TIMOTHY 4:3 NIV

*K*arli and the other first grade girls assembled on the soccer field for one of their first games. Cheering parents stood or sat along the sidelines. The girls' focus wasn't on the game as much as it was on the ball. With the exception of the goalkeepers (who had a tendency to practice pirouettes or pick dandelions), both teams hovered around the soccer ball. If a bystander couldn't see the ball, she or he could rest assured it was somewhere in the swarm of twenty players on the field.

"I call it herd ball," remarked one dad.

Several minutes into the second half, an airplane flew over the soccer field. The entire herd—including the goalkeepers—stopped and looked up. One overachiever grabbed her chance and kicked the ball up the field with the determination of a world-class soccer star. None of the herd was focused any longer on the ball. Except her—and all the screaming parents.

Sometimes we Christians follow after things like a herd. A new preacher, a new book, a new Bible study carries us all down the field—until the next novelty comes along. We need to heed the words in today's verse and prayerfully "keep [our] head in all situations" (2 Timothy 4:5 NIV).

Keep me focused on You and Your Word, Lord. Amen.

Sophisticated Sin

Do I not hate those who hate you, O LORD,
and abhor those who rise up against you?
PSALM 139:21 NIV

*D*o we hate what You hate, Lord? Or does wickedness attract us because it looks appealing? We need to ask ourselves these questions.

When David penned Psalm 139, he had to deal with just his day-to-day contacts in ancient Israel. He didn't have to contend with multiple forms of media and people across the world denying God's name. Even his royal court—the height of elegance in his day—looks fairly primitive compared to the sophisticated world we face today. But none of that changes the value of David's message—God's message to us.

The world tells us how wonderful sin is, and the message is so attractively packaged that sometimes it is really tempting, even to those of us who remain faithful. We often would like to believe that there is nothing wrong with sins that appeal to our senses.

David's condemnation of sin isn't popular, and it's not pretty. But sin isn't pretty, either, and prophets aren't slick salespersons. David didn't package a one-minute message approved by his PR firm. God was the only One he sought to please. And despite their lack of popularity, his words are true.

Make God's truth a major priority in your life.

Chic, refined, stylish, urbane—sin gets called all those "sophisticated" things,
Lord. But it's still sin. And You still hate it. Help me to hate it, too. Amen.

PERSEVERING THROUGH ADVERSITY

"But if it is from God, you will not be able to stop these men; you will only find yourselves fighting against God." His speech persuaded them. They called the apostles in and had them flogged. Then they ordered them not to speak in the name of Jesus, and let them go. The apostles left the Sanhedrin, rejoicing because they had been counted worthy of suffering disgrace for the Name.
ACTS 5:39–41 NIV

*J*oseph, sold into slavery, found himself in prison. Ruth and Naomi lost their husbands then headed out to another country without protection. David, though anointed as the next king, lived in exile. Esther spent most of her life as an orphan dependent on the goodness of her relatives. The apostles experienced violent persecution.

Scripture overflows with stories of God's beloved children undergoing extreme hardships. Just because we have faith, hope, and trust in the Lord does not mean that life will be easy. Instead, God's love for us means that He will provide a way *through*, not around, adversity, resulting in His greater glory.

Everyone experiences tough times. The goal, however, is not to find relief. It is to live in a way that shows how well we love and trust the Lord.

Father God, I know that no matter how troubled my life is, You can provide me a way to persevere. Help me to trust Your guidance and love. Amen.

EXPECT TROUBLE

These things I have spoken unto you, that in me ye might have peace. In the world ye shall have tribulation: but be of good cheer; I have overcome the world.
JOHN 16:33 KJV

*W*hy do bad things happen to good people? It is an age-old question. Sometimes we expect God to surround us with an invisible shield that keeps us from all harm and disease, all hurt and disappointment. As nice as this might sound, it is simply not how life works. Christians are not exempt from trials.

In the Gospel of John, we read that Christ told his followers to *expect* trouble in this world. The good news is that we do not have to face it alone. When trials come, remember that Jesus has overcome this world. Through Him, we, too, are overcomers. Draw upon the promise that through Christ you can do all things. The children's song says it this way: "Jesus loves me, this I know, for the Bible tells me so. Little ones to Him belong. They are weak, but He is strong."

Expect trouble, but refuse to let it defeat you. Trials strengthen our faith and our character. No one gets excited about a trial, yet we can be assured that God is still in control even when trouble comes our way.

Lord Jesus, be my strength as I face trouble in this life. Walk with me. Hold my hand. Assure me that in my weakness, You are strong. Amen.

HEAR NO EVIL

Do not pay attention to every word people say, or you may hear your servant cursing you—for you know in your heart that many times you yourself have cursed others.
ECCLESIASTES 7:21–22 NIV

Sitting in the pew at church or at your desk at work, you hear two people talking. The mention of your name snags your attention and you're hooked. You have to listen.

You might hear something pleasant. Maybe your friends are planning a birthday party. Maybe someone mentions you as a good resource for a work problem or as a potential volunteer for a church project. They highlight your good qualities, gifts, and knowledge. You like to overhear that kind of conversation even if it ruins a surprise.

Then again, you might overhear something less pleasant. Maybe someone criticizes your work performance. Maybe someone you thought was a friend complains about something you've done. You feel they're cursing you, and a splinter infects the relationship.

Solomon warns against listening in. In an ideal world, no one would speak badly of us, and we would never gossip about someone else. But in the real world, it happens. We have all said things that never should have entered our minds, let alone come out of our mouths. The best defense against hurt feelings is an intentional ignorance.

The next time we overhear our name, we should keep on walking.

Lord, teach us to put a guard on both our lips and our ears.
Close our ears to the gossip that swirls around us. Amen.

WHAT IS A TRUE FRIEND?

There are "friends" who destroy each other,
but a real friend sticks closer than a brother.
PROVERBS 18:24 NLT

In today's world we use the term *friend* loosely. Unable to describe a hypothetical, indefinable somebody, we often say, "I have a friend who. . ." The person usually is a distant acquaintance, but because we are unable to determine what to call them, we clump them into the multifaceted category of friend.

An ancient proverb, however, captures the essence and beauty of true friendship. It says, "Ah, the beauty of being at peace with another, neither having to weigh thoughts or measure words, but spilling time out just as they are, chaff and grain together, certain that a faithful hand will keep what is worth keeping and with a breath of kindness, blow the rest away."

Friends find the good in us and dismiss the rest. We can be ourselves in their presence and not worry about misunderstandings or saying the wrong thing.

Jesus is that kind of friend. He sticks close by us at our most undesirable, least lovable moments. We can tell Him anything and He understands. In fact, He knows everything about us and loves us anyway. Like a true friend, Jesus enhances our good qualities and, with a breath of kindness, blows the rest away.

Dear Jesus, thank You for loving me even when I fail, encouraging
me in my discouragement, and sticking close to me during tough times.
May I be as good a friend as You are. Amen.

DO WE NEED TO DO IT ALL?

I have glorified thee on the earth:
I have finished the work which thou gavest me to do.
JOHN 17:4 KJV

*O*n the night before He was crucified, our Lord offered a bold prayer to the heavenly Father. He prayed for Himself, His disciples, and us. In that prayer, He declared that He had finished the work the Father gave Him to do, and in so doing, He glorified the Father.

Although Jesus did all the Father required, did Jesus do it all?

No.

Jesus did not heal every crippled, blind, or demon-possessed person He encountered. Nor did He save everyone who came to Him. More than once the unbelieving departed, and He let them go.

Early in Jesus' ministry, He explained His method: He could do nothing of Himself; He worked where He saw the Father working. He never went rashly ahead of the Father.

This should be our pattern.

We women often think that because we *can* do something, we *should* do it. We listen to the world's chant that we "can do it all."

Simply because we can do all things through Christ doesn't mean He is calling us to do everything.

If we would be like Jesus, we will do only the work the Father gives us, not all the work we can do.

Dear Father, give me eyes to see where You are working so that I
may work with You. Help me rebuff the world's temporal demands
so that I can focus on heavenly duties that bring eternal rewards. Amen.

SOWING THE WIND

"They sow the wind and they reap the whirlwind."
HOSEA 8:7 NASB

*A*dmit it. Sometimes our jam-packed days leave us feeling as if we're running around like chickens with our heads cut off. From the first drop of morning coffee to the last sip of evening tea, our days reel by in fast motion. The next thing we know, a year has passed. Then two, then three. And what have we done? Where are we?

What is the point of our days? Are we chasing after foreign idols, proudly wearing a badge of busyness, worshipping the almighty dollar, determined to keep one step ahead of the Joneses?

That's what the Israelites were doing when Hosea wrote, "They sow the wind and they reap the whirlwind." In sowing the wind, nothing of everlasting value is produced, and we end up with arms filled with temporal nothings.

As followers of Christ, we are to reap righteousness, keeping our eyes on Jesus, for He is our ultimate prize—not that new car, new house, or new wardrobe.

Don't lust for earthly idols that keep you from sowing the right seeds—those of righteousness. Take a deep breath. Take a long walk. Depart from the rat race. Relax in God's arms. Keep your eyes on Christ instead of worldly goods, and you will reap not the earthly whirlwind but heavenly treasure.

God, keep my eyes on the right prize—Your Son, Jesus Christ.
Help me to slow down, walk in Your will, and become a
blessing in this world, always looking toward the next. Amen.

DIAL DOWN ANGER

A gentle answer turns away wrath, but a harsh word stirs up anger.
PROVERBS 15:1 NIV

*W*hat implications could Proverbs 15:1 have for world peace? National harmony? Personal relationship improvement? Responding in anger is a natural thing for fallen humanity; and statesmen, politicians, and average people of every sort have all opened their mouths too quickly and said words that invited a fierce response.

When we react wrathfully, it's unrealistic to imagine that the person we just verbally flamed will not take it badly. No one wants to become another's emotional punching bag. So the anger keeps increasing on both sides.

But God calls us to end anger by returning fury with love. It's not easy to speak the first peaceful word. Our fallen natures call out a warning that we'll be taken advantage of. We don't want to appear to be the one who backed down—we'd lose face.

But keeping face isn't a Christian concept, and as we follow God's advice and speak gently, amazing things happen. Instead of escalating the argument, we allow tensions to die down. Suddenly, an opponent can hear what we say—if we allow some decompression time and a few moments for thought.

Facing another's anger? Try taking God's advice. You'll be amazed at the response!

Lord, help me dial down anger and spread Your love instead. Amen.

PERFECT GUIDANCE

May the Lord direct your hearts into the love
of God and into the steadfastness of Christ.
2 THESSALONIANS 3:5 NASB

A woman recalls the day she passed her driver's test many years ago. "My dad handed me the car keys and kissed me on the cheek. I said, 'What was that for?' He laughed and said, 'Because, as bad as your sense of direction is, I'll probably never see you again!' "

This is our predicament when we try to operate without the Spirit of God. It's like trying to drive our car to an unfamiliar destination without a map or GPS. We end up making wrong turns and poor decisions. We drive around and around in circles, and we don't bother to stop to ask for directions.

Even before Jesus sent His Holy Spirit to indwell believers, God used a variety of means to guide His people. He spoke to Israel through the prophets. He gave certain individuals dreams and visions. God even gave the Israelites a pillar of clouds by day and a pillar of fire by night in which God's Spirit dwelled to lead them out of Egypt into the Promised Land.

Thanks to GPS technology in our automobiles, we need never be lost on the road. Praise be to God for giving us His Spirit, who resides in us so that we need never lose our direction as we navigate our way through life.

Thank You, Jesus, for sending Your Holy Spirit to lead me in the right direction.
Amen.

DAYBREAK

"As your days, so shall your strength be."
DEUTERONOMY 33:25 NKJV

The morning star is a bright light that appears in the eastern sky just before sunrise. It is a sign that the darkness is nearly over and daybreak is on its way. It offers hope and encouragement to weary travelers who pressed on through the night to reach their destiny and were beginning to feel that perhaps they had lost their way.

There are times in life when we feel that the night season we're facing will last forever and a new morning will never come. During that time, dreams have faded and hope is dim. We look for a flicker of encouragement, holding tightly to any sign that the night will soon pass.

For those particularly dark seasons of your life, you don't have to look to the east to find the morning star, but instead find that morning star in your heart. Allow the hope of God's goodness and love to rekindle faith. With the passing of the night, gather your strength and courage. A new day is dawning and with it new strength for the journey forward. All that God has promised will be fulfilled.

*Heavenly Father, help me to hold tightly to faith,
knowing in this situation that daybreak is on its way. Amen.*

I CAN'T
HEAR YOU

Faith comes by hearing, and hearing by the word of God.
ROMANS 10:17 NKJV

*I*ntentional listening is essential in the Christian life. But why do we so often falter in following Jesus' frequent admonition, "He who has ears to hear, let him hear"? The Gospels alone record ten instances of Jesus repeating these important words. Of course, He's talking about spiritual ears, not physical ears, although we often manage to block incoming messages to our spiritual ears as if we were wearing cotton plugs.

How can our faith grow if we don't unplug our ears and actively listen to the Word of God?

Sometimes the flow of words cascading from our own mouths drowns out the incoming message, effecting a hearing impairment created of our own devices. How many times have we tuned out the still, small voice of God because obeying His message would cause us too much effort, inconvenience, or even embarrassment?

God's Word often acts as an alarm clock to wake us up spiritually. We can hit our snooze button and ignore the warnings, or we can listen with our spiritual ears and allow scripture to pierce us like a two-edged sword—a sword that slices through the thick padding of complacency with which we have insulated ourselves and exposes the rough gristle of our stubborn inner selves clinging to our old, sinful natures.

Yes, words are powerful. They cut. They heal. They confirm. God uses His Word to help us, to mold us, to make us more like Him. But only if we *hear* it.

Lord, speak to my heart today. My spiritual ears are open. Amen.

CONFIDENCE

And now, little children, abide in him; that, when he shall appear,
we may have confidence, and not be ashamed before him at his coming.
1 JOHN 2:28 KJV

*S*omeday each one of us will stand before our Maker. It is difficult to imagine how we will react. Will we run to Him with open arms or shrink back with embarrassment? Will we desire to sit at His feet or retreat to a far-off corner of heaven? Our reaction then will depend on our relationship with Him now.

We have the opportunity to enter into a personal relationship with our heavenly Father through Jesus Christ. The acceptance of this invitation by faith assures us of eternal life. Yet many people who profess faith in Jesus never grow in their relationship with Him. They stick their ticket to heaven in their back hip pocket, never realizing there is so much more!

Jesus came to give us eternal life in heaven as well as abundant life on earth. As we allow His Word to speak to our hearts, we grow in our relationship with Him. He becomes our friend, our confidant, our Good Shepherd. We know Him intimately. We communicate with Him constantly. We love Him deeply. Let's get to know the Lord now. Then we will anticipate our face-to-face meeting with excitement and confidence!

Dear Lord, help me to pursue my relationship with You now. May I know You
more with each passing day so that I will be excited when we meet face-to-face.
Amen.

God's Business

Be very careful, then, how you live—not as unwise but as wise,
making the most of every opportunity, because the days are evil.
Therefore do not be foolish, but understand what the Lord's will is.
EPHESIANS 5:15–17 NIV

*J*ulia, a ninety-two-year-old woman, lived in an assisted-living center. Although she suffered from a broken back, she often used a walker or a scooter to move around the facility. Her physical ailments did not prevent her from doing God's business. She was often found witnessing to others about the love of Christ through her behavior and words. She did not complain but was a joy to be around as the light of the Lord radiated from her.

Are you about God's business?

God's Word tells us to live as wise people, making the most of our time. We need to understand the Lord's will and then act accordingly. For some people, we may be the only "Jesus" they will see. Because of this, we need to act wisely as we love others with the love of Christ. We need to be deliberate in walking in God's way of truth, justice, and light.

As we look at our culture, it is easy to see that the days are evil; evil permeates earth as Satan is allowed to rule for a short time (Revelation 12:12). We must not waste any time, but daily surrender to God's business, revealing who He is and drawing others to know Him.

Heavenly Lord, please let Your light radiate from
me so that others are drawn to know You. Amen.

MARVELOUS PLANS

*O LORD, you are my God; I will exalt you and praise your name, for in perfect
faithfulness you have done marvelous things, things planned long ago.*
ISAIAH 25:1 NIV

*G*od had marvelous plans for the children of Israel, and they were
blessed by God. God sent bread from heaven each morning in the form
of manna while Israel wandered in the wilderness. When the people
complained they had no meat, God sent quail. When the people
complained they had no water, God gave water from a rock.

Amazingly, everything the people needed, God provided in the
wilderness over and over again. Yet when they came to the Promised
Land, only Joshua and Caleb believed that God would help them
conquer the land. Everyone else was afraid and complained—again.
Because of their faith, Joshua and Caleb were the only ones God
allowed to move into the Promised Land.

God has a "promised land" for us all—a marvelous plan for our
lives. Recount and record His faithfulness in your life in the past,
because God has already demonstrated His marvelous plans to you
in so many ways. Then prayerfully anticipate the future journey
with Him. Keep a record of God's marvelous plans in a journal as
He unfolds them day by day. You will find God to be faithful in the
smallest aspects of your life and oh so worthy of your trust.

*Oh Lord, help me to recount Your faithfulness, record Your faithfulness,
and trust Your faithfulness in the future. For You are my God,
and You have done marvelous things, planned long ago. Amen.*

WHERE DID SUNDAY GO?

By the seventh day God had finished the work he had been doing; so on the seventh day he rested from his work. And God blessed the seventh day and made it holy, because on it he rested from all the work of creating that he had done.
GENESIS 2:2–3 NIV

*K*ate remembered that when she was growing up stores were closed on Sunday. It was as if the whole country held that day as sacred. Sunday even felt different, a day set apart.

But now? Kate lamented one afternoon, while trying to find a parking spot at the mall, that Sunday felt like any other day. Overscheduled, overcommitted, running from church (if sporting events didn't preclude it) to the grocery store. Too often she woke up tired on Monday mornings—not tired from lack of sleep but from a relentless pace.

"And God blessed the seventh day and made it holy," the Bible says. *If God rested on that day, shouldn't I?* Kate wondered. And if it was meant to be a blessed day, was Kate missing something God had in store for her?

From that afternoon on, Kate didn't go to stores on Sunday. By planning ahead, she could have Sunday's meals taken care of and at least be prepared for Monday school lunches. She noticed that she started the week feeling renewed and refreshed, just the way the Lord intended a Sabbath to be: a blessed day.

Lord, You gave us an example of Sabbath rest for our good—spiritually and physically. May we faithfully set aside Your day for worship and rest. Amen.

THY WILL
BE DONE

"Your kingdom come, your will be done on earth as it is in heaven."
MATTHEW 6:10 NIV

$\mathcal{W}$e pray it. We say it. But do we really mean that we want God's will to be done on earth as it is in heaven? Submitting to God's will is difficult. Jesus struggled with submission in the Garden of Gethsemane. We wrestle with it most days. Unfortunately, most of us assume that we know best. We want to call the shots and be in control. But following God's path requires trusting Him, not ourselves.

Many times submitting to God's will requires letting go of something we covet. We may be called to walk away from a relationship, a job, or a material possession. At other times God may ask us to journey down a path we would not have chosen. Venturing out of our comfort zone or experiencing hardship is not our desire.

Embracing God's love enables us to submit to His will. God not only loves us immensely, but He desires to bless us abundantly. However, from our human perspective, those spiritual blessings may be disguised. That is why we must cling to truth. We must trust that God's ways are higher than ours. We must believe that His will is perfect. We must hold fast to His love. As we do, He imparts peace to our hearts, and we are able to say with conviction, "Your will be done."

Dear Lord, may I rest secure in Your unconditional love. Enable me to trust You more. May I desire that Your will be done in my life. Amen.

RECIPROCAL ENCOURAGEMENT

*Let us consider how we may spur one
another on toward love and good deeds.*
HEBREWS 10:24 NIV

*S*ometimes when we read the Bible, we become preoccupied with inward reflection. We think about how we are supposed to be living, what we are supposed to be doing, where we are supposed to be going. We ask God to help mold and change us, and we have faith that He will transform us into the people He wants us to be.

While these practices are good, the author of Hebrews intimates that we should take note of what is going on in the lives of our brothers and sisters. We all need encouragement, but we all must learn to *give* encouragement as well. We also must rely on our brothers and sisters; if we encourage them, we believe that they, in turn, will encourage us.

In this day and age, we have a myriad of tools for encouragement at our fingertips. A note left on the passenger seat, an unexpected hug, a random e-mail, an unanticipated phone call—these are just a few of the many ways we can encourage each other. The point is, we must think about our brothers and sisters in Christ. How can we spur them on? The options are limitless—be creative! But encourage, encourage, encourage!

*Dear Lord, please help me to encourage others toward love and good deeds.
Please also raise up brothers and sisters who will encourage me. Amen.*

Voice Recognition

"His sheep follow him because they know his voice."
John 10:4 niv

Katie sensed that she needed to pray for a young couple she had recently met at her church. The couple, getting ready to go overseas as missionaries, were expecting their first child.

She had only briefly met them. She had not heard of them before nor seen them since that day they spoke at her church. But suddenly Katie felt compelled to pray—but why? For what?

"Their unborn baby."

God's still, small voice was clear. Katie didn't know any details. She didn't even know the baby's due date. But she recognized her Lord's voice. So she prayed. For weeks she felt compelled to pray for the expectant couple. Then, abruptly, that compulsion evaporated. What could it mean?

Katie sent the couple a letter, telling them about her experience and asking about the pregnancy.

"Thank you so much for praying," the reply came back. "After we visited your church, our baby was diagnosed with a heart deformity on a prenatal sonogram. But to our doctor's amazement, she was born completely healthy!"

Every mother knows her own baby's cries. Children know the voice of Mom and Dad. When we keep our ears tuned to listen and obey, what delight can follow our obedience to God's voice!

Lord, You recognize my voice when I call on You. Give me ears to listen and a heart to respond in obedience when You call to me. Amen.

GOD IN DISGUISE

*"For I was hungry, and you fed me. I was thirsty, and you gave me a drink.
I was a stranger, and you invited me into your home. . . . And the King
will say, 'I tell you the truth, when you did it to one of the least
of these my brothers and sisters, you were doing it to me!' "*
MATTHEW 25:35, 40 NLT

What does it mean to be a missionary? Wholehearted service to God. A heart for others. A desire to lead people to a relationship with Jesus.

A missionary can be a mother, a teacher, an office worker, an emergency medical technician, or a salesperson. God instructs His followers to "go into the world"—across borders—to tell people about Him. But "go" can also mean walking across the street or driving down the road to visit another person.

What is keeping you from your mission field? The details and to-do lists of day-to-day life easily take away time for daily service to others. Sometimes we can become so concerned with serving God that we forget that God is served *when* we serve people. Just as it is possible to have head knowledge *about* God without having a relationship *with* God, so can people interact with others without ever meeting a person's real need.

Jesus met people's immediate needs, but He didn't stop there. He fed and healed people, but he also invited them to accept him and follow him. It's all too easy to overlook people. Sometimes they don't even look like they need help. Although we cannot force someone to accept our help, we can make a point to offer it.

Lord, open my eyes to see those who need care. Amen.

TIMELY WORDS

The LORD God gives me the right words to encourage the weary.
ISAIAH 50:4 CEV

*J*ean felt lower than she had in years. The job she had coveted, fought for, and won had disappeared. After initial success, her second project failed to meet expectations. The company downgraded her job responsibilities, and once again she was relegated to entry-level duties.

Across the country in another state, Helen didn't know about Jean's job situation, but God prodded her. *"Write to Jean. Tell her how much you appreciate her and what a good job you think she did when you worked together."* Helen obeyed. It didn't take much time to send a few brief sentences through cyberspace.

Helen's timely words arrived at the time Jean most needed encouragement. Many of us can testify to similar experiences.

God has given us tongues and fingers to communicate timely words to the weary around us. Perhaps it is a simple matter of complimenting someone on a new blouse. Perhaps it is time to send a card through the mail or to pick up the phone and call a friend you haven't seen for a while. Perhaps you need to set aside your plans for the evening and visit a friend in the hospital.

When God prompts us to speak, we become part of His answer.

*Lord God, You have given us gifts that can lift up the weary when
they most need it. Teach us to listen for Your instructions. Amen.*

PRACTICALITY VS. PASSION

Leaving her water jar, the woman went back to the town and said to the people,
"Come, see a man who told me everything I ever did. Could this be the Christ?"
JOHN 4:28–29 NIV

*L*eaving her water jar. . ." One might overlook the phrase; nevertheless, the act was important enough to be included in John's Gospel.

Fetching water was part of the Samaritan woman's daily routine. What caused her to abandon the task, lay down her jar, and run into town?

We don't know much about this woman. We do know, like many women today, that she was searching for fulfillment in all the wrong places. She had had five husbands and was living with a man to whom she was not married. But everything changed the day she met a man at the well and He asked her for a drink of water. Then, although they had never met before, He told her everything she had ever done. He offered her living water that would never run dry.

Practicality gave way to passion! She knew this man was the Messiah, and sharing that good news became a priority. The woman tossed aside her water jar. She took an extreme measure, for she was responding to an extreme interruption in her lost existence. She had met Jesus.

Do you live with such passion, or do you cling to your water jar? Has an encounter with Christ made an impact that cannot be denied in your life?

Lord, help me to lay down anything that stifles my passion
for sharing the Good News with others. Amen.

FINDING BALANCE

Hope deferred makes the heart sick,
but when the desire comes, it is a tree of life.
PROVERBS 13:12 NKJV

*O*ur minds are full of the things we are trying to fix in our lives—strained relationships, financial worries, stress, health concerns.

Too much too fast is overwhelming. Looking for balance can leave us lost, not knowing which way to turn. The best way to gain balance is to stop moving and regain focus.

Jesus is your hope! He stands a short distance away bidding you to take a walk on water—a step of faith toward Him. Disregarding the distractions can be hard, but the rough waters can become silent as you turn your eyes, your thoughts, and your emotions to Him.

You can tackle the tough things as you maintain your focus. Let Him direct you over the rough waters of life, overcoming each obstacle one opportunity at a time. Don't look at the big picture in the midst of the storm, but focus on the one thing you can do at the moment to help your immediate situation—one step at a time.

Lord, help me not to concentrate on the distractions, but to keep
my focus on which step to take next in order to reach You. Amen.

IDENTITY CRISIS

Charm can be deceiving, and beauty fades away,
but a woman who honors the LORD deserves to be praised.
PROVERBS 31:30 CEV

"Identity crisis" is a term used to describe a person who is suffering stress or anxiety over her role in society or how she is viewed by others. The world places much superficial value on charm, beauty, and feminine wiles. Scripture, however, makes it clear that those things will fade away.

Some people interpret Proverbs 31:30 as meaning that the charm of a cunning woman can be deceiving to others. But the original Hebrew wording gives a fuller picture of what is actually being taught in this verse. The warning is not that charm is deceiving to *others*; it is that it is deceiving to *you*! When you trust in something that will fade away, such as charm or beauty, you have deceived yourself into a false sense of security.

As a believer in Christ, your identity is that you are a child of the King, an heir to the kingdom of God, and a part of the body of Christ. You are His. Let that identity solve your crisis and, from now on, place no more value on your charm or beauty than He does. Your Father sees you through the blood of His Son, Jesus, and He finds you perfect.

Thank You, Jesus, for my true identity. Please help me to remember
not to get caught up in the unimportant things that will fade away,
and to nurture the parts of me that bring glory to You. Amen.

TIME FOR PRAISE

And a voice came from the throne, saying, "Give praise to our God,
all you His bond-servants, you who fear Him, the small and the great."
REVELATION 19:5 NASB

A kindergarten teacher wanted to infuse her school day with opportunities to praise God. She realized that she walked into her storage room numerous times during the day, collecting such things as art supplies, kickballs for recess, and tissues for runny noses, and so she decided that in these brief moments she would lift up an offering of praise to God.

"Thank You, Lord, for giving me wisdom today," she would whisper right after the bell rang in the morning.

"Great is the Lord and greatly to be praised!" she said as she put on her sweater to go outside.

"Your loving kindness is better than life," she would hum as she grabbed an extra box of chalk later in the day.

What a wonderful idea this teacher had! We can follow her example, examining our daily routines for snippets of time in which to offer up praises to the Almighty. A stay-at-home mom might praise the Lord at traffic lights as she is running her errands. An office worker might find her moments of praise in the break room. The more we praise God, the more we will feel the joy of His presence in the ordinary moments of our day-to-day lives.

Jesus, You are worthy to be praised; help me to
making praising Your name a lifelong habit. Amen.

WOMEN
WRESTLERS

Epaphras. . .a servant of Christ Jesus. . .is always wrestling in prayer for you,
that you may stand firm in all the will of God, mature and fully assured.
COLOSSIANS 4:12 NIV

A group of women gather weekly, giving up a morning when they
could be doing something more exciting. Yet over the years, the living
room has become holy ground as they kneel. They meet to wrestle
in prayer for the needs of other believers. This is their ministry to
the body of Christ. Their hearts listen during regular contact or
conversations throughout the week. And people tell them of needs,
knowing that these women are serious about their intercession.

When someone is in need of wisdom, strength, or provision, they
know who to call. This side of heaven, no one will know the full impact
these women have on the lives of others. But we can thank God for
pray-ers that plead for the needs of those we know and love, praying
for their salvation, assurance, and maturity. We can stand in the gap for
others knowing that our faithful God hears our prayers.

Mighty God, teach me to pray effectively, interceding for others' needs
that they—and I—might stand firm and sure in our faith. Amen.

REALISTIC
EXPECTATIONS

O LORD, how manifold are thy works!
in wisdom hast thou made them all:
the earth is full of thy riches.
PSALM 104:24 KJV

*W*orking, cleaning, cooking, attending meetings, calling people, going places—life is full of business, things we have to accomplish. We often make lists to help us remember what we need to do and when, or we fill in the daily agenda on our calendar or PalmPilot. At the end of the day, we can look back and see what we have finished and what is left to juggle into tomorrow's schedule.

If the unexpected happens, our schedule is thrown off. We struggle to find the time to do everything we have listed to do. We become stressed. Sleeping becomes difficult. Our health suffers. Friends and relatives may note a change in our demeanor.

God worked hard to create all the wonderful world around us, yet He did so with wisdom and proper timing. He didn't do everything in one day. Instead, He had a plan and accomplished all He needed to do in that time frame.

Consider what is important in life. Start your day with God; then list your agenda in order of importance. As we let God lead, His wisdom will make us have realistic expectations. Our well-being and attitude will improve.

Thank You, Lord, for Your example. Please guide me.
Show me what is important in my day.
Help me to depend on Your wisdom. Amen.

THE BLAZING FURNACE

*"If we are thrown into the blazing furnace, the God we serve is able
to save us from it, and he will rescue us from your hand, O king."*
DANIEL 3:17 NIV

God wouldn't actually let these three godly men, Shadrach, Meshach, and Abednego, be thrown into the furnace, would He? Their bold declaration surely was just an act of defiance to King Nebuchadnezzar's tyrannical order to worship his golden statue. Surely God would provide a way of escape.

But He didn't. Or at least not in the way they had probably hoped— by avoiding that furnace. Imagine their thoughts as Nebuchadnezzar's fury was unleashed and he ordered the furnace to be heated seven times hotter than usual. Imagine how they felt as they were bound, in highly flammable clothing, and carried to the furnace. Imagine the terror they felt as the guards who were ordered to throw them into the furnace perished from its heat!

Had God abandoned Shadrach, Meshach, and Abednego? Hardly!

Nebuchadnezzar looked into the furnace and found the three men walking around, unbound and unharmed, along with a fourth man. Scholars believe this was Jesus, preincarnate.

Too often we think that our faith should keep us out of the furnace: a health crisis, financial worries, troubling situations with our kids. But being in the furnace doesn't mean that God has abandoned us. As promised in Hebrews 13:5 (NKJV), "I will never leave you nor forsake you." He will be right there in the furnace with you.

*Lord God, thank You that I can count on You to be with me in every
circumstance. Though evil threatens, You hold me in Your loving hands. Amen.*

A FRESH,
NEW HARVEST

Do not rejoice over me, my enemy; when I fall, I will arise;
when I sit in darkness, the LORD will be a light to me.
MICAH 7:8 NKJV

*P*ast mistakes and failures are like dried pits in the bottom of a bowl of cherries. As you enjoy the fresh fruit of your life in Christ, there are times when you reach into the bowl and touch a dried, dead seed of the past.

The truth is that God has made all things new through your salvation. You may be challenged with the consequences that remain from past life choices, but God is busy turning past mistakes into future successes.

The enemy of your soul wants you to consider each failure and dwell on the past, fully intending to rob you of your future. But God wants you to take that seed of hope that seems to have died and bury it in His garden of truth—trusting Him for a new harvest of goodness and mercy.

Once you have buried that seed deep in the ground of God's love, it will grow and become a part of His destiny for your life. Maybe you have fallen and spilled a bowl of your dreams. Pick them up and plant them in God's love. Over time you will have a harvest of goodness, and your enemy will have no reason left to celebrate.

Lord, help me not to focus on the past but to look to You every step of the way.
Amen.

STIRRING IT UP

*This is why I remind you to fan into flames the spiritual
gift God gave you when I laid my hands on you.*
2 TIMOTHY 1:6 NLT

*T*he campers at the campsite always appreciated the warmth of an early morning fire. But no matter how hot the fire was the night before, by morning there were only ashes until someone stirred it. Underneath, the embers smoldered, glowing orange. It took a gentle stirring, a consistent blowing of air, to rekindle the flames. More wood piled on top kept the fire dancing all morning.

So, too, we need to awaken our latent gifts. Left unused, they cool down and lay dormant and neglected. Paul urges us to rekindle our talents, fan the flame, and keep our gifts burning and active for God and His people. Prayerfully seek ways to share your talents with those around you. Joy is yours when your gifts are used, and they are a blessing for those you have given to. When you keep that fire burning, God is honored, you are more fulfilled, and the body of Christ is more complete.

*Giver of gifts, show me creative ways to use my gifts.
Help me to be a good steward of the gifts You have given me by
using them for others, igniting them to live more for You. Amen.*

PRISCILLA AND AQUILA:
GOD'S TEAM

When Aquila and Priscilla had heard, they took him unto them,
and expounded unto him the way of God more perfectly.
ACTS 18:26 KJV

$\mathcal{P}$riscilla and Aquila, a Jewish couple, moved to Corinth because Emperor Claudius expelled all Jews from Rome. There they met the apostle Paul, a man who would change their lives. The three shared the same vocation: tent making. They began to work together. As they cut, stitched, and sold their wares, Paul followed Jesus' revolutionary pattern of teaching women, instructing both Aquila and Priscilla. These close friends sailed with him to Ephesus. When Paul had to leave, he trusted Priscilla and Aquila to nurture the fledgling church there.

When Apollos, a follower of John the Baptist, began to speak in an Ephesian synagogue, the couple took him home for dinner. Together, husband and wife shared the full gospel with Apollos and helped him grow spiritually. Apollos became a strong advocate for Jesus Christ and helped spread the gospel.

Priscilla and Aquila found it natural to welcome Apollos into their home for fellowship and instruction. Later, back in Rome, they would host another developing church, working as a team to build Christ's kingdom.

Priscilla's challenging life reminds us that we can grow spiritually and share our faith amid business deals, meals, and meetings. In the everydayness of life, God does extraordinary things!

Lord Jesus, thank You that Priscilla thought outside the box. You used her
to fan the flame of the Spirit in the early church. Please use me as well. Amen.

Make Every
Effort

Make every effort to keep the unity of the Spirit through the bond of peace.
Ephesians 4:3 niv

*T*he church renovation project was near completion. For more than two years, the committee labored together with minimal conflict, swallowing minor differences and dislikes for the sake of forward movement on the project. Subtle discord sneaked in the back door of conversations, crept into e-mails, and lingered after backhanded comments were made. Soon rumbles were abundant, "Well, if the leaders just would have done. . ." Leaders defended themselves by saying, "Well, if the team could stop squabbling, we could. . ." The conflict was ripe with dissension—the antithesis of what Christ wants for the body of Christ.

Regrouping, the members spent time in prayer. The Word reminded them to make every effort to preserve the unity, be diligent, work hard, and strive earnestly for oneness. Harmony with others isn't always easy. Differences can chafe at patience. Grievances may need to be delayed until a proper time. Restraint from pressing one's own agenda may need to be exercised. A willed choice of acting in love is needed instead of a rash response that may feel good at the time but further divide the group. Only when peace is restored can believers experience how good and pleasant it is to dwell in unity.

Prince of Peace, help me to make unity my focus. Enable me to make
every effort to preserve oneness with fellow believers. Then with
one heart and one mouth we can glorify You. Amen.

A Little Time
with God

"I thank You and praise You, O God of my fathers;
You have given me wisdom and might."
DANIEL 2:23 NKJV

*S*usan headed out of her house in the same way she always did—in a hurry, guiding two children before her, double-checking their backpacks as she went and reminding them of chores and practices scheduled for that afternoon. "Remember, 3:30 is ballet; 4:00 is soccer. I'll pick you up school, but I have to go back to work, so—"

She stopped as her coat snagged on a bush. "What?—" She looked down to find her hem caught firmly by a cluster of thorns. As she stooped to untangle the cloth, the stem bent suddenly, and Susan found herself nose-to-petal with a rose. It smelled glorious, and she paused, laughing.

When Susan had planted the bush, a friend had asked why. "You never stop long enough to enjoy even what God drops in front of you. What makes you think you'll care about a rose?"

Susan glanced up toward the sky. "Thanks for grabbing me. I guess I should spend a little more time with You."

God blesses us every day in both great and simple ways. Children, friends, work, faith—all these things form a bountiful buffet of gifts, and caring for them isn't always enough. We need to spend a little time with the One who has granted us the blessings.

Father God, You have given us so much to be grateful for. Show me a way to
spend more time with You, and help me to grow closer and know You better.
Amen.

One Day at a Time

Blessed be the Lord, who daily loadeth us with benefits,
even the God of our salvation.
PSALM 68:19 KJV

*T*here's a reason why the Lord's Prayer teaches us to ask for daily bread. We tend to forget about yesterday's provision in the crunch of today's needs. God calls us to a childlike faith, one that basks in the provisions of the moment and forgets yesterday's disappointments and tomorrow's worries.

Think about small children. A toddler may cry when another child knocks him down and takes away his ball. The tears disappear when his mother hugs him and gives him a kiss. His joy in the expression of his mother's love obliterates his disappointment about the toy. Later he returns to the ball with fresh enthusiasm. He lives in the moment.

God always provides for us. Benefits overflow the shopping carts of our lives every single day. But He only gives us what we need for today, not for tomorrow. He knows that we need those benefits like a daily vitamin. By tomorrow, even later today, we may forget all that God has done for us. The Bible verse that spoke to us this morning feels empty by afternoon.

God gives us blessings every day so that we still have what we need after we have spent ourselves on life's disappointments.

Father, You give us bread daily. We praise You for Your constant care and ask
that You will train our eyes to focus on Your blessings, not on our failings.
Amen.

COMFORTINGLY CLOSE

The LORD is close to the brokenhearted;
he rescues those whose spirits are crushed.
PSALM 34:18 NLT

*J*anice walked into the room full of people, still shaken from the death of her father. Her mind was filled with the memory of his laughing face; her hand yearned for his touch. Barely a day went by when she wasn't welling up with tears at some reminder of him. *When will this pain end?* she wondered.

As Janice continued across the room, she realized that everyone had stopped talking. She looked up, and the others turned away, as if they were embarrassed, not knowing what to say or do.

Janice longed for someone to say something, anything. To act normal whether she smiled or cried. She needed so much comfort. To whom could she turn? Then Janice heard a voice. *"Turn to Me, child. I am here. I am always here. Take My hand. I long to comfort you."*

When others turn away from us, we know we can always rely on our eternal Father, the One who will never leave or forsake us. He is close to us in the best and the worst of times. He rescues us when we are crushed. Take His hand. Rest in His arms. Let Him love you.

God, thank You for always being there. Heal my broken heart,
my crushed spirit. Hold my hand in Yours. With every breath I take,
may I know You are right here beside me, loving me. Amen.

NOTHING BUT THE TRUTH

God is not a man, that he should lie; neither the son of man,
that he should repent: hath he said, and shall he not do it?
or hath he spoken, and shall he not make it good?
NUMBERS 23:19 KJV

*B*alaam, a professional enchanter, had been summoned by Balak, the worried king of Moab. Balak feared the huge company of Israelites who had just wiped out the Amorites. Now they were pitching their tents in his country! Balak figured that Balaam could provide the supernatural help needed to get rid of them.

However, Balaam and his donkey had just encountered God's angel holding a sword. The donkey understood, but it took Balaam a while to comprehend God's warning. He meant to bless Israel, not curse them. Balaam told his employer, "Even if you give me your house full of silver and gold, I must say what God wants. I must bless Israel!"

When the desperate king took him to three different places to perform a curse on Israel, Balaam's message did not change—because it was God's message: He would bless His people. Those who worshipped idols, including Balak and the Moabites, would fall.

Unlike the words of human beings, God's words can be trusted. What a comfort to know He who has promised us salvation, strength for daily living, and a glorious future means what He says!

Holy Lord, in a day when truth is hard to find,
You won't change Your mind about me. Thank You! Amen.

INFINITE AND PERSONAL

Am I a God at hand, saith the LORD, and not a God afar off? . . .
Do not I fill heaven and earth?
JEREMIAH 23:23–24 KJV

*B*ack in the 1950s, the Union of Soviet Socialist Republics sent up its first satellite, *Sputnik*. At that time, communism held Russia in its tightfisted grip. Everyone who was anyone in the USSR was a communist and an atheist. Not long after *Sputnik*, the Russian cosmonauts circled planet Earth. After their return to earth, one cosmonaut made this announcement to the world: "I saw no God anywhere."

When U.S. astronauts finally made it into space some months later, one remarked, "I saw God everywhere!"

Our worldview determines the way we see reality. The cosmonaut didn't expect to see God, and he didn't. The astronaut didn't see anything more or less than his Russian counterpart, but he came away with an entirely different response. God says that He is both close at hand and over all there is. The late theologian and philosopher Francis Schaeffer called Him the infinite-personal God.

Whether your day is crumbling around you or is the best day you have ever had, do you see God in it? If the "sky is falling" or the sun is shining, do you still recognize the One who orders all the planets and all your days? Whether we see Him or not, God tells us He is there. And He's here too—in the good times and bad.

Lord, empower me to trust You when it's hard to remember that You are near.
And help me to live thankfully when times are good. Amen.

GODLY LIVING IN A GODLESS WORLD

For the grace of God that bringeth salvation hath appeared to all men, teaching us that, denying ungodliness and worldly lusts, we should live soberly, righteously, and godly, in this present world.
TITUS 2:11–12 KJV

One of the most difficult tasks mothers have in the twenty-first century is teaching children godliness. How can we hope to swim even a yard against the rising tide of materialism, self-centeredness, and self-indulgence that has swept over the world?

We cannot go to a mall without being bombarded by ungodliness and worldly lusts. Innocence vanishes at the first lingerie store. The ubiquitous television and vile cable channels are a constant threat, as is the Internet with its "perversion on demand."

What's a woman to do?

Some have tried separation through home education. Others have cut the cable and filtered the Internet. Some avoid malls.

This is not enough. Keeping children unstained from the world alone will not foster godliness. Godliness comes from within, from a deep desire to please and obey our Lord. It is developed in children by careful, consistent training. Children must learn to obey parents, first time, every time, so that their hearts are ready to obey Christ.

Such training takes time and commitment. But it is our best investment against the ungodliness of the world.

Father, I put too much emphasis on the externals. I think that keeping the world out will develop godliness within. Give me the strength to do the hard job of consistently training my children in obedience. Let me give them a pattern of obedience to follow. Amen.

TOUGH FAITH

These people of faith died not yet having in hand what was promised, but still believing. How did they do it? They saw it way off in the distance, waved their greeting, and accepted the fact that they were transients in this world.
HEBREWS 11:13 THE MESSAGE

Sometimes Renee felt that she could not stand one more day of her complicated life. Her husband, Tony, spent Sundays racing stock cars instead of going to church. Their daughter struggled at school. Renee had run out of ideas to help her. Although Renee's siblings lived nearby, too, her elderly parents always seemed to call Renee for a ride to the doctor's office. Even the dog dragged his dish to her! Renee tried hard to balance her days in a godly way. Whatever happened to the abundant life that was supposed to be hers as a Christian?

Renee—and most of us—want to identify with the triumphant heroes listed in Hebrews 11, the "Faith Chapter." God protected them as they succeeded in doing great things for Him. We would rather forget others mentioned who did not achieve their goals during their lifetimes, suffering injustice and hardship. But God has not forgotten them—or Renee and other heroines who faithfully follow Him. They may see few results from their obedience, but their great reward will last an eternity.

Father, when I am sick and tired of doing good, help me to say good-bye to earthly expectations and wave hello to Your forever love. Amen.

BE STILL

Be still, and know that I am God.
PSALM 46:10 NIV

From the minute the alarm clock goes off in the morning, we are busy. Many women rush off to work or begin their tasks around the house without even eating breakfast. Most of us keep hectic schedules, and it is easy to let the day pass by without a moment of peace and quiet.

In Psalm 46:10 the command to *be still* is coupled with the result of *knowing that He is God*. Could it be that in order to truly recognize God's presence in our lives, we must make time to quiet ourselves before Him?

Sitting quietly before the Lord is a discipline that requires practice. Just as in our earthly relationships, learning to be a good listener as we converse with our heavenly Father is important. If prayer remains one-sided, we will miss out on what He has to say to us.

Although God may not speak to us in an audible voice, He will direct our thinking and speak to our hearts. Stillness allows us to dwell on God's sovereignty, His goodness, and His deep love for us. He wants us to remember that He is God and that He is in control, regardless of our circumstances.

Be still. . .and know that He is God.

God, so often I do all the talking.
Quiet me before You now.
Speak to my heart, I pray. Amen.

THINKING OF OTHERS

Do nothing out of selfish ambition or vain conceit, but in humility consider others better than yourselves. Each of you should look not only to your own interests, but also to the interests of others.
PHILIPPIANS 2:3–4 NIV

The apostle Paul, along with Timothy, founded the church at Philippi. Paul's relationship with this church was always close. The book of Philippians is a letter he wrote to this church while he was imprisoned for preaching the gospel.

Paul knew the Philippians had been struggling with jealousy and rivalry. He encouraged them in his letter to think of others. He reminded them that this was the attitude of Jesus, who took on the role of a servant and humbled Himself for us, even to His death on the cross.

In the final chapter of Philippians, we read the well-known verse that says, "I can do everything through him who gives me strength" (Philippians 4:13 NIV). We can do *everything* through Christ Jesus who gives us strength. That includes putting others before ourselves. That includes replacing "I deserve. . ." with "How can I serve?"

When you start to look out for "number one," remember that your God is looking out for you. You are His precious daughter. As you allow Him to take care of you, it will free up space in your heart and allow you to look to the needs of others.

Father, You have made me to be a part of something much larger than myself. Focus my attention on those around me and not only on my own needs. Amen.

REFRESHING GIFT

For we have great joy and consolation in your love,
because the hearts of the saints have been refreshed by you, brother.
PHILEMON 1:7 NKJV

*U*nsure whether she could continue in the race, the woman looked ahead. A small stand wasn't far down the road. She could see the line of cups at the edge of the table—drinks set out to refresh the runners. The sight encouraged her enough to give her the needed confidence to finish the race.

Encouragement is a wonderful gift. Simple gestures mean so much to those around us. We don't have to make big, splashy scenes to give someone a boost. Our smile can lift someone who is discouraged. A sincere thank-you or a quick hug conveys a wealth of love, gratitude, and appreciation. We all have the opportunity to make small overtures to those around us.

Jesus always took the time for those who reached out to Him. In a crowd of people, He stopped to help a woman who touched him. His quiet love extended to everyone who asked, whether verbally or with unspoken need.

God brings people into our path who need our encouragement. We must consider those around us. Smile and thank the waitress, the cashier, the people who help in small ways. Cheering others can have the effect of an energizing drink of water so that they will be able to finish the race with a smile.

Jesus, thank You for being an example of how to encourage and refresh others.
Help me to see their need and to be willing to reach out. Amen.

WALK AND PRAY

And pray in the Spirit on all occasions with all kinds of prayers and requests.
With this in mind, be alert and always keep on praying for all the saints.
EPHESIANS 6:18 NIV

Their friendship began when their daughters played on the same soccer team. Leaning against their cars, they chatted and waited for practice to end, both realizing after a couple of conversations that they had more in common than two energetic thirteen-year-old girls. They shared a common faith in God, and both women were experiencing the growing pains that come with parenting adolescents.

One day the women decided to start wearing their workout gear to practice so that they could talk and pray for their daughters as they walked the perimeter of the soccer field. By the end of the season, both women were encouraged and strengthened, and they had forged a deep friendship. The added bonus was their increased fitness levels derived from these long walks.

Jesus said, "For where two or three come together in my name, there am I with them" (Matthew 18:20 NIV). Real power is available when friends get together for fellowship and prayer, because Christ Himself is right there with them. Along with gaining another's insight and perspective, anytime we share a burden with a friend, our load instantly becomes lighter.

Is there a friend you might call today to join you in a prayer walk?

Heavenly Father, thank You for faithful friends,
and thank You for Jesus, the most faithful friend of all. Amen.

MUTUAL DELIGHT SOCIETY

He brought me forth also into a large place:
he delivered me, because he delighted in me.
2 SAMUEL 22:20 KJV

$\mathcal{D}$id you know you are part of a mutual delight society? If you're a Christian, God delights in you, and you delight in Him, too (Psalm 37:4). Over and over, scripture refers to this two-sided enjoyment. How could anyone, believer or not, have missed it?

Sadly, non-Christians don't understand this mutual-delight organization. They think Christians spend their time moping and complaining or sitting in church. All they can see are the things Christians don't do and no longer enjoy or the things they, as unbelievers, wouldn't like doing. The faithless miss out on the larger picture: Sin is no longer fun for those who delight in God. It's more wonderful to live for Him than engage in the sin.

If a sliver of the light of Christian joy pierces the unbelievers' lives, Satan blocks it so they can't see what they might be missing. He can't let them know that loving God can be fun!

The one who delights in God has God delighting in her, too. His plans for her future are beautiful because she has experienced His salvation. No good thing will He deny her (though her definition of a good thing and His may differ at times).

Do you delight in God? Then share the news. Help others join this mutual delight society today.

Thank You, Lord, for inviting me to share Your delights. Amen.

GIVE THANKS

"Give thanks to God. . . . Shout to the nations, tell them what he's done, spread the news of his great reputation!"
ISAIAH 12:3 THE MESSAGE

*C*ommon courtesy grows more uncommon in our society with the passing of each generation. Finding someone who puts others first and uses words like *please* and *thank you* is like finding a rare gem. Most people hurry to their next task with little thought of others crossing their paths.

Every favor and earthly blessing that we experience is given to us by God. It is nothing we have accomplished in our own right. All that God has done since the beginning of creation, He did for humankind. You are His greatest treasure.

Give thanks to God today for giving you life—the very air you breathe. He has given you the ability to make a living, to feed your family, and to give to others. He is a good Father—he won't withhold anything good from you.

What has God done for you lately? What doors of opportunity has He opened? Give Him the credit, tell others of His goodness, and thank Him! It blesses God to hear you express your gratitude, and it will do your heart good as well.

God, I am thankful for all You have given me and for who You made me to be. Help me to have a grateful heart and to express my appreciation to You in everything! Amen.

No-Compromise Lifestyle

*"Turn from all your evil ways.
Obey my commands and decrees."*
2 KINGS 17:13 NLT

*O*bedience is a long walk in the same direction. Flirtation with sin is like wandering in aimless circles. Each public or private action, no matter how large or small, plays a key role in moving you either toward or away from personal integrity, an intact marriage, healthy friendships, joyful and productive collegiality, and harmony in your relationship with God.

Disobedience is an age-old problem. Just read through 2 Kings. Over and over, kings did evil in the sight of the Lord and suffered grave consequences (see, *e.g.*, 15:5). Amid a long string of evil kings, we periodically read with relief about kings who did do "right in the sight of the LORD." However, they still failed to remove the "high places" or altars of sacrifice to foreign gods (see, *e.g.*, 15:3–4). So, as it turns out, the "almost good" kings were only "almost obedient," and "almost obedient" behavior doesn't cut it with the Lord.

Though the Lord saved His people from Egypt and provided guidelines for living, He warned His people over and over again against offending Him. He defined righteous behavior and forbade worship of idols. However, the people "stiffened their necks" and stubbornly would not listen. The consequence was that the Lord removed His people from His sight (2 Kings 17:7–18). God requires a no-compromise lifestyle.

*Oh Lord, forgive me. You know the evil in my heart,
my shortcomings, my failures. Help me live a life of integrity
and moral purity, a no-compromise lifestyle. Amen.*

JUST SAY NO

Submit yourselves therefore to God.
Resist the devil, and he will flee from you.
JAMES 4:7 KJV

The antidrug slogan "Just say no" sounds easy. Yet if that is the case, why are so many people addicted to drugs? For the same reason we struggle with sin. Temptation is great. We are weak. An adversary is out to destroy us, but our hearts will be encouraged as we focus on greater truth.

Jesus defeated Satan at the cross when He died and rose victorious. He imparts that same resurrection power to us. But although the battle has been won, Satan attempts to convince us otherwise. Jesus called Satan the "father of lies" because lying is Satan's primary weapon. We must learn to recognize his subtle attacks on our thoughts. We must choose to listen to God's truth instead of embracing Satan's lies.

Bank tellers learn how to detect counterfeit money by handling large amounts of real money. In the same way, we need to immerse ourselves in God's Word and prayer, which show us how to discern God's voice and recognize the counterfeit. When confronted by our enemy, we need not retreat in fear. We can resist him and stand firm by God's power. Satan must flee in defeat. Let's "just say no" to Satan and say yes to the Lord!

Dear Lord, thank You for the truth of Your Word.
Help me resist the devil by embracing You. Amen.

WEARY DAYS

Why art thou cast down, O my soul? and why art thou disquieted in me? hope thou in God: for I shall yet praise him for the help of his countenance. O my God, my soul is cast down within me: therefore will I remember thee from the land of Jordan, and of the Hermonites, from the hill Mizar.
PSALM 42:5–6 KJV

*I*t's easy for life's responsibilities and commitments to drag us down. Each day seems like a repeat of the day before. The morning alarm becomes our enemy, and the snooze button becomes our considerate companion. Our hard work often goes unappreciated. Nothing feels accomplished. Our souls yearn for something more.

If we accept it, God's constant goodness can be our delight. In the mornings, instead of our groaning and hiding beneath the pillows, God desires for us to communicate with Him. His voice could be the first one that we hear each day. As we roll over and stretch, we can then say, "I love you, God. Thank You for another day of life."

Our willingness to speak with God at the day's beginning shows our dependence on Him. We can't make it alone. It is a comforting truth that God never intended for us to trek through the hours unaccompanied. He promises to be with us. He also promises His guidance and direction as we meet people and receive opportunities to serve Him.

Getting started is as simple as removing our heads from beneath the pillows and telling God good morning.

Lord, refresh my spirit and give me joy for today's activities. Amen.

RELEASE THE
MUSIC WITHIN

Those who are wise will find a time and a way to do what is right.
ECCLESIASTES 8:5 NLT

*M*iss Lilly is a talented woman. Without the luxury of taking one lesson, she plays the violin with grace and ease. Her oil paintings exude warmth, character, and charm. And her ability to retain information would challenge a twenty-year-old college student. But in her eighty years, Lilly has merely dabbled in the gifts God has entrusted to her.

"Never had the time, and too late to start!" she insists, as she discusses her unfulfilled dreams and what she would do differently if she could "do it all over again." So her talents are undeveloped, unused, and unappreciated by a world waiting for Lilly's God-given abilities to touch, bless, and stir them.

It has been said that many people go to their graves with their music still in them. Do you carry a song within your heart, waiting to be heard?

Whether we are eight or eighty, it is never too late to surrender our hopes and dreams to God. A wise woman trusts that God will help her find the time and manner in which to use her talents for His glory as she seeks His direction.

Let the music begin.

Dear Lord, my music is fading against the constant beat of a busy pace.
I surrender my gifts to You and pray for the time and manner
in which I can use those gifts to touch my world. Amen.

No Unfinished Business

My cup runs over.
PSALM 23:5 NKJV

*A*n elderly man was admitted to the hospital after experiencing symptoms of a heart attack. His doctor was making preparations for surgery to repair some of the damage to his heart when the elderly man spoke up and said, "I don't want surgery. I want to go home!"

The doctor laughed, thinking he was a little "out of his head," when the elderly man's daughter spoke up. "Doctor, my dad is a Christian." And pointing up, she continued, "He wants to go to his heavenly home."

The doctor was silent for a moment and then said to the daughter, "Well, you'd better get the rest of the kids in here for any unfinished business with their dad." The elderly man looked at the doctor and smiled, "I have had a wonderful life filled with God's goodness and love. I have five children, and we have no unfinished business between us. There are no regrets, unspoken words, or need for forgiveness. My children all know I love them. They all have a strong relationship with the Creator of heaven and earth. One day we will all be together again."

Imagine living your life with no need to discuss unfinished business with anyone.

Lord, help me to live each day with a pure heart and love for others so that I can rest each day knowing that I have no unfinished business. Amen.

IT'S ALL GOOD

And we know that all things work together for good to them that love God,
to them who are the called according to his purpose.
ROMANS 8:28 KJV

*B*arren for life. A seventeen-year-old girl received news from her doctor that she would never conceive children. Questions flooded her mind: What guy would want to marry me? What about my love of children? Yet amid the questions came a gentle whisper: "We know that all things work together for good to them that love God." She didn't understand how, but she trusted the Lord to fulfill His promise. He did. Over the next thirty years, she became a wife, a mother, and a grandmother.

God can and does use all things in our lives for His good purpose. Remember Joseph in the cistern, Daniel in the lions' den, and Jesus on the cross? The Lord demonstrated His resurrection power in each of those cases. He does so in our lives as well. He brings forth beauty from ashes.

What are you facing that seems impossible? What situation appears hopeless? What circumstance is overwhelming you? Believe God's promise. It is easy to trust God when things are going well. And when we choose to trust Him in uncertain times, we receive a peace that gives us hope that sustains us. We are not disappointed, because God always keeps His promises. Our response is to trust Him.

Dear Lord, thank You that You work all things together for Your good purpose.
May I trust You to fulfill Your purpose in my life. Amen.

SAY WHAT?

Don't fool yourself into thinking that you are a listener when you are anything but, letting the Word go in one ear and out the other. Act on what you hear!
JAMES 1:22 THE MESSAGE

$\mathcal{H}$ave you ever been introduced to someone and immediately forgotten the person's name? Similarly, have you ever tried to talk to someone who is engrossed in a television show? "Yeah, I'm listening," the person replies in a less-than-attentive voice.

James seems to be in a similar situation. He is frustrated by those who pretend to listen and yet do not apply what they have heard. Like a person who sits through a speech and afterward cannot list the main points, so the people to whom James writes have heard the Word of God and cannot—or will not—apply it.

So often we find ourselves tuning out the minister on Sunday morning or thinking about other things as we read our Bibles or sing hymns of praise. We look up at the end of a sermon, a stanza, a chapter, and we don't know what we've heard, sung, or read. We pretend to hear, but we are really letting the Word of God go in one ear and out the other. Our minds must be disciplined to really listen to God's Word. Then we must do the more difficult thing—*act* on what we've finally heard.

Dear Lord, please teach me to be attentive to Your Word. Help me to act on the things You teach me so that mine becomes a practical faith. Amen.

A SACRIFICIAL LIFE

"There is no greater love than to lay down one's life for one's friends."
JOHN 15:13 NLT

Jesus, our Lord, took the form of a human and humbled Himself in coming to earth, not to be served, but to serve (Philippians 2:6–8). In fact, Christ showed His love for us in that while we were still sinners, He died for us (Romans 5:8). We may not be called to literally lay down our lives for someone, but we all are called to lay down our lives in sacrificing our needs and desires for others.

Christ modeled for us daily how to live this sacrificial life. Is there someone in your life today who needs a word of encouragement, a listening ear, or God's truth spoken over her or him? Does someone need a meal prepared, an errand run, a lawn mowed? What physical acts of service can you do for someone in need today?

Serving others may mean that you won't be able to accomplish all the tasks you have on your to-do list. It may mean that you miss lunch because you are running an errand during your lunch break. It may mean that you go to bed late. Whatever the acts of love are, you can be assured that you are modeling this sacrificial life of laying down your own life for the good of others. In living this sacrificial life, you can be certain that Jesus is saying, "Well done, good and faithful servant!" (Matthew 25:21–23).

Lord Jesus, in an effort to follow Your example,
show me someone for whom I can lay down my life today. Amen.

Pack Up!

The Lord had said to Abram, "Leave your native country, your relatives,
and your father's family, and go to the land that I will show you. . . .
I will bless you. . .and you will be a blessing to others."
GENESIS 12:1–2 NLT

"Honey, we're moving!" Kayla's husband called to tell her. His company had offered him a big promotion—in another state. Her response? Fat, sloppy tears. She hoped her weeping would change his mind.

Kayla ended up loving her new home.

In God's wisdom, He likes to shake us up a little, stretch us out of our comfort zone, push us out on a limb. Yet we resist the change, cling to what's known, and try to change His mind with fat, sloppy tears.

God seems to have a fondness for change. His first words to Abram were, "Get packing. Say good-bye to your pals in glitzy Ur. I have something better in mind for you" (my paraphrase).

Are you facing a big change? It might not be a change of address. It could be running for a seat on the school board or going on a short-term mission trip. God wants us to be willing to embrace change that He brings into our lives. Even unbidden change. You may feel as if you're out on a limb, but don't forget that God is the tree trunk. He's not going to let you fall.

Holy, loving Father, in every area of my life,
teach me to trust You more deeply. Amen.

CHOOSING WISELY

Our mouths were filled with laughter.
PSALM 126:2 NIV

*A*manda stared glumly at the rock-hard turkey parked on the kitchen counter. She'd miscalculated defrosting time; it was now Thanksgiving morning, and the entrée of honor was still obstinately ossified.

The twenty-two-pound bird was too large for the microwave, so she tried the blow dryer. Warm air only deflected into her face from the turkey's impenetrable skin. Dunking the bird in a warm bathtub merely cooled the water down, leaving dinner's main course as nonpliable as a cement block.

In a rush of frantic desperation, Amanda grabbed the toolbox from the garage and whacked the turkey with a hammer. It only jarred her budding headache into full bloom.

Lunch was at noon. Guests would soon be arriving. What to do?

We women often plan perfect family events, only to find out how imperfectly things can turn out. The soufflé falls, the cat leaps onto the counter and licks the cheese ball, little Johnny drops Aunt Martha's crystal gravy dish (full of gravy, of course). Our reactions to these surprise glitches can make or break the event for everyone present. Mom's foul mood sucks the joy from the room.

The Bible says that Sarah laughed at the most unexpected, traumatic time of her life—when God announced that she would have a baby at the age of ninety (Genesis 18:12). At this unforeseen turn of events, she could either laugh, cry, or run away screaming.

She chose to laugh.

Lord, give us an extra dollop of grace and peace to laugh about unexpected dilemmas that pop up. And to remember that our reaction is a choice. Amen.

DISASTER!

*I will take refuge in the shadow of your
wings until the disaster has passed.*
PSALM 57:1 NIV

Natural disasters bring about a host of responses from people. Understandably, many individuals weep and mourn. Others look for the silver lining or even some humor in devastation. That was the response of Charlie Jones.

He found his office underwater. Records, machinery, data, personal items—all of it—ruined by flooding. He didn't cry. He didn't scream. He didn't curse. He said he did what most grown men in his situation would do.

He began to suck his thumb.

In that moment, he said later, he heard the voice of God.

"It's okay, Charlie. I was gonna burn it all anyway."

We find little good in the premature loss of things that harbor dear memories for us. But God's Word is filled with promises of renewal and restoration. We may not see it today or next month or even ten years from now. Nevertheless, our Lord's name is Redeemer. He alone can and will redeem the valuable, the precious, the everlastingly worthwhile.

If we find no comfort in the words God whispered to Charlie, we have a sure Word of God that we can hold on to in our tears. "In all their distress he too was distressed" (Isaiah 63:9 NIV).

Lord, You are in control of all things. When I'm overwhelmed with terrible events in my life, draw me close to You for the help I so desperately need. Amen.

DARKNESS
INTO LIGHT

*We can rejoice, too, when we run into problems and trials, for we know
that they help us develop endurance. And endurance develops strength of
character, and character strengthens our confident hope of salvation.*
ROMANS 5:3–4 NLT

When anything unexpected, painful, or trying comes our way, our
first reaction is to run from it. Whether it's an illness, job loss, strained
friendship, or even the everyday challenges that sneak up, we want to find
the quickest way out.

Imagine a person who is afraid of the dark watching a sunset. The
sky darkens and the light fades. Facing her biggest fear, the person
attempts to chase after the sun. But the earth is moving too quickly,
and no one could ever avoid night completely.

Fortunately, we have a loving God who promises to stay beside us
through the darkness. Even though night does come, the quickest way to
see the morning is to take God's hand and walk through the hard times.
In the morning, the sun rises and the darkness fades, but God is still
there.

God never promised that our lives would be easy, but He did
promise that He would always be with us—in the darkness and all
through the night.

*God, thank You for being a constant source
of comfort and dependability in my life. Amen.*

AN EMPTY PROMISE?

Pray without ceasing.
I THESSALONIANS 5:17 NASB

J'll pray for you." Much of the time this is an empty promise.

From the pulpit a pastor once apologized to his congregation for using that empty promise as a way to end long conversations or to fill the void when he had run out of good advice. One day he realized that he rarely actually followed through with prayer. His habits proved either that he didn't have much faith in prayer or that he didn't love and serve his people as he was called to do.

While that must have been a very difficult admission for that sweet, old pastor, it also must have been deeply cleansing and freeing to admit to his human inadequacies. Also, the people who were affected naturally would have been convicted of their own lack of prayer commitment and the insincerity of their own empty promises to pray.

We need to see prayer as the greatest gift we can give, not as a last-ditch effort. Promising that you will keep others in your prayers means that you will continue to pray for them, without ceasing, until you hear of a resolution to their problem. "I'll pray for you" are words that offer hope and life to people who are hurting.

Dear Jesus, please forgive me for all the times I promised prayers in vain, never intending to follow through. Thank You for being bigger than my weaknesses and for meeting needs despite my failures. Call to mind the people I need to bring before Your throne each day. Amen.

GOD'S CURE FOR DISAPPOINTMENT

A man has joy in an apt answer, and how delightful is a timely word!
PROVERBS 15:23 NASB

*H*urts often are soothed with the rich love found in our relationships with others. When a friend faces disappointment, we naturally want to make it better for her. A wonderful way to do that is to offer comfort—an understanding smile, a warm hug, or a few words of affirmation. Maybe she just needs someone who will listen as a gesture of support.

Comfort is not counsel. A friend may not be looking to us to solve the problem or offer advice. She may simply need a shoulder to cry on, a hand to hold, and a heart that desires to understand. She is looking for a strong spiritual relationship in friends she can trust.

Comfort is God's cure for disappointment. Maybe we don't understand exactly what a friend is going through, but we can offer comfort by being honest—letting them know we have never experienced their situation, but we are there to walk with them through the storm and hold them up when they feel weak.

Lord, help me to be aware of the needs of others and help me to find the words to reach out to them. Amen.

Light in the Darkness

*I will lead blind Israel down a new path, guiding them along
an unfamiliar way. I will brighten the darkness before them
and smooth out the road ahead of them.*
ISAIAH 42:16 NLT

In the dim moonlight, we can sometimes find our way in the darkness
of our homes. In familiar places we know the lay of the land. At best we
will make our way around the obstacles through memory and shadowy
outline. At worst, we will lightly stumble into an armchair or a piano
bench. When all else fails, we know where the light switch is and,
blindly groping in the darkness, we can turn on the light to help us
find our way.

But when we walk in the darkness of unfamiliar places, we may
feel unsettled. Not sure of our bearings, not knowing where the light
switch is, we become overwhelmed, afraid to step forward, afraid even
to move. At those times, we need to remember that our God of light is
always with us. Although we may not see Him, we can rest easy, knowing
He is ever-present in the darkness of unknown places, opportunities,
and challenges.

God will never leave us to find our way alone. Realize this truth
and arm yourself with the knowledge that no matter what the situation,
no matter what the trial, no matter how black the darkness, He is ever
there, reaching out for us, helping us find our way. Switch on the light
of His truth in your mind, and walk forward, knowing He is always
within reach.

*Lord, be my Light. Guard me in the darkness of these days.
Make my way straight and the ground I trod smooth.
And if I do stumble, catch me! In Jesus' name, I pray. Amen.*

TREASURES, TIME, AND TALENTS

The children of Israel brought a willing offering unto the LORD, every man and woman, whose heart made them willing to bring for all manner of work, which the LORD had commanded to be made by the hand of Moses.
EXODUS 35:29 KJV

After the Israelites' exodus from Egypt, God showed Moses His plan for an enormous project: the tabernacle. This finely crafted tent would serve as a worship center for His people, reminding them that God dwelt among them.

Many rich materials were needed for its construction and furnishings. When Moses asked for donations, thousands of Israelites came forward with their dearest treasures: gold, silver, bronze, precious stones, acacia wood, spices, olive oil, and incense. Others brought dyed ram skins and sea cow hides for the outer covering of the tabernacle.

Women in those days led very busy lives caring for large extended families—with no McDonald's nearby! Nevertheless, many volunteered to spin blue, purple, and scarlet yarn to be used in embroidered curtains that comprised the tabernacle's walls. Hours of their handiwork also helped create the exquisite garments to be worn by the priests. Other women spun fine linen for the courtyard walls, the perimeter of which would measure approximately 450 feet around the tabernacle.

Despite their heavy daily responsibilities, these women freely offered their time and skills to make something beautiful for God.

Lord, some days I feel fortunate to even brush my teeth! But even in my busiest moments, please help me use all I possess to worship You. Amen.

ASK FOR DIRECTIONS

Day 335

The wicked in his proud countenance does not seek God;
God is in none of his thoughts.
PSALM 10:4 NKJV

$\mathcal{D}$o the laundry, wash the dishes, shop for groceries, cook dinner, work a full day, drive the kids to soccer practice, the list of a busy woman's duties goes on and on. Entwined within those chores are the mental challenges of making wise decisions, dealing with relationships, raising the kids well—again, the list goes on.

Somewhere along the way we got the idea that it is wrong to ask for help. But you can't live the Christian life like that. It's impossible. You can't possibly forge through life alone, managing to make wise decisions while you resist temptations and recover from failures. If you don't ask for help, you won't stand a chance.

Women often tease that men would rather drive around lost for hours instead of stopping to ask for directions. But how often, in your own day, do you stop for a moment and ask the Father for directions? Jesus, knowing that He needed guidance from His Father, constantly sought His will by praying and asking for it. Instead of trying to find His own way through the day, Jesus fully depended on directions from above and actively pursued them.

Jesus, forgive me for my pride and for not asking You for directions.
Please show me the way to go and lead me in it. Help me to
hear Your leading and then to follow it. Amen.

THE GREAT
GIFT GIVER

*Every good and perfect gift is from above, coming down from the Father
of the heavenly lights, who does not change like shifting shadows.*
JAMES 1:17 NIV

Do you know a true gift giver? We all give gifts on birthdays and at Christmas, when we receive wedding invitations, and when a baby is born. But do you know someone with a real knack for gift giving? She finds all sorts of excuses for giving gifts. She delights in it. A true gift giver has an ability to locate that "something special." When shopping for a gift, she examines many items before making her selection. She knows the interests and preferences, the tastes and favorites of her friends and family members. She chooses gifts they will like—gifts that suit them well.

God is a gift giver. He is, in fact, the Creator of all good gifts. He finds great joy in blessing you. The God who made you certainly knows you by name. He knows your tastes and preferences. He even knows your favorites and your dreams. Most important, God knows your needs.

So in seasons of waiting in your life, rest assured that gifts chosen and presented to you by the hand of God will be worth the wait.

*God, sometimes I am anxious. I want what I want, and I want it now.
Calm my spirit and give me the patience to wait for Your perfect gifts. Amen.*

TOO MUCH INFORMATION

The wise don't make a show of their knowledge,
but fools broadcast their foolishness.
PROVERBS 12:23 NLT

 $\mathscr{I}$ ve missed seeing Brad around church," Nicole casually mentioned to her friend, Ashley. "I've seen Julie and the kids but not Brad."

"Brad's struggling with a spiritual issue," Ashley said. "Be sure to keep him in your prayers."

Nicole did, especially since she continued to see Julie but no Brad.

Nicole went to have her nails done several days later. Her manicurist, who was another friend from her church, whispered, "Did you know that Julie's husband, Brad, was caught with porn on his office computer?"

After that, Nicole had more trouble praying for Brad. She could pray for Brad who had a spiritual struggle, but she struggled to pray for a friend who indulged in pornography. In less than a dozen words, she had gotten more information than she wanted—or needed.

Urban adages echo proverbs like the one above. "You don't need to tell everything you know" is how we often hear it. To receive a prayer request without a lot of detail is not a bad thing. Lurid details invite gossip. In painfully private situations, the less information shared, the better—both for those praying and those being prayed for. Sharing of information, even in asking for prayer support, calls for discernment. Knowing not only what to say but when to say it shows us to be wise women.

Give me discernment, Lord, as to when I
should speak and when I should keep quiet. Amen.

FORGIVENESS HURTS

*"And forgive us our debts, as we
also have forgiven our debtors."*
MATTHEW 6:12 NASB

$\mathcal{N}$o one likes being wronged. Whether it's being cut off in traffic by a careless driver, gossiped about by a thoughtless friend, or hurt more deeply, we all have unresolved pain. A common feeling is to want the other person to experience the same pain we felt. Sometimes we follow through on our retaliation; other times no action is taken, but quiet festering and imagining takes place in our minds. We want payback!

Unknown to us, the other person may not realize (or even care) that the wrong had such an effect on us. Sometimes we try to be the "bigger person" and resolve the issue. Other times that person might not want to address the issue, let alone claim any responsibility.

So what do we do? God says that we can do our part to examine the situation, acknowledge our responsibility, and attempt to move forward even if we don't receive an "I'm sorry." We may not forget the issue, but our stress, anxiety, and anger will be lessened because the issue will no longer be our focus. We will once again have the opportunity to live in and enjoy the present rather than concentrate on the past.

God chose to save us by sending His Son. The world reacted to this by abusing and killing Him. The next time hurt springs up, remember that God can especially relate to our feelings of being wronged.

*Lord, thank You for forgiving my sins. Help me
to forgive and love others as You love me. Amen.*

LEAD GOOSE

Jethro replied: That isn't the best way to do it. You and the people who come to you will soon be worn out. The job is too much for one person; you can't do it alone.
EXODUS 18:17–18 CEV

The V formation of flying geese is a fascinating example of aero-dynamics. Each bird flies slightly above the bird in front of it, resulting in a reduction of wind resistance. It also helps to conserve the geese's energy. The farther back a goose is in formation, the less energy it needs in the flight. The birds rotate the lead goose position, falling back when tired. With this instinctive system, geese can fly for a long time before they must stop for rest. This is an example of God's wisdom displayed in the natural world.

We often find ourselves as a lead goose. We have a hard time recognizing signs of exhaustion in ourselves. Even harder is falling back and letting someone else have a chance to develop leadership skills. Deep down we think that no other goose could get the gaggle where it needs to go without getting lost or bashing into treetops.

Jethro, Moses' father-in-law, came for a visit as the Israelites camped near the mountain of God. Jethro found Moses to be on the brink of exhaustion. "You will wear yourself out and these people as well," he told Moses. Jethro recommended that Moses delegate responsibilities. Moses listened and implemented everything Jethro suggested, advice that benefited the entire nation of Israel.

Dear Lord, help me to know when to fall back and rest, letting someone else take the lead. Teach me to serve You in any position. Amen.

LAY IT AT
THE CROSS

"Come to me, all you who are weary and burdened, and I will give you rest.
Take my yoke upon you and learn from me. . .you will find rest for your souls.
For my yoke is easy and my burden is light."
MATTHEW 11:28–30 NIV

*D*oes life sometimes get you down? Often when we experience difficulties that weigh us down, we hear the old adage "Lay it at the cross." But how do we lay our difficulties at the cross?

Jesus gives us step-by-step guidance in how to place our difficulties and burdens at the foot of the cross. First, He invites us to come to Him; those of us who are weary and burdened just need to approach Jesus in prayer. Second, He exchanges our heavy and burdensome load with His easy and light load. Jesus gives us His yoke and encourages us to learn from Him. The word *yoke* refers to Christ's teachings, Jesus' *way* of living life. As we follow His teachings, we take his yoke in humility and gentleness, surrendering and submitting ourselves to His will and ways for our lives. Finally, we praise God for the rest He promises to provide us.

Do you have any difficulties in life, any burdens, worries, fears, relationship issues, finance troubles, or work problems that you need to "lay at the cross"? Jesus says, "Come."

Lord, thank You for inviting me to come and exchange my heavy burden
for Your light burden. I praise You for the rest You promise me. Amen.

HOLY CLOTHING

*Rather, clothe yourselves with the Lord Jesus Christ, and do
not think about how to gratify the desires of the sinful nature.*
ROMANS 13:14 NIV

*J*anie has a terrible time with her wardrobe. She dreams of having a
fashionista come and lay out the clothes she is to wear each morning.
Perfect taste. Perfect color combinations. Perfect accessories. She could
completely allay her mind of all of these worldly demands for which she
has so little natural talent.

What should I wear? Janie thinks each morning. Then comes the
quandary of determining what is clean, what is ironed, what matches. . . .
Yes, a fashion expert would be a fabulous asset to her morning routine.

The Proverbs 31 woman is honored primarily for her godly
character and acts of charity, a focus of inner beauty, not outward
beauty. Jesus spoke about wardrobes on the Sermon on the Mount. In
fact, He said quite specifically not to be anxious about what you will
wear (Matthew 6:27–34). Later Paul tells us, "Clothe yourselves with
the Lord Jesus Christ." Clothing ourselves in holiness, not outward
adornment, should be the foremost focus of our thoughts.

*Lord Jesus, adorn me with Yourself, inside and out.
I desire "holy clothing" that reflects Your beauty. Amen.*

KEEPING A
CLEAN HEART

*Therefore, having these promises, beloved, let us cleanse ourselves from all
filthiness of the flesh and spirit, perfecting holiness in the fear of God.*
2 CORINTHIANS 7:1 NKJV

*H*er new home had white ceramic tile floors throughout. Upon
seeing them, visiting friends and family often asked, "Won't they show
every speck of dirt?"

"Yes, but at least I can tell if I need to clean them," replied the new
home owner, explaining her thinking that the better she could see the
dirt, the better chance she had of keeping them sparkling clean.

"So how often do you have to clean them—once a week?" her
friends asked.

"More like every day," she replied, laughing at their horrified
faces.

Keeping a clean heart requires similar diligence and regular upkeep.
While Jesus Himself cleanses us from all unrighteousness, as believers
we need to be on the lookout for temptations and situations that might
cause us to fall into sin in the first place. Reading the Bible reminds
us that God is holy and that He expects us to strive for holiness in
our thoughts and actions. As we pray daily, God shows us areas in our
character or behaviors that are displeasing to Him and that need a
thorough cleaning.

Like the home owner who enjoyed knowing her floors were clean,
there is joy and peace knowing our hearts can be clean, too.

"Create in me a clean heart, O God, and renew a steadfast spirit within me"
[PSALM 51:10 NKJV]. *Amen.*

TAKE FIVE

The LORD God formed man of the dust of the ground,
and breathed into his nostrils the breath of life.
GENESIS 2:7 NKJV

*H*ow would you describe your physical and mental state today? Are you rested and refreshed, or do you feel weary, worn down by the unrelenting demands and pressures of doing life? We tend to think that the longer and harder we work, the more productive we will be. But when we become fatigued spiritually and emotionally, we eventually reach a point of exhaustion.

You *are* in control and you *can* stop the world from spinning. Even if you know that it is impossible to take a day off, it helps tremendously to make time for a personal "time out."

Pause from whatever you are doing for just a few moments and breathe deeply. Shut your office door, close your eyes, or pause for a second or two in the bathroom. Ask God for a sense of calm and clarity of mind to deal properly with your next assignment. Take time to unwind from a stressful day by taking a few minutes of "me time" in the car as you drive home. If your commute is short, pull over for a few minutes and let the weight of the day fall off.

Sometimes the most active thing we can do is rest, even if for only a short time.

Father, help me not to push myself so hard.
Help me to remember to take five and breathe. Amen.

CREATION'S PRAISE

For you created my inmost being;
you knit me together in my mother's womb.
PSALM 139:13 NIV

God didn't spend six days creating things and then put His creation abilities on the shelf. He is continually creating wonderful things for His people. He created each of us with a special design in mind. Nothing about us is hidden from Him—the good parts or the bad.

Before you had a thought or moved a muscle, God was working out a plan for your existence. Maybe He gave you brown hair and a sweet smile or good genes for a long life, or He gave you dark hair and clever fingers that are artistic. Perhaps He gave you a musical voice that worships Him daily in song. Whatever His gifts, He designed them just for you, to bring ministry to His hurting world.

When we look at the six days of Creation, let's thank God that He didn't set things working and then walk away. Adam and Eve were important to Him, but so are we. He has personally created everything in this wonderful world—including us.

Do we need any more reason to praise the Lord who brought into existence every fiber of our beings?

Thank You, Lord, for detailing every piece of my body, mind, and spirit.
I'm glad nothing that happens to me or in me is a surprise to You.
Help me use all Your gifts to Your glory. Amen.

REJOICING TO COME

He who continually goes forth weeping, bearing seed for sowing,
shall doubtless come again with rejoicing, bringing his sheaves with him.
PSALM 126:6 NKJV

*W*ork had become a drain on one woman. One of her coworkers hated Christians. Every day the person would make some snide remark about the worthlessness of Christianity. The coworker derived great enjoyment in pointing out faults of Christians in the news.

The woman prayed about the situation, leaving for work each day with renewed hope, trusting the Lord to get her through—to keep her from becoming like her acquaintance. By quitting time, she would be drained emotionally and spiritually. Yet she continued going to work each day and interacting with her coworkers, although hurting from the barbs.

Jesus has always been under assault from those who don't believe in Him. When He lived as a man, He endured great trials. The insults and ridicule didn't stop after His death but continue on today. Still, He faced even the cross for the joy that was to come.

With Jesus as our example, we can carry on, even when we're hurting and discouraged. Being belittled for our faith is tough, but we have hope, knowing what is to come. We can go out with seed for sowing, knowing there will come a time of great rejoicing.

Jesus, thank You for being the example I can follow. Help me to have the courage to face each day, knowing my joy is in You and my hope is in heaven. Amen.

BEHAVE YOURSELF!

I will behave myself wisely in a perfect way.
O when wilt thou come unto me?
I will walk within my house with a perfect heart.
PSALM 101:2 KJV

*H*ome is where the heart is.

Home is a refuge, a place of rest.

Home is the smell of fresh-baked bread, the sound of laughter, the squeeze of a hug.

Because home is a place of comfort and relaxation, it is also the place where we are most likely to misbehave. We would never think of yelling at family members in public, for example, but if one of them pushes our buttons *just once* at home, we will instantly level her or him with a verbal machine gun.

David himself knew the danger of walking unwisely at home. He was home—not in battle—when he saw Bathsheba on the rooftop. His psalm cited above reminds us that we must behave wisely all the time, but especially at home.

Because more is caught than taught, our families must see mature behavior from us. We must model integrity—we must keep our promises and act the way we want those around us to act. Hypocrisy—"Do as I say, not as I do"—has no place in the home of a mature Christian woman who has been made complete in Christ.

May God grow us up into mature women, and may we walk accordingly, especially at home.

Father God, how often I fail at home. Make me sensitive to the Spirit
so that I will recognize when I am straying from the path of maturity.
I'm the adult here; help me to act as one. Amen.

DIFFICULT PEOPLE

Do not turn your freedom into an opportunity for the flesh,
but through love serve one another.
GALATIANS 5:13 NASB

In the classic movie *An Affair to Remember*, Deborah Kerr asks Cary Grant, "What makes life so difficult?" to which he responds, "People?"

Yes, people tend to make our lives difficult. But they also make life worth living. The trick is not to let the biting words or nefarious deeds of others become glaring giants that make us flee or weigh us down with hate and resentment.

The only way David stood up to the giant Goliath was by turning his problem over to the Lord and relying on His strength and power. Then, acting in faith, David prevailed with the weapons at hand—a slingshot and one smooth stone.

Sometimes, like David, we need to turn our skirmishes with others over to the Lord. Then, by using our weapons—God's Word and a steadfast faith—we need to love and forgive others as God loves and forgives us.

Always keep in mind that, although we may not like to admit it, we have all said and done some pretty awful things ourselves, making the lives of others difficult. Yet God has forgiven us *and* continues to love us.

So do the right thing. Pull your feet out of the mire of unforgiveness, sidestep verbal retaliation, and stand tall in the freedom of love and forgiveness.

The words and deeds of others have left me wounded and bleeding.
Forgiveness and love seem to be the last thing on my mind. Change my heart,
Lord. Help me to love and forgive others as You love and forgive me. Amen.

CREATED VS. CREATOR

"And when you look up to the sky and see the sun, the moon and the stars—all the heavenly array—do not be enticed into bowing down to them and worshiping things the LORD your God has apportioned to all the nations under heaven."
DEUTERONOMY 4:19 NIV

The sun, moon, and stars are not to guide our lives, regardless of the power their light seems to have over us or the horoscopes people have concocted. God placed those lights in the sky with the touch of His little finger and could turn them off again, if He so chose, with less effort than it would take to flip a switch. They are beautiful creations, but they do not compare with the Creator!

Once in a while nature takes our breath away. We marvel at snowcapped mountains or get caught up in the colors of a sunset. Our heavenly Father is like a loving parent on Christmas Eve who arranges gifts beneath the tree, anticipating the joy those gifts will bring to his children.

When God fills the sky with a gorgeous sunset, it is not just about the colors and the beauty. Those colors reflect His love. He paints each stroke, each tiny detail, and mixes purples with pinks and yellows so that you might *look up!* When you look up to find the bright lights that govern our days and nights, or the next time you see a sunset, remember the Creator and give Him glory.

Father, thank You for the beauty of Your world.
Remind me to stand in awe of the Creator, not the created. Amen.

TOUGH QUESTIONS

Nothing in all creation is hidden from God's sight. Everything is uncovered and laid bare before the eyes of him to whom we must give account.
HEBREWS 4:13 NIV

*Th*ree-year-old Austin peered into the incubator where his new baby sister lay in the hospital's intensive care nursery. Dan, his father, held him up to see his sister for the first time.

"There's Maddie," his dad whispered. "That's your new sister."

Austin looked at their newest family member bundled snuggly under miniature blankets. For several seconds he remained quiet, studying her with a perplexed look on his face.

"Where are her legs?" he asked.

"They're there," his dad assured him. "They're just covered up."

"Does she play games?"

"Well, mostly she sleeps."

Maddie's nurse came to update Dan on Maddie's condition. Dan knew his premature daughter occasionally needed to be gently stimulated. She would stop breathing and experience "blue spells."

"She's been good today," the nurse told Dan. "She hasn't been turning colors."

Austin's eyes widened. "What color is she *supposed* to be?"

Often we hear people say they have some questions they are going to ask God some day. After Job lost everything, he had some questions. But God thundered back dozens of questions of His own. The first: "Who is this that questions my wisdom with such ignorant words?" (Job 38:2 NLT). Someday God is going to be the One asking the tough questions. Let's live humbly before our all-wise God in that truth.

Father, You understand all things. I don't. Help me to trust You even when I don't understand everything that's happening in my life. Amen.

TAKE TIME TO
TAKE TIME

Remember how short my time is.
PSALM 89:47 KJV

You stroll a sandy, white beach as a warm breeze sweeps across your face. Broken waves froth against your bare feet and seagulls soar above. You breathe in the fresh sea air. . .and then reality interrupts the daydream.

"Time and tide wait for no man," reads one quote. As surely as the tide rises and falls, time passes swiftly. Like a wet bar of soap slipping through our fisted hand, we lose grip on time as good intentions fall prey to crowded schedules. Our busy pace deters us from taking a walk on the beach, having lunch with a friend, or making a date with our significant other.

King David recognized the brevity of life when viewed through the window of eternity. Often we fool ourselves into thinking that we have plenty of time; meanwhile, months and years pass by seemingly without notice.

Is time passing you by? Have you allowed other things to rob you of much-needed time apart? It's never too late to take time for yourself.

Dear Lord, time flies and I've let it pass me by. I want to use the time You've given me more effectively. I want to enjoy life. Help me to take time out for myself and for others. Amen.

HAVE YOU BEEN WITH JESUS?

*Now when they saw the boldness of Peter and John, and perceived
that they were uneducated and untrained men, they marveled.
And they realized that they had been with Jesus.*
ACTS 4:13 NKJV

A young woman grew up in the Deep South but attended college in
another part of the country. With time, she began to lose her Southern
drawl. When she returned to her hometown for extended visits, however,
she found herself picking up the regional dialect again. Her friends
would tease her, saying, "We can tell you've been down South again!"
Words like *y'all* and phrases such as *fixin' to* made it apparent that she
had spent time with her family. This didn't bother her, though. The
woman was proud of her Southern roots.

In Acts we read that Peter and John healed a crippled man and,
when questioned by the authorities, boldly responded that the healing
had been done in Jesus' name. They went on to preach the gospel.
Extraordinary courage was seen in these ordinary men. The rulers were
astounded. They took note that Peter and John *had been with Jesus.*

When we meditate on scripture and seek the Lord in prayer
regularly, we naturally become a little more like Him. Just as slow
Southern speech points clearly to a particular region on the map, may
our lives undeniably reflect that we have been with the Son of God.

Jesus, make me more like You today. Amen.

THE PRACTICE
OF PRAISE

Bless the LORD, O my soul; and all that is within me. . . . Bless the LORD,
O my soul, and forget not all his benefits: who forgiveth all thine iniquities;
who healeth all thy diseases; who redeemeth thy life from destruction.
PSALM 103:1–4 KJV

*T*rials come to all of us, and when they do, it's easy to forget all that God has done for us in the past. Often our adverse circumstances sabotage our efforts to praise God in every situation.

The psalmist practiced the power of praise as he acknowledged God's faithfulness to forgive, heal, and restore. He blessed the Lord with his whole heart because he trusted in God's divine plan.

Positive acclamations of our faith produce remarkable results. First, praise establishes and builds our faith. It decrees, "No matter what is happening, no matter how I feel, I choose to praise God!" Second, praise changes our perspective. As we relinquish control, praise redirects our focus toward God rather than on our problems. And third, praise blesses the heart of God. It brings God joy for His children to acknowledge His presence and power through praise.

The Bible admonishes us to praise God in every circumstance, saying, "In every thing give thanks: for this is the will of God in Christ Jesus concerning you" (1 Thessalonians 5:18 KJV). To bless the Lord in all things is to receive God's blessings. Begin the practice of praise today!

Heavenly Father, You are worthy of all my praise. I thank and praise You for
my current circumstances, knowing that You are at work on my behalf. Amen.

CHANGING
DIRECTION

*Later they were warned in a dream not to return to Herod,
and they went back home by another road.*
MATTHEW 2:12 CEV

$\mathcal{W}$ise men, having seen a shining star in the east, headed to Jerusalem, where they asked King Herod about the birth of the King of the Jews. Herod, a cruel and crafty tyrant, sent the wise men to Bethlehem, telling them to search for this Child and, after finding Him, to come back and bring him word.

So the wise men left Herod, continued to follow the star, and eventually were led to Jesus' house, where they presented Him with their gifts. Then, being warned by God in a dream not to go back to Herod, they returned home by another way.

Do *we* listen to God that well? Are we able to change direction at God's prompting? Or are we bent on following the route we have set before us and then are somehow surprised when we come face-to-face with a Herod?

We would do best to become wise women, daily presenting ourselves to Jesus, asking Him to lead us on the right path, and keeping a wary eye on the heavenly sky. Then, alert for God's directional promptings, we will avoid the Herods of this world.

By following God's direction—in a dream, His Word, your quiet time, or conversations with others—you will be sure to stay on the right path and arrive home safely.

*Jesus, I present myself to You. Show me the right path to walk with every
step I take. Keep me away from evil and lead me to Your door. Amen.*

ASK AND YOU SHALL RECEIVE

*Then she said, "Give me a blessing; since you have given me
the land of the Negev, give me also springs of water." So he
gave her the upper springs and the lower springs.*
JOSHUA 15:19 NASB

$\mathcal{T}$hroughout the Bible, women often appear on the scene as the voice of practicality. Abigail appealed to David's understanding of God; the daughters of Zelophehad petitioned Moses for fairness (Numbers 27:1–8). And here Achsah, the daughter of Caleb, asks her father for water. Caleb had just awarded Achsah and her new husband a generous piece of land, but she knew that in the middle of a desert they needed more than land; they needed water.

In our overwhelming schedules today, as we try to balance all the different pieces of our lives, we should never overlook a very reasonable solution to our need for more time in the day and more hands for the work: Ask for help. It is biblical, practical, and understandable. And, in doing so, we just may be blessed by the kind of help God brings into our lives.

*Lord, I know I can always turn to You for help. Let me remember that I can
also rely on believers around me in a way that will bring blessings to us all.
Amen.*

FOLLOW YOUR HEART

"When Moses the servant of the LORD sent me from Kadesh Barnea to spy out the land. . .I brought back word to him as it was in my heart."
JOSHUA 14:7 NKJV

Sometimes when we speak our hearts, we come against opposition. This is nothing new. The same thing happened to Caleb when he and the other Israelites were sent to spy out the land of Canaan. When the spies came back to Moses and the people, everyone but Joshua and Caleb gave a bad report. Those driven by fear said there was no way Israel could take possession of the land. The current tenants—giants, to be exact—were too strong for God's people to overcome.

Yet Caleb and Joshua, the men whose spirits witnessed with God's Spirit, knew the truth of the matter. They alone stood against the bearers of bad report. They spoke the truth in their hearts—truth that was met by the tears and mourning of the Israelites who feared the giants, were disgusted with their leaders, and rejected God.

Don't let naysayers mislead you. Walk uprightly and speak the truth in your heart (see Psalm 15:2). Although the going may get rough—with giants and unbelievers obstructing your path—by following your heart and God, you will never lose your way on your journey to the land of milk and honey.

God, give me the courage to speak from my heart. Stand beside me, lead me in the right direction, and grant me Your wisdom as I step out from among the crowd. Amen.

WELL-SEASONED
SPEECH

*Let your conversation be always full of grace, seasoned with salt,
so that you may know how to answer everyone.*
COLOSSIANS 4:6 NIV

Cassie was a horrible cook! Her food was bland, flat, and boring to
the extreme—no zest, no zing to tempt you for a second helping. Oh,
she'd try to please people with what they wanted, but the result was
pathetic.

As pale and uninviting as Cassie's food was, her conversations were
the exact opposite: full of life, spiced with the hope of the gospel, meaty
with truth, and sprinkled with kindness and love. People were drawn
to her and would linger in conversation, savoring the sweet aroma of
Christ that bubbled from within her. She didn't preach or use Christian-
ese. Instead, she used words that encouraged, challenged, or piqued
you for more. When asked about this, she admitted to making every
effort to choose words that build up people, make them laugh, or give
truths to chew on when they walk away—a practice of longer-lasting
value than cuisine acclaim.

*Word Giver, may Your words of truth and life be on my lips.
Help me to sprinkle the salt of grace on those I converse with,
making them want more of You. Amen.*

KEEPING
CHRISTMAS

"For there is born to you this day in the city
of David a Savior, who is Christ the Lord."
LUKE 2:11 NKJV

Christmastime comes. It comes every year right after Thanksgiving. It comes with noise and crowds and gift wrap. It comes with fudge and mistletoe and shopping—lots of shopping—whether we are ready for it or not. December brings a new type of "busy" into our days. It is a busy that is pine-scented and sparkly and, if we are lucky, snow-blanketed.

Christmas goes. It goes as quickly as it came, with crumpled tissue paper and leftover ham. It goes with the last surprise, the final carol, and the taking down of lights. It goes out to the curb, pine-scented still—but over.

This Christmas season, among the wonderful hustle and bustle of one more party and one more gift to purchase, take time to rest in the true meaning of the celebration. God's only Son was born in Bethlehem and laid in a manger, sent from heaven to save us from our sin and give us everlasting life.

This year let Christmas stay. As December melts into January and a new year begins, *keep Christmas*. Let the Christ of Christmas make every day a little happier, a little brighter, a little bigger. Make *life* the special occasion, not just December 25.

Keep Christmas this year—all year.

Father, thank You for the gift of Your only Son, sent that I might have
life instead of death. Help me to keep the spirit of Christmas in
my heart and celebrate Jesus all year long. Amen.

SHARING OUR BLESSINGS

Divide your investments among many places,
for you do not know what risks might lie ahead.
ECCLESIASTES 11:2 NLT

$\mathcal{D}$aphne stacked the boxes of canned goods against the pantry wall, singing praise songs while she worked. God had transformed the bare-boned Christmas that she expected into an overwhelming abundance. First her church and then her workplace brought box after box of food and gifts. The last, crowning gift came from her husband's workplace, a leftover Christmas tree. Green branches and Christmas cards replaced the strands of light she had hung on the front window.

Many of us have experienced times when God's people have stepped in with a much-needed gift of transportation or food or a car repair.

Maybe that's why God tells us to give as much of ourselves and our belongings to as many people as possible. We need the grace of giving *and* receiving.

Later Daphne had more to offer. An abused woman stayed in her home. She invited friends over for holiday meals and bought gifts for needy children. She started small during that memorable Christmas. There was so much more than she could use. One out of every ten cans went to a local food bank.

As we have freely received from God's goodness, may we freely give.

Father, You provide for our needs. Use us to provide for others.
Give us wisdom as to how and to whom to give. Amen.

In Receiving, Give

Mary treasured up all these things and pondered them in her heart.
LUKE 2:19 NIV

Sarah dropped her suitcase in the motel doorway and stared at her husband in disbelief. "We didn't pack the box in our closet?" He slowly shook his head.

"Oh, no!" Sarah dropped her head into her hands. "We forgot all of Bethany's presents, and the roads are iced over. Tomorrow's Christmas—what will we do?"

Sarah racked her brain. A catastrophe of miscommunication and an ice storm en route to Grandma's house. . . How could Jesus' birthday still be special to ten-year-old Bethany with no gifts, family meal, or twinkling tree?

That frosty Christmas morning, they took turns reading Luke's account of the Christmas story. Then, using the markers and sketch pad Bethany took everywhere, the family drew scenes of crowded Bethlehem, a bedraggled couple, a frustrated innkeeper, a rustic stable, shepherds on a hillside, a glorious star, angels praising God, and of course, a newborn baby in a manger.

Pausing for breath while gustily singing Christmas carols, the family could hear the faint but jubilant strains of "Joy to the World" in the distance. The excited family bundled up and followed the sound to a tiny church up the hill and joined hands and voices with the dozen members who were serving Christmas lunch to the homeless.

One look at Bethany's glowing face as she served mashed potatoes to a hungry man assured Sarah that, this Christmas, *giving* instead of *getting* was the best gift her daughter ever could have received.

*Prince of Peace, we celebrate Your birth. Fill us with
the beauty and simplicity of that first holy Christmas. Amen.*

I Have Arrived

*"Who knows but that you have come to
royal position for such a time as this?"*
ESTHER 4:14 NIV

*Y*ou may have experienced a time in your life when you thought, *I'm
precisely where God destined me to be at this point in my life.* Did you feel as
if you had arrived—or that you had found the very thing you were
created to do?

Maybe you felt complete after the first week at a new job. Perhaps
you found your niche in volunteering at church or for a worthy organization. Maybe you had the opportunity to stay home with your children,
something you always dreamed of doing. In that season, God equipped
you to fulfill your purpose, but even greater moments are awaiting you.

There is coming a day in which each one of us will truly be able
to say, "I have arrived!" When we reach heaven and are able to worship
God face-to-face, then we will be able to say that we are doing what we
were destined to do—worship the very One who created us.

Then we will look around and say, "I have arrived!"

*Heavenly Father, thank You for giving me a dream and a destiny.
I want to serve You in the very purpose You created me for—
today and into all of eternity. Amen.*

BE REAL

I cry aloud to the LORD; I lift up my voice to the LORD for mercy.
I pour out my complaint before Him; before him I tell my trouble. . . .
You desire truth in the inner parts.
PSALM 142:1–2; 51:6 NIV

*W*riting in a private journal is risky. If someone reads it, the writer is exposed by what and how she wrote. So it is with the psalmists. Their hearts are exposed, showing how very real they were with God. They put on no spiritual face when writing their prayers, thoughts, and songs. They are very real. They complain. They cry out. They vent in anger, weep in remorse, ask deep questions, sing with joy, and dance in celebration. Their honesty before God is refreshing. That is why for so many people, Psalms is their favorite book of the Bible. How gracious of God to include this book for the comfort of His people.

As Psalms demonstrates, God wants genuineness and truth in our hearts. He can handle it. He is not surprised to find anger or questions aimed at Him. Truth sets us free—be honest in examining your heart. See and accept things for what they are. New levels of communion with God are the result of an honest heart, deepening your walk with your Creator. Vibrancy and authentic joy bubble from within a heart that is clean, open, and entwined with God.

Gracious Savior, strip me of any pretenses that hinder genuine communion
with You. Let my thoughts and prayers be truthful and real,
that we can walk in oneness. Amen.

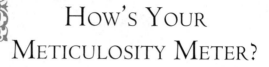

HOW'S YOUR METICULOSITY METER?

Nothing is completely perfect, except your teachings.
I deeply love your Law!
PSALM 119:96–97 CEV

*A*re you a perfectionist? Do you scramble to clean the breakfast dishes, run the vacuum, toss in laundry, and give a visual overview of the house before leaving for work? Does the sight of grass scaling over two inches or unruly weeds growing from the crevices of your driveway drive you crazy? For perfectionists, checking one's meticulosity meter is necessary to maintain balance.

Martha was a woman who also struggled with meticulosity. She and her easy-going sister, Mary, invited Jesus to their home for dinner. Martha, the perfect hostess, frantically scurried with preparations in a one-woman race for Homemaker of the Year. Mary, on the other hand, ignored her sister's busyness and chose to sit at Jesus' feet, absorbing His every word.

Meanwhile, Martha seethed. After she complained to Jesus, the Lord responded, saying, "Martha, Martha! You are worried and upset about so many things, but only one thing is necessary. Mary has chosen what is best" (Luke 10:41–42 CEV).

Perfection is not so perfect. Nothing is. We live in a flawed world no matter how much we work and strive. As Jesus instructed Martha, He instructs us today. To love God's life-giving words is the closest we will ever come to achieving perfection here on earth.

So how's your meticulosity meter?

Dear Lord, nothing is as important as listening to Your voice and reading Your Word. Please remind me of that when my quest for perfection overwhelms me.
Amen.

GOD'S WASH DAY

*If we confess our sins, he is faithful and just to forgive us our sins,
and to cleanse us from all unrighteousness.*
I JOHN 1:9 KJV

$\mathcal{W}$e women know all about wash day: the piles of clothes sorted for color and type; the detergent, softener, and bleach; the time it takes to wash, dry, and fold. It's a big production. Most of us probably work it in around other chores to make the most of our time, but it still doesn't happen quickly. And if we have to go to a coin-op laundry and wait, it seems to take forever. But even when we do our best, sometimes a few items don't come out quite clean and need rewashing.

Did you realize that God does laundry, too? But He needs nothing out of a box or bottle, because His cleansing works not on fabric but on human hearts. The "detergent" is the blood of His Son.

Ironically, blood is something that causes a stain that is hard to remove from clothes. But the blood of Jesus eradicates all the dirt on human hearts, removing every stain of sin. Though we receive it once, it is ever effective. No matter how often we fail, we can return, and a simple confession will renew the cleansing.

Need a wash? Look to God.

Thank You, Lord, for washing my heart clean with Your own blood. Don't let me forget what it cost You, and help me turn to You whenever I fail. Amen.

ETERNAL GOALS

*"For I know the plans I have for you," declares the L*ORD*, "plans to prosper you and not to harm you, plans to give you hope and a future."*
JEREMIAH 29:11 NIV

*A*s she considered the excitement generated by the upcoming New Year's celebration, the woman sat down with paper and pencil. She wanted to jot down her goals for the year. As she wrote, she realized some of the objectives would be easily accomplished, while others would take much longer. She ended up dividing her list into short-term and long-term goals.

Looking at our aims or desires for life can give us a picture of what is most important to us individually. Do we first pray and ask God what He wants for us in the coming weeks, months, or years? Have we considered what God's plans are for our lives and allowed room for change if His will doesn't align with ours?

Although God's plans may be different than what we might have chosen, His ideas for us are perfect. They are intended to complete us, to give us hope and a future with Him.

As we think tomorrow of what the coming year will bring, we must remember that the things of earth are very temporary. We need to set goals with eternity in mind. Think beyond long term.

Lord, I thank You for the plans You have for me.
With You I can have a future full of hope and promise. Amen.

BE STRONG AND COURAGEOUS

"Have I not commanded you? Be strong and courageous. Do not be terrified; do not be discouraged, for the LORD your God will be with you wherever you go."
JOSHUA 1:9 NIV

*I*n Joshua 1:9, God commands Joshua to "be strong and courageous," a phrase that is repeated five more times in the book of Joshua. When God repeatedly commands something, we would do well to pay attention. But are we listening to God, or are we letting the fears of this world paralyze us?

Many things in this world can terrify us—the state of the economy, terrorist threats, the current crime rate, another car swerving into our lane of traffic—the list goes on and on. But we are to take courage and be strong. We are *commanded* to do so.

Someone has calculated that the words *fear not* appear exactly 365 times in the Bible. How wonderful to have this affirmation available to us every day of the year! Praise God that with Christ the Deliverer in our lives, we are no longer threatened by the world around us. He has overcome all! Now all *we* need to do is believe it!

Believe that God is with you every moment of the day. Believe that He has the power to protect and shield you from the poisonous darts of the evil one. Believe that He has overcome the world. Believe that with Him by your side, you can be stronger than the world's most powerful army. Believe that you have the courage to face the unfaceable. Nothing on this earth can harm you.

Today, Lord, I will not fear. No matter what comes against me, I am strong and courageous, able to overcome any foe—because You are by my side! Amen.

CONTRIBUTORS

Biggers, Emily: Days 24, 28, 55, 83, 89, 113, 119, 123, 144, 157, 182, 197, 227, 238, 266, 269, 271, 277, 295, 313, 314, 336, 348, 351, 357

Emily Biggers is a gifted education specialist in a north Texas public school district. She enjoys travel, freelance writing, and serving in a local apartment ministry through her church.

Coty, Debora M.: Days 1, 45, 79, 107, 133, 185, 247, 285, 328, 359

Debora M. Coty is an events speaker, columnist, author of *The Distant Shore* and *Hugs, Humor, and Hope for Harried Moms*, contributor to *Heavenly Humor for the Woman's Soul*, and coauthor of *Grit for the Oyster: 250 Pearls of Wisdom for Aspiring Writers*.

Douglas, Katherine: Days 2, 22, 33, 38, 68, 78, 94, 106, 134, 148, 151, 161, 174, 186, 205, 213, 229, 248, 260, 274, 292, 310, 329, 337, 349

Author and speaker Katherine Douglas started writing creatively in the third grade. Her publications include six books and dozens of articles. You may visit her Web site at www.katherinedouglas.com.

Elacqua, Tina C., Ph.D.: Days 9, 40, 59, 80, 105, 120, 136, 152, 203, 232, 243, 249, 287, 326, 340

Tina Elacqua teaches, writes, and publishes journal articles, books, conference papers/presentations, and technical reports/presentations. She has held roles of research scientist, professor, and consultant in industrial/organizational psychology.

Farrier, Nancy: Days 6, 27, 48, 69, 84, 112, 137, 169, 199, 224, 245, 300, 315, 345, 364

Nancy J. Farrier is the author of twelve books and numerous articles and short stories. She is married and has five children. She lives with her family in Southern California.

Fisher, Suzanne Woods: Days 23, 39, 61, 102, 108, 121, 132, 171, 206, 215, 244, 289, 301, 327, 339

Suzanne Woods Fisher's debut novel, *Copper Star*, was released in 2007. The sequel, *Copper Fire*, was released in May 2008. Fisher is a contributing editor to *Christian Parenting Today* magazine.

Franklin, Darlene: Days 19, 47, 66, 103, 131, 147, 154, 156, 208, 216, 261, 278, 294, 307, 358

Darlene Franklin lives in Englewood, Colorado. She is the author of *Romanian Rhapsody* and the "Dressed for Death" mystery series, as well as numerous articles. You may visit her Web site at www.darlenehfranklin.com.

Gregor, Shanna D.: Days 4, 25, 32, 44, 77, 92, 101, 139, 150, 173, 179, 200, 209, 240, 242, 250, 265, 284, 296, 302, 318, 323, 343, 360

With a passion to see the gospel touch lives through the written word, writer and editor Shanna Gregor helps ministries and publishers develop books that express God's voice for today through the doors of opportunity He sets before her. www.gregorswrite.com.

Hetzel, June, Ph.D.: Days 20, 41, 67, 73, 109, 149, 166, 172, 192, 202, 231, 262, 288, 319, 341

June Hetzel is professor of education at Biola University. She enjoys the roles of wife, friend, author, editor, and professor. She and her husband, Geoff, reside in Southern California.

Keller, Austine: Days 13, 50, 64, 115, 129, 163, 159, 175, 194, 237, 259, 283, 298, 316, 342

Austine Keller resides in Tampa, Florida, writing and publishing as ministry to others as well as for her own enjoyment. She also enjoys a newly emptied nest and fishing with her husband.

Tina Krause is an award-winning newspaper columnist and author of the book *Laughter Therapy*. She is a wife, mom, and grandmother of four. Tina and her husband, Jim, live in Valparaiso, Indiana.

P. J. Lehman lives in Valrico, Florida, with her husband and three children. She enjoys children's ministry, photography, animals, being outdoors, and—her all-time favorite—a hammock with a good book!

Donna K. Maltese is a writer, editor, and the author of *Power Prayers to Start Your Day*. She is married, has two children, and resides in Silverdale, Pennsylvania.

Pamela McQuade has been a book and magazine editor and has written numerous Christian books. When not writing or reading, she's often quilting or giving belly rubs to her basset hounds.

Helen Widger Middlebrooke is a freelance columnist and the author of *Lessons for a Supermom*. She is a homemaker, home educator, and the mother of nine.

Mandy Nydegger lives with her husband, David, in Waco, Texas. She loves Christmas, snow, and the Indianapolis Colts.

Nicole O'Dell, a devoted wife and mother, is an accomplished writer of books, devotions, and Bible studies. She has been a Bible study leader and teacher for more than ten years.

Rachael Phillips (www.rachaelwrites.com) is the author of four Barbour biographies and is an award-winning fiction and humor writer. Rachael and her husband live in Indiana.

Julie Rayburn is a public speaker and an area director for Community Bible Study. She lives in Atlanta with her husband, Scott. They have two grown children and one granddaughter.

Ramona Richards is an award-winning author whose books include *Secrets of Confidence* and *A Murder among Friends*.

Kate E. Schmelzer graduated from Taylor University in 2008 with a double major in professional writing and counseling and a minor in Christian education. She hopes to be an author, counselor, and missionary.

SCRIPTURE INDEX

Old Testament

New Testament

Be sure to check out these other titles from Barbour Publishing

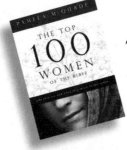